Reality TV

Reality TV restores a crucial, and often absent, element to the critical debate about reality television: the voices of people who watch reality programmes. Annette Hill argues that much can be learned from listening to audience discussion about this popular and rapidly changing television genre. Viewers' responses to reality TV can provide invaluable information to enhance our understanding of both the reality genre and contemporary television audiences.

Do audiences think reality TV is real? Can people learn from watching reality TV? How critical are viewers of reality TV? *Reality TV* argues that audiences are engaged in a critical examination of the development of popular factual television. The book draws on quantitative and qualitative audience research to understand how viewers categorise the reality genre, and how they judge the performance of ordinary people and the representation of authenticity within different types of reality programmes, from *Animal Hospital* to *Big Brother*. The book also examines how audiences can learn from watching reality programmes, and how viewers think and talk about the ethics of reality TV.

Annette Hill is Professor of Media, and Research Centre Director, School of Media, Arts and Design, University of Westminster. She is the co-author of *Shocking Entertainment: Viewer Response to Violent Movies* (1997) and *TV Living: Television, Audiences and Everyday Life*, with David Gauntlett (1999), and the co-editor, with Robert C. Allen, of *The Television Studies Reader* (Routledge, 2003). Her current research interests include television audiences and factual programming, and companion animals and the media.

Reality TV

Audiences and popular
factual television

Annette Hill

Routledge
Taylor & Francis Group

LONDON AND NEW YORK

First published 2005
by Routledge
2 Park Square, Milton Park, Abingdon, Oxon OX14 4RN

Simultaneously published in the USA and Canada
by Routledge
270 Madison Ave, New York, NY 10016

Routledge is an imprint of the Taylor & Francis Group

© 2005 Annette Hill

Typeset in Palatino by
Rosemount Typing Services, Auldgirth, Dumfriesshire

Printed and bound in Great Britain by
MPG Books, Bodmin, Cornwall

All rights reserved. No part of this book may be reprinted or
reproduced or utilised in any form or by any electronic,
mechanical, or other means, now known or hereafter invented,
including photocopying and recording, or in any information
storage or retrieval system, without permission in writing from
the publishers.

British Library Cataloguing in Publication Data
A catalogue record for this book is available from the British
Library.

Library of Congress Cataloging in Publication Data
A catalog record for this book has been requested.

ISBN 0–415–26151–1 (hbk)
ISBN 0–415–26152–X (pbk)

PN
1992.8
. R43
H 55
2005

To Don Butler, and my family, for taking care
of business

Contents

Acknowledgements

I am indebted to the people who have supported and encouraged my research over the past few years. The audience research project 'Quantitative and Qualitative Audience Research in Popular Factual Entertainment' was funded by the Economic and Social Research Council, the Independent Television Commission, and Channel 4. I thank these organisations for their financial support. The audience research project also benefited from the help and support of the Broadcasting Standards Commission, the BBC, Five, and the British Film Institute. The project greatly benefited from a steering group, who offered practical advice and valuable ideas regarding the research design, data collection and analysis. In particular, I would like to thank Bob Towler and Pam Hanley from the ITC, Andrea Millwood Hargrave from the BSC, Janet Willis from the BFI, Claire Grimmond from Channel 4, Andrea Wills from the BBC, and Susanna Dinnage from Five. Nicholas Garnham and Brian Winston offered sound advice in the early stages of the project design. I would like to thank Sarah Selwood for helpful comments in early stages of the quantitative research design. I would also like to thank Vincent Porter for being so supportive about the project from the beginning to the end. The research benefited enormously from the assistance of Caroline Dover, who was quite simply the best research assistant I could have hoped to work with, and who made this project far more interesting and innovative than it would have been if I had done it on my own – many, many thanks.

This book could not have been written without the support of the University of Westminster, and the School of Media, Arts and Design. I would in particular like to thank my colleagues in the Department of Journalism and Mass Communication for their encouragement and support. I would also like to thank the Research Office for doing such a good job of managing everything at the University. Over the past few years students on the Media Consumption module and the Communication Research Methods module have been patient enough to listen to me talk about my research on many occasions – thanks for listening, and for giving me good ideas for this book.

A number of colleagues have offered their help and support over the years. Thanks must go to Robert C. Allen, Minna Aslama, Charlotte Brunsdon, Hanne Bruhn, Ian Calcutt, Nick Couldry, Peter Dahlgren, Jon Dovey, Jan Ekecrantz, David Gauntlett, Jostein Gripsrud, Richard Kilborn, Sonia Livingstone, Peter Lunt, Ernest Mathjis, Lothar Mikos, Gareth Palmer, Liina Puustinen, Elizabeth Prommer, Clive Seale, Henrik Søndergaard, and the talented group of audience researchers at YLE, Finland. In particular, I need to thank John Corner, John Ellis, Derek Paget, Jane Roscoe, and anonymous readers for their expert advice on the proposal and final manuscript. John Corner also provided invaluable advice at every stage of the research project and the writing of this book, and therefore became my guiding light throughout the research – John, I'm your number one fan. I would like to thank Rebecca Barden for being so patient and encouraging, and Kate Ahl and Lesley Riddle for overseeing the final stages of the manuscript.

And finally, I would like to thank the television viewers who agreed to take part in this project, and who are represented in this book. Without your comments and reflections on watching reality TV, I would be out of a job. In particular, I wish to thank the families who were so welcoming and generous, and who took the time to get to know us, and allowed us to get to know them. It's been a pleasure.

Chapter 1

Understanding reality TV

Welcome to *Reality TV*. It's Friday night and I'm watching the finale of *Teen Big Brother*. It's an emotional experience. The remaining housemates sit around a table, choosing who will win the first *Teen Big Brother*. Commissioned by 4 Learning, the educational wing of Channel 4 in the UK, *Teen Big Brother* is an experiment in the reality genre. Part observational documentary, life experiment, educational programme, gameshow and soap opera, this reality programme has hit the headlines for being the first UK *Big Brother* to feature sex. 'Bonk on Big Bruv', says the *Sun*. 'Horny Teens Show Big Bruv Way to Go', adds the *Daily Star*. Love it or hate it, the programme is a popular topic for public debate. I'm watching *Teen Big Brother* to see what all the fuss is about. I missed the tears and tantrums, the backbiting and bedroom antics, only to tune in to the last ten minutes of the final programme. I'm gripped. The housemates explain why they should win. They go around the group, each one speaking with tightness in their throat. Everyone says the same thing: 'I should win because I've been myself – what you see is what you get.' Everyone cries. Everyone votes. The winner bursts into tears of gratitude, excitement and something else known only to them. And I watch with mixed feelings – fascination, anticipation, and scepticism. As I watch I'm enjoying the drama of the moment, and judging the reality of what I see on my television screen. This is my viewing experience of *Teen Big Brother*.

During the course of writing this book, I have watched a lot of reality TV, from *Cops* to *Children's Hospital*, *UK's Worst Toilet* to *Survivor*, *Celebrity Detox Camp* to *When Good Times Go Bad 3*. I've seen all of these programmes, and more. But I also watched a lot of reality TV *before* writing this book. And will continue to watch reality TV long after the publication of this book. So, is this a book about my experience of watching reality TV? Like many viewers of reality TV, I only watch certain types of programmes. I like watching *Animal Hospital* because I'm an animal lover, but I dislike *When Animals Attack* because I think it's tacky. I enjoy *Temptation Island* because it is melodramatic, but I don't enjoy *The Bachelor* because it isn't dramatic enough. I love *The Edwardian Country*

House because the characters are engaging, but I have fallen out of love with *Big Brother* because the characters are not engaging enough. If this book were about my personal taste in reality programmes then you might learn a lot about me, but little about the social phenomenon of reality TV.

So, what is this book about? *Reality TV* is about the development of a television genre often called reality TV. Reality TV is a catch-all category that includes a wide range of entertainment programmes about real people. Sometimes called popular factual television, reality TV is located in border territories, between information and entertainment, documentary and drama. Originally used as a category for law and order popular factual programmes containing 'on-scene' footage of cops on the job, reality TV has become the success story of television in the 1990s and 2000s. There are reality TV programmes about everything and anything, from healthcare to hairdressing, from people to pets. There are reality TV formats sold all over the world, from the UK to Uruguay. There are people who love reality TV, and people who love to hate reality TV. Whatever your opinion of *Cops*, *Neighbours from Hell*, *Big Brother*, or *Survivor*, reality TV is here to stay. Rupert Murdoch, the man who gave us Fox TV and *Cops*, even has a channel devoted to the genre – Reality TV – with plans for further popular factual channels in the future. Where Murdoch leads, others follow.

Reality TV is also about the viewing experience of a developing factual television genre. It is commonly assumed that audiences cannot tell the difference between entertainment and information, or fiction and reality in popular factual television. With such concern regarding audiences and reality TV it is necessary to explore the development of this genre, and audience relationships with these types of popular factual output. If this book is about exploring the genre of reality TV, then what audiences have to say about their experience of watching reality programmes is paramount. Audience responses to reality TV can provide invaluable information and analysis for understanding the transitional terrain of the reality genre, and can enhance critical understanding of contemporary television audiences.

RATING REALITY TV

The reality genre has mass appeal. Popular series such as *American Idol* in the USA or *I'm a Celebrity …* in the UK have attracted up to and over 50 per cent of the market share, which means more than half the population of television viewers tuned into these programmes. To achieve such ratings these reality series have to be all round entertainers. The proposed reality cable channel, Reality Central, has signed up more than thirty reality stars to appear on and promote the channel in 2004. According to

Larry Namer, the co-founder of E! Entertainment and Reality Central, there is a large base of reality TV fans: 'to them reality TV is television. It's not a fad.'[1]

In 2000, the reality gameshow *Survivor* rated number one in American network prime time (27 million viewers) and earned CBS during the final three episodes an estimated $50 million in advertising revenue. In 2002, the finale of the reality talent show *American Idol* (Fox, USA) attracted 23 million viewers, and a market share of 30 per cent, with almost half the country's teenage female viewers tuning in to watch the show.[2] In January 2003, *American Idol* drew nearly 25 million viewers two nights running, making it 'the most watched non-sports show in the network's history'.[3] By February 2003, Fox had another winner, this time with the finale of reality dating show *Joe Millionaire*, which drew 40 million viewers, making it almost as popular as the broadcast of the Academy Awards, and 'the highest series telecast on any network since CBS' premiere of *Survivor II* in January 2001'.[4] In comparison, only 15 million viewers watched the number one crime drama series *CSI: Crime Scene Investigation* (CBS), or sitcom *Friends* (NBC), during the same period. Reality programmes regularly win the highest ratings for the majority of half-hour time slots during primetime American television.[5]

Reality TV is just as popular in the UK. In 2000, over 70 per cent of the population (aged 4–65+) watched reality programmes on a regular or occasional basis (Hill/ITC 2000). The types of programmes watched most often by the public in 2000 were: police/crime programmes (e.g. *Police Camera Action!*, ITV1) watched either regularly or occasionally by 72 per cent of adults and 71 per cent of children; 'places' programmes (e.g. *Airport*, BBC1) watched by 71 per cent of adults and 75 per cent of children; and home/garden shows (e.g. *Changing Rooms*, BBC1) watched by 67 per cent of adults and 84 per cent of children. Amongst the under 16s (in particular, the under 13s), pet programmes (e.g. *Animal Hospital*, BBC1) were as popular as the categories cited above – watched by 83 per cent of children and 63 per cent of adults (Hill/ITC 2000). All of these reality programmes have performed strongly in peaktime schedules, and have attracted up to and over a 50 per cent market share.

The highest rated series, such as reality talent show *Pop Idol* (ITV1) or reality gameshow *I'm a Celebrity ... Get Me Out of Here!* (ITV1), attracted over 10 million viewers, which makes such reality series almost as popular as established soap operas such as *Coronation Street* (ITV1). *I'm a Celebrity ...* was so successful it single-handedly changed the profile of its sister digital channel, ITV2, from the 'must not watch channel' to 'the second most-watched channel in multichannel homes at that time after ITV1'.[6] The third series of *I'm a Celebrity ...* attracted record ratings, with a 60 per cent market share for particular episodes (over 15 million viewers). The broadcaster charged approximately £90,000 per 30 second advert, compared to its normal charges of between £40,000 and £50,000 for a similar peaktime advertising slot.[7] Littlewoods, the major gambling organisation in the UK, has signed a five-year interactive television deal with ITV, anticipating that reality series such as *I'm a Celebrity* ... will provide high-level gambling revenues for interactive TV gaming and betting (estimated £2.8 billion per year in total revenue).[8] Television producer Simon Fuller, the creator of *Pop Idol*, 'shot up an astounding 500 places in the *Sunday Times* Rich List [2003], thanks to his £90m fortune, which has grown by £40m' as a result of the success of this reality format and its spin-off music products.[9] *Big Brother* gave Channel 4 its most popular ratings in the history of the UK channel, attracting nearly 10 million viewers in 2000; the second series of *Big Brother* averaged 4.5 million viewers, giving Channel 4 more than a 70 per cent increase on their average broadcast share (Hill 2002). *Big Brother 3* generated over 10 million text messages, and attracted 10 million viewers for its finale.[10] A 30 second advertising spot during *Big Brother 3* cost £40,000, over three times more than for any other show on Channel 4 in 2003 (for example, *Frasier*'s cash value was £14,000 for a 30 second spot).[11]

The picture is the same in many other countries around the world. In the Netherlands, the first *Big Brother* 'became one of the country's top-rated shows within a month, and drew 15 million viewers for its climax on New Year's Eve 1999'.[12] In Spain, more people tuned in to watch *Big Brother* in 2000 than the Champions League semi-final match between Real Madrid and Bayern Munich (Hill 2002). The finale of *Expedition Robinson* (the Swedish version of *Survivor*) was watched by half the Swedish population in 1997.[13] In Norway, a country with a population of 4.3 million, *Pop Idol* (2003) received 3.3 million SMS votes.[14] *Loft Story*, the French version of *Big Brother*, was a ratings hit in 2003 with over 7 million viewers, despite regular demonstrations by 'Activists Against Trash TV' calling for the series to be banned, and carrying placards which read 'With trash TV the people turn into idiots'.[15] The pan-African version of *Big Brother*, produced in Malawi, involved ten contestants from ten different countries and, despite calls by Church groups in several African countries for it to be banned, the show remained popular with viewers who praised it for bridging cultural gaps.[16] The Russian reality gameshow *The House* (*Dom*) enthralled Russian television viewers in 2003, as they watched contestants build a £150,000 five-bedroomed house (the average wage in Russia is less than £150 a month).[17] When a woman won *Big Brother 3* in Australia, Channel Ten attracted twice as many viewers as its main rival, Channel Nine, the number one rated channel (2003).[18] More than 3 million people, about half the population of television viewers in Australia, tuned into the hit reality property series *The Block* on Channel Nine. The series featured the renovation of apartments in Sydney by four couples, who were given a budget and eleven weeks to renovate their properties. After twelve weeks the apartments were auctioned, and the couple with the highest bid won. The conclusion to *The Block* was 'Australia's most watched TV show since the 2000 Sydney Olympics. Only the funeral of Princess Diana drew a bigger audience for a non-sport related program.'[19] The format has been sold to the US Fox network, ITV1 in the UK, TV2 in Denmark, as well as being picked up by broadcasters in Belgium, France, the Netherlands and South Africa. The *Herald-Sun* called *The Block* 'a runaway smash that shows no sign of losing steam'.[20]

There are hundreds of reality TV websites devoted to keeping viewers informed about a range of reality programmes, related merchandise, news, and fan activities. RealityTVplanet.com has a reality TV calendar with up-to-the-minute scheduling information on the latest reality programmes on US television, plus episode summaries, news, a 'what's hot' gossip column, various games, e-cards and bulletin boards. Similarly, realitytvworld.com contains up-to-the-minute schedules, news items, and polls about a range of US reality series. Sirlinksalot contains a site for the reality television genre with selected news items, and websites devoted to US reality series and selected reality series around the world. In the USA alone, sirlinksalot lists a total of 130 reality TV series (during November 2003): 17 reality TV series for ABC, 15 for CBS, 22 for NBC, 25 for Fox, and 20 for MTV, as well as 31 series for other cable channels such as WB Network, UPN, and HBO. Each series has its own list of selected official and unofficial websites. For example, Fox's *Joe Millionaire* (first and second series) has over fifteen sites listed, including Fox's official site, and several fan forums devoted to debate about 'who will he choose?' and Joe's 'manly thoughts'.

One of the reasons the reality genre has been so powerful in the television market is that it appeals to younger adults in particular. For example, reality gameshows and talent shows in the USA are especially popular with 'young viewers who have watched reality shows in far bigger numbers than anything else on television and are the consumers most coveted by advertisers'.[21] Fox reality specials, such as *World's Worst Drivers Caught on Tape 2*, specifically attract males aged 18–49, a coveted demographic group for advertisers.[22] In the UK, reality gameshows such as *Big Brother* specifically attract upwardly mobile, educated viewers aged 16–34, the target audience for Channel 4 who shows the series (Hill 2002). A national survey conducted in 2000 indicated that 16- to 34-year-olds were twice as likely to have watched *Big Brother* as older viewers. In addition, viewers with higher income jobs, college education and access to the internet were more likely to watch *Big Brother* than those with lower incomes, no college education or access to the internet (Hill 2002).

Economic change in the US syndication market is another factor in the success of reality programming. As a result of the deregulation of the financial interest and syndication rules during the past decade, larger corporations have bought up many local stations. Local stations provided a significant revenue source for independent producers, who would sell programmes specifically made for local stations, and/or programmes that had previously been aired on network stations. Stacey Lynn Koerner, executive vice-president and director of global research for Initiative, commented:

> Syndication is a victim of big corporate mergers and ever-expanding station groups. This makes it pretty hard for independent producers to get new programmes on the air because there are so few time periods to be filled by programming not already locked in by their owners.[23]

One result of these changes to ownership of local stations is that less non-network drama is being made for syndication. Reality programming provides a cheap alternative to drama. Typically, an hour-long drama can cost approximately $1.5m (£875,000) per hour, whereas reality programmes can cost as little as $200,000 (£114,000) per hour.[24] Reality programming is cheaper to make than drama because it involves a smaller production crew for non-scripted programming, few scriptwriters or professional actors, and non-unionised crews.[25] Reality programmes are therefore economically attractive to local stations and networks. For example, the ratings success of the reality makeover format *Queer Eye for the Straight Guy* on Bravo (a small cable channel) ensured its crossover to network NBC (its parent company). For NBC, *Queer Eye for the Straight Guy* is a win–win situation, as it is relatively cheap to make compared to drama, and has proved itself in the cable/network marketplace.

According to the *New York Times*, reality programming is so popular it has changed the economics of the television industry. The ratings success of network reality series such as *Americal Idol* or *Joe Millionaire* has ensured that some television executives are 'ready to embrace plans for a radical restructuring of the network business.'[26] Such restructuring may involve the provision of new programming fifty-two weeks of the year, a reduction in scripted series by Hollywood studios, and an increase in product placement within programmes. As television writer Stephen Godcheaux points out 'you have a playboy bunny being dipped into a vat of spiders. What kind of fictitious script can compete with this?'[27] Network executives are publicly cautious about their commitment to reality programming. Leslie Moonves, president of CBS Television, warns 'reality programming has been called the crack cocaine of programming. It gives you a quick fix but it depends on the quality of the program and the longevity of the program.'[28] But, the *New York Times* suggests, 'even as executives scorn the genre, TV networks still rely on reality' to rescue ailing network television.[29] Catherine Mackay, regional chief executive US, Australasia and Asia for Freemantle Media, claims

> the networks in the US have realised that a reality show can grab a primetime audience just as effectively as a good drama or comedy, but sometimes at half the price. Reality shows are a lot cheaper to make, and yet they are getting just as many eyeballs in many instances and, sometimes, even more because of the event nature of these shows.[30]

DEBATING REALITY TV

Since the early days of reality programming, critics have consistently attacked the genre for being voyeuristic, cheap, sensational television. Articles such as 'Danger: Reality TV can Rot Your Brain', 'Ragbag of Cheap Thrills' or 'TV's Theatre of Cruelty' are typical of the type of commentary that dominates discussion of reality programming.[31] With series such as When Animals Attack advertised with the image of a snarling dog and the words 'Lassie He Ain't', reality programmes are targets for all that is thought to be wrong with commercial television.[32] In a UK report for the Campaign for Quality Television in 2003, reality TV was singled out by Michael Tracey of the University of Colorado as the 'stuff of the vulgate', encouraging 'moral and intellectual impoverishment in contemporary life'.[33] Robert Thompson of Syracuse University suggests that reality TV is popular 'because it's stupid and moronic'.[34] Broadcaster Nick Clarke argues in his book The Shadow of a Nation that the popularity of reality TV has led to a dangerous blurring of boundaries between fact and fiction, and as a result reality TV has had a negative effect on modern society. As one critic commented: 'In essence, this may as well be network crack: reality TV is fast, cheap and totally addictive ... the shows [are] weapons of mass distraction ... causing us to become dumber, fatter, and more disengaged from ourselves and society.'[35] The mixed metaphors of drug addiction and war indicate how the reality genre is often framed in relation to media effects and cultural, social and moral values.

Such criticism of reality TV fails to take into account the variety of formats within the reality genre. To say that all reality TV is stupid and moronic is to ignore the development of the genre over the past decade. There are infotainment formats, such as 999, that contain stories of emergency services rescue operations as well as advice to the public regarding first aid; there are surveillance reality formats, such as House of Horrors, that contain investigative stories of consumer-based issues; there are fly-on-the-wall docu-soap formats, such as Airport, that show behind the scenes of people's everyday lives in an international airport; there are lifestyle formats, such as *Changing Rooms*, that contain stories of do-it-yourself (DIY) makeovers as well as ideas on interior design; there are reality game formats, such as *Survivor*, that show ordinary people in emotionally and physically challenging situations; there are reality life experiment formats, such as *Faking It*, that contain stories of personal and professional transformation; there are reality talent formats, such as *Popstars*, that transform ordinary people into celebrity performers; there are celebrity reality formats, such as *I'm a Celebrity …* , that transform D-list celebrity performers into C-list celebrity performers; and there are reality clipshow formats, such as *When Animals Attack*, that show spectacular stories of crime, accidents and near-death experiences. The type of reality programming that was associated with the genre in the early 1990s (unscripted, on-scene footage of crime and emergency services) has expanded to include a range of formats with distinctive programme characteristics.

The development of reality programming within different broadcasting environments is also significant to our understanding of the genre as a whole. In the UK, the strong historical presence of public service broadcasting and documentary television has ensured that certain types of reality formats are related to public service and documentary ideas and practice. The same can be said of other Northern European countries with public service and documentary traditions (see Kilborn 2003; Winston 2000). In comparison, the strong historical presence of commercial broadcasting and the weak historical presence of documentary television in the USA has ensured that certain types of reality formats are related to commercial and entertainment ideas and practice. Although this is a crude comparison, it serves to highlight the culturally specific nature of reality programming, and the development of particular formats within different broadcasting environments. Even when reality formats such as *Big Brother* are bought and sold in the global marketplace, the individual series are located in specific cultural and production contexts. Different types of reality formats may share programme characteristics, such as caught on camera footage, or stories about ordinary people, but the reality genre is made up of diverse and distinctive subgenres, that are 'evolving … by a process both of "longitudinal" subgeneric developments and intensive cross-fertilization with other formats' (Corner 2002b: 260).

In addition, whilst certain reality programmes perform well in the ratings, others do not. For example, *Joe Millionaire* was very successful, but *Married by America*, a similar reality relationship format, was 'consigned … to a ratings coma'.[36] *American Idol*, brainchild of Simon Fuller, was also a ratings winner, but his spin-off reality talent format *All American Girl* was met with 'wholesale rejection' by the American public.[37] According to one critic of *All American Girl*: 'we've seen enough reality shows to expect a certain amount of smoke and mirrors. What I – and America – will not tolerate is a programme that treats us with more contempt than its own contestants.'[38] Reality TV may be popular, but audiences are able to make distinctions between what they perceive to be good and bad reality programming. After public protest about a proposed real-life version of *The Beverly Hillbillies*, CBS president Les Moonves admitted there are limits to public taste in reality programming.[39] When audiences watch reality TV they are not only watching programmes for entertainment, they are also engaged in critical viewing of the attitudes and behaviour of ordinary people in the programmes, and the ideas and practices of the producers of the programmes. As John Ellis points out, audiences of reality programming are involved in exactly the type of debates about cultural and social values that critics note are missing from the programmes themselves: 'on the radio, in the press, in everyday conversation, people argue the toss over "are these people typical?" and "are these really our values?" '.[40]

Scholarly research on reality TV has been somewhat thin on the ground until recent years. Early studies into the then emerging phenomenon of reality TV focused primarily on the definition of the genre, and its relationship with other types of television genres. Work by Bill Nichols (1994), John Corner (1995, 1996) and Richard Kilborn (1994, 1998) on the status of reality programming within factual television is particularly useful in highlighting early debates about the factual and fictional elements of the reality genre. In many ways, such early debates about the 'reality' of reality TV raised important questions about actuality and the epistemology of factual television that have still not been answered today. Much of the work of Nichols, Corner and Kilborn was related to positioning an emergent and hybrid genre within the arena of documentary television, and within existing academic debates about documentary studies. For Corner and Kilborn the issues they raised about the characteristics of reality programming and the impact of popular factual television on the future of documentary television are issues they have continued to address in their contemporary work. Both scholars have written extensively about the changing nature of audio-visual documentation, and the role reality TV has to play in opening up debate about the truth claims of factual television (Corner 2002a, 2002b; Kilborn 2003). Although Corner and Kilborn are critical of aspects of reality programming, they recognise that its popularity over the past decade cannot be ignored by scholars in documentary studies.

Recent work by scholars in documentary studies and cultural studies suggests that the reality genre is a rich site for analysis and debate. Brian Winston (2000) in his book *Lies, Damn Lies and Documentaries* addresses the legal and ethical framework to documentary television, and argues for greater responsibility for the making and regulating of factual programmes. Jon Dovey (2000) in his book *Freakshow* considers genres such as true confessions and docu-soaps as examples of first-person media, a type of media that often foregrounds private issues at the expense of wider public debate about social and political issues. John Ellis (2000, 2002) in his book *Seeing Things* argues that genres such as chat shows or documentaries invite us to witness the modern world, and through this process understand the world around us. John Hartley in his book *The Uses of Television* (1999) suggests that popular factual programmes can teach us how to become do-it-yourself citizens, how to live together in contemporary society. Gareth Palmer (2003) in his book *Discipline and Liberty* considers the surveillance context to many popular factual programmes, and argues that television's use of CCTV raises important issues about our civil liberties. Jane Roscoe and Craig Hight (2001) in their book *Faking It* examine mock-documentary as an example of popular factual forms that play with boundaries of fact and fiction, and question the status of audio-visual documentation. Su Holmes and Deborah Jermyn (2003) in their edited collection *Understanding Reality Television* examine the economic, aesthetic and cultural contexts to the genre.

These selected examples of research in the emerging genre of reality TV illustrate how debate about the genre need not be dominated by arguments about dumbing down, or voyeur TV. Whilst these debates can be found in media discussion of reality TV, many academic scholars have moved the debate to fresh terrain. Along with a variety of other scholars in media studies, such as Arild Fetveit (2002), Nick Couldry (2002), Frances Bonner (2003) and Ib Bondebjerg (2002), discussion about reality TV is now rich and varied. With edited collections such as those by Friedman (2002), Mathjis *et al.* (2004), and Holmes and Jermyn (2003) on a range of reality programmes the stage is set for further directions in the reality TV debate.

My own research contributes to the body of existing work on the production, content and reception of reality TV. My previous research in crime and emergency services reality programming (Hill 2000b, 2000c), along with an edited collection on *Big Brother* (Hill and Palmer 2002; Hill 2002), represents a move to situate the audience in debate about reality TV. In this sense, this book follows directly on from my previous interests in the critical reception of reality programmes. Throughout this book I situate my own research in audiences of reality programming in relation to existing knowledge and debate about the reality genre in documentary, media and cultural studies. My hope is that the research findings, as outlined in this book, provide a useful contribution to the thoughtful and illuminating research by other scholars that I have already briefly mentioned. The focus of this book is to examine the viewing experience of reality TV. Just as there is a range of programmes and formats that make up the reality genre, so too is there a range of strategies and responses that make up the viewing experience of different types of reality programmes. What is often missing from the great debate about reality TV, and its impact on television and its audience, are the voices of people who watch reality programmes. There is much to learn from listening to audience discussion about a popular and rapidly changing television genre. To that end I draw upon my own research in television audiences and reality programming in order to foreground the role of the audience in our understanding of reality TV.

RESEARCHING REALITY TV

The research presented in this book is drawn from a multi-method research project I conducted during 2000–2001. The research aim was to provide information and analysis regarding viewing preferences and strategies across all age ranges for a variety of reality programming, available on terrestrial, satellite, cable and digital television in the UK. The research was funded by the public organisation the Economic and Social Research Council, the regulatory body The Independent Television Commission (now Ofcom), and the television company Channel 4. The research also received support from the Broadcasting Standards Commission (now Ofcom), the BBC, and Channel 5 (now Five). I used quantitative and qualitative audience research methods, in conjunction with analysis of the scheduling, content and form of reality programmes. The data from the quantitative survey, conducted using the national representative sample (over 9,000 respondents aged 4–65+) of the Broadcasters' Audience Research Board (BARB), enabled me to gather a large amount of information on audience preferences for form and content within reality programming, and audience attitudes to issues such as privacy, accuracy, information and entertainment. On the basis of what I learnt about audience attitudes towards and preferences concerning reality programming in the survey, I used qualitative focus groups to explore key issues such as authenticity and performance, information and entertainment, and the social context to watching reality programming. I used quota sampling to recruit (self-defined) regular viewers of a range of reality programming. There were twelve groups, consisting of male/female viewers, aged 11–44, in the social category C1C2DE (skilled and working class, and lowest level of subsistence), living in the south-east of England. I also conducted family in-depth interviews over a six-month period, observing family viewing practices, and the relationship between scheduling, family routine, and content of reality programmes. There were four visits to ten families living in the south-east of England. Appendices 1 and 2 provide more detailed discussion of research design, data collection and analysis.

BOOK OUTLINE

The book is organised according to the central theme of the viewing experience of reality TV. Chapter 2 charts the rise of reality TV at a time when broadcasters were looking for quick solutions to economic problems within the industry. The chapter uncovers the roots of the reality genre in tabloid journalism, popular entertainment, and in particular documentary television, which has struggled to survive in a commercially driven broadcast environment. The chapter defines the main formats within the reality genre – infotainment, docu-soaps, lifestyle and reality gameshows – and critically examines how these various hybrid formats have ensured high ratings in peaktime schedules. Chapter 3 provides an overview of the various ways the television industry, scholars and audiences classify reality TV. The chapter argues that there is no one definition of reality programming, but many competing definitions of what has come to be called the reality genre. The chapter draws on discussion by members of the television industry about classifying reality programming, by scholars about the development of reality programming, and by audiences about the viewing experience of reality programming in order to suggest it is vital to differentiate between the rapidly expanding range of programming that comes under the category of reality TV, and to locate the reality genre within a broader understanding of general factual, and indeed fictional, television.

Chapters 4 and 5 focus on audience discussion of the twin themes of performance and authenticity, and information and entertainment within reality programming. Chapter 4 argues that contemporary reality programmes, especially reality gameshows and docu-soaps, are concerned with self-display. These reality programmes encourage a variety of performances from non-professional actors (as contestants, as TV personalities) and this level of self-display ensures that audiences perceive such programmes as 'performative'. The manner in which ordinary people perform in different types of reality programmes is subject to intense scrutiny by audiences. Most viewers expect ordinary people to 'act up' for the cameras in the majority of reality programming. These expectations do not, however, stop audiences from assessing how true or false the behaviour of ordinary people can be in reality programmes. The chapter analyses how speculation about the performance of ordinary people can lead to critical viewing practices, in particular regarding the authenticity of certain types of reality programming. Chapter 5 critically examines the changing role of information in popular factual television. The chapter assesses how audiences judge the informative elements in popular factual television, and whether information is valued in hybrid formats which draw on fictional or leisure formats for entertainment. The chapter argues that reality formats can provide practical and social learning opportunities within an entertainment frame. However, viewers make a distinction between more traditional types of reality programming and contemporary reality programming, and overall are critical of the idea of learning from watching reality programming.

The next two chapters are concerned with family viewers of reality programming. Chapter 6 examines the relationship between ethics and reality TV. Ethics is about how we ought to live our lives, and much reality programming is concerned with good and bad ways to live. The chapter focuses on a particular type of ethical reasoning, an ethics of care, that has its origins in traditional moral philosophy about care of the self, and modern ethical writing on social ethics and rights ethics. The chapter outlines the concept of an ethics of care, and examines an ethics of care as it is developed in the content of certain popular reality formats, and as it is discussed by family viewers. Chapter 7 is an extended case study of one popular example of reality programming for family viewers – pet programmes. The chapter explores reality programming concerned with the ill health, ill-treatment, recovery, and in extreme cases, death of companion animals, and argues that the central address of pet programmes relates to an ethics of care. Families, especially children and mothers, watch pet programmes in order to understand socially acceptable treatment of pets. The sentimental stories of pets in crisis highlight the morally charged arena of human–animal relations, and mark the transformation of the cultural meaning of pets in the late twentieth century from 'lifestyle accessories' to valued 'members of the family'. In addition, such stories of pets in crisis raise ethical issues concerning the politics of animal suffering, and the politics of viewing animal suffering on television.

The concluding Chapter 8 presents an overview of key concepts, issues and arguments discussed throughout the book. The chapter examines the tensions and contradictions in the way audiences respond to a reality genre in transition. In particular, the chapter argues for greater understanding of the categorisation of reality programming, the idea of learning from reality programming, and the relationship between ethics and reality programming. The chapter also outlines the role of critical viewing within audience responses to different types of reality programming, and suggests that audience debate about reality programmes can only be healthy for the development of the reality genre and its relationship with other types of factual and fictional television.

Chapter 2

The rise of reality TV

Successful reality TV series such as *Survivor* or *Big Brother* are marketed as 'all new' – new concepts, new formats, new experiences. Few television shows are 'all new'. But it is certainly the case that reality programmes draw from existing television genres and formats to create novel hybrid programmes. 'Factual entertainment' is a category commonly used within the television industry for popular factual television, and the category indicates the marriage of factual programming, such as news or documentary, with fictional programming, such as gameshows or soap opera. Indeed, almost any entertainment programme about real people comes under the umbrella of popular factual television. Reality TV is a catch-all category, and popular examples of reality programming, such as *Changing Rooms* (BBC, 1996–), *Cops* (Fox, 1988–), *Animal Hospital* (BBC, 1993–), *Airport* (BBC, 1996–), *Popstars* (ITV, 2001–), or *The Osbournes* (MTV, 2002–), draw on a variety of genres to create ratings winners. It is no wonder that media owner Rupert Murdoch has launched a reality TV channel – there is something for everyone in the reality genre.[1]

The historical development of popular factual television is multifaceted and worthy of a book-length study. There is a growing body of literature that provides excellent analysis of crime reporting (e.g. Fishman and Cavender 1998; Palmer 2003), tabloid journalism (e.g. Langer 1998), documentary (e.g. Nichols 1994, Winston 1995, Corner 1995, Bruzzi 2000, Kilborn 2003, amongst others), docu-drama/drama-doc (e.g. Paget 1998), and mock documentary (e.g. Roscoe and Hight 2001), all of which have a role to play in the development of reality programming. In this chapter, I can only touch on historical, cultural and industrial contexts, as my main intention is to provide an overview of the rise of reality TV throughout the 1990s and 2000s. Out of necessity, my overview is selective, and more detailed discussion of specific formats and theoretical insights into popular factual programming occur in later chapters.

THE ORIGINS OF REALITY TV

Where did reality TV come from? There is no easy answer to this question. The genealogy of popular factual television is convoluted, as the type of hybrid programming we have come to associate with reality TV is difficult to categorise, and has developed within historically and culturally specific media environments. There are three main strands to the development of popular factual television, and these relate to three areas of distinct, and yet overlapping, areas of media production: tabloid journalism, documentary television, and popular entertainment. Production of tabloid journalism and popular entertainment increased during the 1980s. This growth was partly a result of the deregulation and marketisation of media industries in advanced industrial states, such as America, Western Europe and Australasia, and partly a result of an increasingly commercial media environment, where convergence between telecommunications, computers and media ensured competition amongst network, cable and satellite channels for revenue (Hesmondhalgh 2002). This media environment was one within which documentary television struggled to survive. In this chapter, I briefly outline these three main areas of media production, providing nationally specific examples in order to highlight the rise of reality TV within different countries and media industries.

Tabloid journalism

There are particular elements of reality programming which draw on the staple ingredients of tabloid journalism, such as the interplay between ordinary people and celebrities, or information and entertainment. A series such as *America's Most Wanted* (USA, Fox, 1988–) is an example of the type of reality programming often classified as tabloid TV. It is difficult to define tabloid journalism as, like reality TV, it relies on fluidity and hybridity in form and content. John Fiske describes tabloid news as follows: 'its subject matter is that produced at the intersection between public and private life; its style is sensational … its tone is populist; its modality fluidly denies any stylistic difference between fiction and documentary' (1992: 48). The intersections between the public and the private, fact and fiction, highlight how tabloid journalism relies on personal and sensational stories to create informative and entertaining news.

Elizabeth Bird points out: 'journalism's emphasis on the personal, the sensational, and the dramatic is nothing new. Street literature, ballads, and oral gossip and rumor all contribute to the development of news' (2000: 216). For example, true crime stories were distributed through broadsheets, pamphlets and popular ballads during the early modern period in the UK. Trial pamphlets sensationalised the criminal, such as one of 1606 that told of a female robber who 'ripped open the belly of a pregnant woman with a knife and severed her child's tongue' (Biressi 2001: 45–6). *The Newgate Calendar*, first published in 1773, collected such pamphlets into bound volumes, and became so popular it outsold authors such as Charles Dickens. Execution narratives were especially popular because they contained 'something for everyone'; these narratives typically contained true accounts of 'sorrowful lamentation and particulars extracted from press reports or police intelligence' and broadsheets 'carrying details of the trial, confession, execution, verses, woodcut portraits or gallow scenes' (2001: 60). Broadside ballads were sold by street pedlars at markets and fairs, and often contained commentaries on current affairs, and crime in particular. These cheap ballads, (songs that tell a story) were very popular, with thousands in circulaton, and large print runs of specific songs. For example, the 'broadside of William Corder's confession and execution (for the "Red Barn" murder) sold over 1,650,000 copies'.[2] These personal and sensational 'real-life' stories were distributed to the general public through popular media and oral storytelling, and particular cases would become part of everyday conversation and speculation.

The tabloid style of storytelling has come to dominate much popular news. Although news reporting varies from country to country, the success of supermarket tabloids in the USA, or tabloid papers such as the *Sun* in the UK, is an example of how the human-interest story has become a central part of popular journalism. For some critics, such as Glynn, 'tabloid television is the electronic descendant of the déclassé tabloid newspapers that surround US supermarket checkout counters' (2000: 6). Bird (2000: 213) argues that the 'tabloid audience' has moved on from tabloid papers to tabloid TV shows. The popularity of personal storytelling in both television news and print media has contributed to the proliferation of reality programming. As John Langer points out, the 'impulse towards tabloidism' resides in the recirculation of traditional story forms, such as ordinary people doing extraordinary things (1998: 161). It is no surprise therefore to see an impulse towards tabloidism in popular news and popular factual television. Indeed, readers of tabloid papers and viewers of reality TV sometimes mix and match their consumption of news and reality programmes, turning to tabloid news in order to learn more about reality TV series, such as *Big Brother* or *I'm a Celebrity ... Get Me Out of Here!*

Tabloid TV did not develop in a vacuum. In America, early network television gave little consideration to popular news. It was after the quiz show scandals during the 1950s that network newscasts attempted to reach a wider audience, by increasing news and current affairs output and focusing on visual and narrative interest in news stories. During the 1960s 'network news held a privileged and profitable position', but during the 1970s 'local news emerged as a potentially profitable product, evolving into a popular hybrid of traditional hard news and gossipy chat that was often preferred by viewers' (Bird 2000: 214). Developments in technology, such as satellites and Minicams, ensured that local news bulletins could ' "transport" their audiences to the scenes of crimes in progress, unfolding hostage situations, urban shooting sprees, raging fires, and the like' (Glynn 2000: 23). This reliance on raw footage would become a staple ingredient of reality programming. When Rupert Murdoch took advantage of deregulation policies during the Reagan administration and launched the Fox Television Network in the late 1980s, the channel featured programmes, such as *America's Most Wanted* or *Cops*, which took advantage of the growth of popular journalism, especially in local news. Although Kilborn (1994: 426) points out that 'NBC were the first company to get in on the reality act with their *Unsolved Mysteries* (1987–)', it was Fox TV that produced a range of reality programming based on the police and emergency services. Indeed, Fox 'redefined US network practices' (Glynn 2000: 28) by producing cheap reality programming, which could compete in a competitive environment of network, cable and independent broadcasting. By the early 1990s, reality programming was an established part of peaktime network schedules, and other countries were beginning to take note.

Documentary television

In the UK, the rise of reality TV was connected with the success of American tabloid TV and the demise of documentary television. In the 1960s and 1970s, early magazine-style series, such as *Tonight* (BBC, 1957–1965) or *Nationwide* (BBC, 1969–1984), provided a mixture of news and humorous or eccentric stories. These magazine-style programmes were forerunners for much contemporary popular factual television (Brunsdon *et al.* 2001: 51). But it was the introduction of British versions of American reality programming in the early 1990s that began a trend in what was commonly referred to at the time as 'infotainment'. For example, *999* (BBC, 1992–) was modelled on *Rescue 911* (CBS). The difference between *999* and its American cousin is significant in that *999* is made by the BBC, a public service channel that promotes itself as a platform for serious factual programming. As Kilborn points out:

> Given their major preoccupation with the human interest aspect and with their overriding concern with action-packed entertainment, reality programmes such as *999* run the risk of being seen as tabloid television. At a time when the BBC has publicly committed itself to

high-quality, less populist forms of programming, the tabloid label is
one which they will wish to avoid.

(1994: 433)

The BBC's interest in popular factual programming in the early 1990s
was a response to political pressure from the Conservative government in
the 1980s and early 1990s to be a public, i.e. popular, service. This move
from public to popular represented a major threat to the traditional
relationship between documentary and public service broadcasting:

> Public service broadcasting (PSB) traditionally assumed that a
> responsibility to the audience was of more importance than, say, a
> commercial duty to shareholders. In this context, documentary, as a
> quality 'duty genre', flourished even though (or perhaps exactly
> because) it did not achieve mass appeal anywhere until the later
> 1990s. The relaxation and reformulation of PSB allowed broadcasters,
> however funded, to become more like other businesses. It became
> clear, as the ratings became more paramount, that documentary
> presence in the schedules was a real mark of public service
> commitment.
>
> (Winston 2000: 40)

The 1992 Broadcasting Act opened up competition from independent
producers and placed pressure on the BBC to deliver cheaper
programming to the general public. The emergence of reality
programming in the early 1990s came at a time when documentary, along
with news and current affairs, was already under performing in the
ratings. Popular factual programming became a key weapon in the BBC's
successful ratings and scheduling war with its commercial rival ITV.
Reality TV filled a gap in the schedules, but at the expense of more
traditional documentary and current affairs. Indeed, as Kilborn points
out, the BBC's use of its digital channel BBC4 as a space for documentary
suggests that the success of popular factual television on mainstream
channels such as BBC1 is at the expense of 'more challenging types of
documentary work' which have been relocated to digital channels (2003:
48). Another way of looking at the popularity of reality TV is to argue that
its success is possibly the 'price of survival' for contemporary
documentary (Winston 2000: 55). It is certainly the case that the
performance of reality programmes in peaktime schedules has
encouraged schedulers to place some popular documentaries, such as
Jamie's Kitchen (Channel 4, 2002), in peaktime slots to great success.

The relationship between documentary television and reality TV is
cause for concern amongst documentary practitioners and scholars, as the
form and content of programmes such as *999* are somewhat removed

from traditional documentary values. The primary aim of much reality programming is 'that of diversion rather than enlightenment'; and although some makers of reality programmes argue that certain formats can provide social value, it is the case that the reality genre as a whole is designed for entertainment value (Kilborn 2003: 11). And yet it is also the case that popular factual television owes a great deal to documentary television. How does the form and content of documentary television connect with reality programming? There is a relationship between the development of documentary television and the development of reality programming. Although this may be an uneasy relationship, it is nevertheless the case that we cannot understand reality TV without considering its place within the context of other types of audio-visual documentation. Even the category of 'documentary' can be related to the category of 'reality TV' as both categories defy simple definitions. Just as reality TV is a broad category that is difficult to define, the category of documentary also 'escapes any tight generic specification', and 'what we understand by "documentary" is always dependent on the broader context of the kinds of audiovisual documentation currently in circulation' (Corner 2002a: 125).

The types of documentary television directly relevant to reality programming include documentary journalism, documentary realism, and, in particular, observational documentary. Documentary journalism addresses topical subjects in a series format, using journalistic conventions, and usually involving the '"quest" of a presenter/reporter ... "delving behind the headlines"' (Corner 1995: 84). This type of documentary was popular with broadcasters in the 1960s and 1970s because it performed a public service, and programmes could become flagship productions for particular channels, for example *Sixty Minutes* (CBS) in America, or *World in Action* (ITV) in the UK. There are links between tabloid journalism and documentary journalism, as the latter too suffered from the popularity of magazine-style news bulletins and infotainment.

Documentary realism is central to understanding the values of documentary practice. Corner (2001a: 127) outlines two practices within documentary that rely on notions of realism: observational realism, which is a 'set of formal markers that confirm to us that what we are watching ... is a record of an ongoing, and at least partly media-independent, reality', and expositional realism, which is a '"rhetoric of accuracy and truth" that many television documentaries variously draw on'. Both types of realism ask the audience to register the techniques used to observe real life (for example, hand-held cameras), or the way in which an argument is presented to us (for example, the interpretation of evidence). The issues of realism, accuracy and truth in documentary are complex, in terms of both production and theory; and key books, such as

Representing Reality (Nichols 1991) or *Claiming the Real* (Winston 1995), address the epistemological claims of documentary to 'represent real life'. In terms of reality programming, the extent to which programmes such as *Cops* or *Survivor* address issues of realism, accuracy and truth is significant precisely because these programmes do not eschew such values, and yet at the same time are unable to stay within the conventions of documentary realism due to their reliance on entertainment formats, such as soap opera or gameshows.

Popular factual television's conflicting relationship with documentary is especially apparent when we consider observational documentary. This type of documentary emerged from 'direct cinema' in 1960s America, 'cinema vérité' in 1960s France, and 'fly-on-the-wall' documentary television in 1970s Britain. Stella Bruzzi comments that observational documentary relies on the use of lightweight, portable cameras and 'tends to deal with current events, events that are unfolding in front of the camera' (2001: 130). This technique clearly influenced the 'fly-on-the-wall' feel of docu-soaps. Documentaries such as *An American Family* (Craig Gilbert, USA, 1972), or *Police* (Roger Graef, UK, 1982) are antecedents to docu-soaps such as *The Real World* (USA, MTV, 1991–), or *The Cruise* (UK, BBC, 1998). As Winston (2000: 55) remarks: 'the docusoap technique represents a bastardisation of television's usual vérité bastardisation'. There are even traces of observational documentary in reality gameshows such as *Big Brother*, although its claims to observe real life are heavily subsumed within the gameshow format.

Other types of documentary have influenced reality programming, such as reflexive/performative documentaries, docu-drama and mock documentaries. Reflexive documentaries contain a self-conscious reference to generic conventions; performative documentaries blur boundaries between fact and fiction (Nichols 1991, 1994). Both types of documentary rely on dramatic techniques, including parody and irony, to question the genre. Docu-drama and mock documentary take this questioning of the documentary genre one stage further. Docu-drama uses a fictional setting in order to present a sequence of events as truthful, by drawing on generic conventions within documentary (Paget 1998). Mock documentary takes 'a fictive stance towards the social world, while utilising documentary aesthetics to "mock" the underlying discourses of documentary' (Roscoe and Hight 2001: 44). Reflexivity, performance, and boundaries between fact and fiction are all hallmarks of reality programming, and are discussed in more detail in later chapters.

Popular entertainment

As with tabloid journalism and documentary television, popular entertainment defies categorisation. It is an umbrella term that includes a collection of programmes that come from different industrial contexts, and which are primarily entertaining. For my purposes, popular entertainment refers to programmes such as talkshows, gameshows, sports and leisure programming, all of which are part of the development of popular factual television. These popular entertainment programmes include interaction between non-professional actors and celebrities, although increasingly non-professional actors are often treated as celebrities in their own right in such programmes. Many of these programmes also contain interactive elements, drawing a studio audience, and viewers at home, directly into a programme, usually as respondents or judges to the activities of the non-professional actors/celebrities. In addition, talk shows, gameshows, sports and leisure programming often perform well within the international broadcasting market, with successful formats sold worldwide, and locally produced to nationally specific requirements. Perhaps one of the best-known examples of a popular entertainment series about ordinary people is *Candid Camera* (CBS, 1948–), which began on radio, and transferred to TV to become one of the top ten US network shows during the 1960s, spawning imitators around the world. *Candid Camera* was also a format familiar to UK audiences in the 1950s, presented by Jonathan Routh in the early years of ITV, the first commercial channel in the UK.

Beginning with the talk show, the celebrity talk show has been a staple of late night programming in America since the success of *The Tonight Show* (NBC, 1954–) in the 1950s. Its offspring, the confessional talk show, has dominated daytime American TV since the 1980s. It is the celebrity talk show's interaction with the studio audience that is most relevant to reality programming, especially in the way 'it allows for a seemingly "democratic" moment as average people are given a similar treatment to the celebrity guests' (Shattuc 2001a: 83). As the celebrity guest gave way to 'average people', the studio audience became even more active in the 'issue-orientated', emotionally laden stories that became a trademark of confessional talk shows, such as *The Oprah Winfrey Show* (NBC, 1984–). Confessional talk shows encapsulate a 'tension between commercial tabloid exploitation and the politicisation of the private sphere' (Shattuc 2001b: 84). This tension between entertainment imperatives within television programming and the use of personal stories within public debate is also apparent in reality programming. There are connections between a format such as *The Jerry Springer Show* (1991–) and a format such as *Big Brother* as both formats focus on interpersonal conflict, emotion and sexual titillation (Shattuc 2001b).

The gameshow has long been a staple of television schedules for two reasons: it is 'cheap and easy to produce' and is 'extremely exportable' (Boddy 2001: 80). The example of *Who Wants to be a Millionaire?* (UK, ITV, 1999–) illustrates the gameshow's potential to dominate schedules around the world, and generate huge profits for broadcasting channels – the format, which originated in Britain, was sold to more than seventy countries in the space of a few years (2001: 81). The gameshow format contains several aspects which work well when transported to popular factual programming: 'the various television quiz formats turn around different calibrations of luck, knowledge and skill, and almost all offer the spectacle of ordinary people facing life-transforming decisions in extended real time' (2001: 80). A series such as *Survivor* (UK, ITV, 2000–) relies on contestants facing life-transforming decisions in order to 'survive', both physically, emotionally and in relation to the game. The format for reality gameshows is also highly exportable. For example, the Dutch format house Endemol have sold the format for *Big Brother* worldwide, to countries including Germany, Spain, America, Argentina, South Africa and Australia.

'Sports television does not constitute a single genre, but rather a mix of different forms of television production practice' (Brookes 2001: 87). These production practices include live sports events, sports journalism, sporting advertisements and other kinds of promotion. According to Brookes a typical sports event will combine a range of television production practices, from 'introductory titles through an opening video segment, to a news feature segment on the teams or individuals involved … to expert discussion panels, into the game proper, and finally interviews with the participants' (2001: 88). A similar mixture of production practices can be found in reality gameshows such as *Survivor*, which features introductory titles through an opening video segment of the participants in survival mode, news on the latest actions of the participants, discussion by expert psychologists and other commentators, the challenges proper, and finally interviews with the winner and losers. In addition to the use of similar production practices to sporting events, reality programming draws on the drama and excitement of sports television, highlighting particular characters, or personalities, and their actions within the spectacle of the reality programme. Mike Darnell, producer of Fox TV specials such as *World's Scariest Police Chases* and *Surviving the Moment of Impact*, deliberately draws on sports television to generate adrenaline in viewers when watching his reality programmes.[3]

Leisure programming refers to a strand of television usually associated with daytime television. Historically, daytime television arose out of a commercialised interest in domesticity during the 1950s, and addressed a female viewer about domestic duties and leisure interests (Hartley 2001a). Brunsdon *et al.* (2001) discuss the relationship between leisure programming and popular factual television. In Britain, leisure and instructional programming in the 1970s were generally about gardening, cooking, dress making and DIY, 'all of which imply a narrative of transformation' which is associated with 'skills acquisition' (Brunsdon *et al.* 2001: 54). Contemporary lifestyle programming picks up on this 'narrative of transformation', subordinating the instructional address in order to foreground the responses of 'real people' to this transformation: 'thus the viewer is shown how to perform certain operations but the emphasis of the programme, what the producers call "the reveal", is when the transformed person or place is shown to their nearest and dearest and the audience' (2001: 55). Indeed, 'the affective close-up … comes from gameshows', and is further instance of the interconnections within popular entertainment and popular factual television (ibid.).

One final area of television production to address here is popular fictional programming such as soap operas or melodrama. Although these fictional genres do not technically fit within the category of popular entertainment as it includes non-fictional programming, they are nevertheless significant popular and entertaining genres that have been influential on the development of reality programming. Briefly, soap operas are serial narratives. The core feature of soap opera is its ability to package 'the experience of fiction over an extended period of time, in segments' (McCarthy 2001: 47). Two different traditions of soap opera, that of realist soap opera in Britain (e.g. *Coronation Street*) and melodramatic soap opera in America (e.g. *The Young and the Restless*), have had an impact on reality programming. The way in which realist soap opera attempts to represent social realities within popular television can be directly related to the docu-soap, a reality format that combines observational documentary techniques with serial narrative techniques of soap opera. The way in which melodramatic soap opera attempts to represent heightened or sensational realities within popular television can be directly related to reality gameshows about relationships, such as *Joe Millionaire*, that combine observational documentary techniques with sensational narrative techniques of soap opera. Docu-soaps and reality gameshows encourage participants to 'indulge in gossipy, soap-like forms of interchange' and 'maintain narrative pace and interest' by switching 'the focus of attention from one group of characters to another' (Kilborn 2003: 82). In addition, other types of fictional genres, such as crime genres or hospital genres, have also been influential on reality formats (see Chapter 7 for a discussion of the influence of medical drama on animal-based reality programming).

To summarise, popular factual television has developed during a period of cross fertilisation with tabloid journalism, documentary television and popular entertainment. The late 1980s and 1990s were a period of increased commercialisation and deregulation within the media industries. As audiences have shopped around, channel surfing between terrestrial, satellite/cable and digital channels, broadcasters (and narrowcasters) have looked to produce cheap, often locally made, factual programming which is attractive to general (and niche) viewers. The development of reality programming is an example of how television cannibalises itself in order to survive, drawing on existing genres to create successful hybrid programmes, which in turn generate a 'new' television genre.

REALITY TV ARRIVES

Although examples of reality TV can be found throughout the history of television, reality programmes arrived *en masse* in peaktime television schedules during the 1990s. The first wave of reality programming was based upon the success of crime and emergency services reality TV, or 'infotainment', and travelled from America to Europe and beyond in the late 1980s to early 1990s. The second wave of reality programming was based upon the success of popular observational documentaries, or 'docu-soaps', and lifestyle programming involving house and garden makeovers, and travelled from Britain to Europe and beyond in the mid- to late 1990s. The third wave was based upon the success of social experiments that placed ordinary people in controlled environments over an extended period of time, or 'reality gameshows', and travelled from Northern Europe to Britain, America and the rest of the world during the early 2000s. The current wave of reality programming is a free-for-all, with America leading the way with crime and relationship reality programming, Britain and Australia forging ahead with lifestyle and social experiment reality programming, and Northern Europe developing variations of the reality gameshow.

Infotainment

To begin at the beginning, infotainment, also called 'tabloid TV', began life as one-off programmes in various countries, but became popular on American network television after NBC aired the 'on-scene' reality series *Unsolved Mysteries* in 1987. Raphael (1997: 107) notes 'the international spread of Reali-TV cannot be explained as the outcome of US product innovation, since many European and Japanese programs pre-dated their US counterparts'. For example, *Crimewatch UK* (BBC) was first aired in 1984, and was in turn modelled on the German programme *AktenzeichenXY … Ungelöst* (ZDF, 1967–). Although *Crimewatch UK* was successful (in 1984 it commanded audiences of over 9 million) and inspired imitators, it did not create a landslide in reality programming. In America, on the other hand, producers of reality programming quickly grasped the potential of infotainment to boost ratings at home, and increase foreign export revenues (Raphael 1997). After the success of

Unsolved Mysteries, other networks followed suit. By 1991, *Variety* estimated there were over thirty reality programmes on air:

> At any time of the day or night, a viewer can tune in to emergency rescues, sex scandals, re-enactments of grisly crimes, unwary bystanders stumbling into practical jokes recorded by hidden cameras, and salacious pseudo-gameshows centred on none-too-subtle sexual voyeurism ... the broadcast networks are scheduling more of them than at any other time in TV history, mainly because an hour-long reality series typically costs about $500,000 an episode, only half of what the networks pay in license fees for a 60 minute dramatic series.
>
> (Dempsey 1991: 32)

The downsides to reality TV – low profits in off-network syndication markets and cautious advertisers (Raphael 1997) – were more than compensated for by economic and ratings success. In the 1991–1992 US season, viewers could tune into *America's Most Wanted* and *Cops* on Fox, *Rescue 911* and *Top Cops* on CBS, *Unsolved Mysteries* and *Expose* on NBC, and *FBI: the Untold Stories* on ABC (Raphael 1997: 109). The majority of these reality series were not deficit-financed which represented a major turnaround from the deficit-financed drama productions of the mid-1980s, when producers lost up to $100,000 per episode for half-hour shows (1997: 103). The economic success of reality TV ensured that producers developed new variations on existing formats. For example, the format for emergency services reality programming was popular in the mid-1990s, with reality series such as *Coastguard*, about adventures on US waterways, or *Extreme*, about a mountain rescue team in Utah, competing alongside familiar series such as *Rescue 911*.[4] Kilborn calls these types of reality programmes Accident and Emergency (A & E) formats, as they contain recurring stories of heroism and bravery by ordinary people who work for accident and emergency services (2003: 55).

European broadcasters were quick to pick up on the success of infotainment in America. Some American programmes were acquired by European broadcasters, such as *Rescue 911* which was aired in Germany and Denmark. More often formats were sold, or copied, in order to make locally produced versions of American reality TV. Kilborn (1994: 430) notes that local resistance to 'American-style reality' TV ensured 'styles and forms ... evolved which are more in tune with national or cultural priorities'. The success of European versions of American reality formats illustrates reality TV's strong performance within the global television market.

To illustrate how reality TV formats 'have legs', I want to profile its early arrival in the UK, marked by the launch of *999* by the BBC in 1992.

I have discussed this series elsewhere, and its reception by the press and viewers (see Hill 2000b, 2000c). The reality series *999* uses reconstructions and found footage to tell stories of rescue operations by emergency services personnel and ordinary people. The series combines a public service address to the viewer concerning information about first aid with a melodramatic narrative of accident and rescue. Peter Salmon was part of the original production team for *Crimewatch UK*, which he described as 'a Frankenstein's monster', and became the producer of *999*, arguably the bride of Frankenstein (Murrell 1992: 48). Critics looked on with horror as the BBC created *999* in order to popularise its factual output; press reviews commented on the programme's 'lust for gore' and even BBC executives questioned the use of sensational stories of accident and rescue in a public service broadcasting factual series (Hill 2000b: 196). An article in *Television Week* commented on the arrival of *999* in relation to other reality programmes:

> Fly-on-the-wall, or vérité, documentary has been with us for decades, and *Crimewatch UK* is approaching its tenth series, but BBC Bristol's *999*, which launched last week, the *Crimewatch* spin-off *Crime Limited*, and Michael Winner's *True Crimes* from LWT suggest that, as a scheduling tool, reality television has now arrived.
>
> (Murrell 1992: 48)

These types of programmes mainly attracted older, low-income viewers, unlike US reality TV that 'cut across a lot of demographics'.[5] They were also not cheap to produce. For example, *999* cost double the amount of *Rescue 911*, approximately £100,000 per 45-minute episode. But with ratings as high as 11 million, television producers were willing to pay the price (ibid.).

If we compare ten years of factual output from 1984 to 1994, we can see the ripple effect created by the introduction of *999*. In 1984, the top rated factual programmes were natural history specials such as *Survival* (ITV/Anglia, 11.3 million) and *The Living Planet* (BBC, 9.9 million). The other types of top-rated factual programmes included the clip show *Automania* (ITV/Central, 9.7 million), the observational documentary *28 Up* (ITV/Granada, 9.4 million), and the infotainment series *Crimewatch UK* (BBC, 9.1 million), all of which were in-house productions. In 1994, the top-rated factual programmes were dominated by infotainment series such as *Police Stop!* (ITV/Carlton, 13.4 million), *Police Camera Action!* (ITV/Carlton, 13.2 million), *999 Lifesavers* (BBC1, 10.2 million), *Crimewatch UK* (9.7 million), and *Special Babies* (ITV/Carlton, 9.3 million), three of which were independent productions.[6] In 1984, there was only one factual series in the top 20 about emergency services (*Crimewatch UK*), by

1994 there were twelve.[7] Not only did infotainment dominate factual output from the BBC, it also dominated commercial networks. Phillips noted the number of tabloid-style series on offer from ITV during a period of decline in factual output:

> ITV transmitted 71 peaktime documentaries in 1996–1999, fewer than one a fortnight. On average they were seen by 7.19 million viewers, an audience share of 32 per cent, which is six percentage points below ITV's overall share on the nights they appeared … in reality most of the more successful programmes are not Prix Italia candidates. Nine of the Top 20 are in the *From Hell* occasional series: catalogues of conduct-unbecoming from different sources, which sometimes offered advice to victims but more often merely wallowed in the awfulness.
>
> (2000: 42)

With markets shares of up to 50 per cent for the *From Hell* series (neighbours, holidays, nannies, builders, drivers, traffic jams, and even garages from hell!), it would take a brave controller to limit the number of infotainment shows in factual programming. As we have seen, during the mid-1990s, public service and commercial channels were more than happy to place popular factual programmes in peaktime schedules (Phillips 2000).

Docu-soap and lifestyle

The docu-soap emerged as an alternative, in some ways complementary, popular factual slot to infotainment in the UK. Docu-soaps, also called 'fly-on-the-wall' documentaries, 'soap-docs', or 'reality-soaps', became the 'motor of peaktime' during the mid- to late 1990s (Phillips 1999a: 23). There were as many as sixty-five docu-soaps broadcast on the main channels between 1995 and 1999, attracting audiences of up to 12 million. Docu-soaps were so popular that the term even made it into the *Oxford Dictionary* (1999a: 22). The docu-soap is a combination of observational documentary, and character-driven drama. One TV producer explained: 'We'd seen that flashing bluelight documentaries could work, but many of the latest ones are factual soaps, very character-led … nothing seems to be too mundane. It's the technique of a soap opera brought into documentaries' (Biddiscomb 1998: 16). Although there had been predecessors to the docu-soap, namely Paul Watson's *The Family* (BBC, 1974) or Craig Gilbert's *An American Family* (PBS, 1973) it was its 'prioritisation of entertainment over social commentary' that made the docu-soap so different from observational documentary, and perforce popular with general viewers (Bruzzi 2001: 132).

It was the BBC who, once again, became the driving force in the production of docu-soaps. A year after the arrival of *999*, the BBC aired *Children's Hospital*, a fly-on-the-wall documentary which had all the hallmarks of a docu-soap (see Hill 2000c for further discussion). Its personal, melodramatic stories appealed to viewers, with more than 8 million tuning in to the first series, despite widespread criticism from the press (Hill 2000c). In 1995, the BBC aired *HMS Brilliant* which attracted a 40 per cent share during midweek, and proceeded to swamp the peaktime schedules with half-hour docu-soaps, which usually aired between 8pm and 9pm. Docu-soaps filled the hole left behind by the decline in comedy and light entertainment during this period, and, once commercial channels entered the field, became ammunition in a ratings war, where even television drama – the 'dreadnoughts and destroyers' of peak time – took direct hits from the docu-soap.[8] At their peak, docu-soaps fought each other head on for the coveted '8–9 slot'. Dovey, in a brief analysis of the schedules during 1998, counted 36 per cent of peaktime factual programming during one week, and concluded that 'right across the peaktime schedule the pattern is the same: light entertainment, sitcom and drama have been replaced by popular factual entertainment programmes' (2000: 19).

Industry analyst William Phillips (1999a: 23) commented: 'never in this writer's experience has a class of programming risen and fallen so fast'. Numbers expanded from four docu-soaps on the BBC and ITV in 1995 to twenty-two in 1998. In the top 50 docu-soaps between 1995 and 1999, the highest series, *X Cars* (BBC, 1996) managed a 51 per cent market share of the audience (12.3 million), and the lowest, *HMS Splendid* (BBC, 1999), a 21 per cent share (4.8 million) (ibid.). The BBC and ITV produced two identical series about airports, and still managed to get both series in the top 10 docu-soaps from 1995 to 1999 – ITV's *Airline* attracted 11.4 million viewers (50 per cent share), and BBC's *Airport* 10.7 million (44 per cent share) during 1998. Compare this with the number one Saturday night drama series for 1998 – *Casualty* (BBC, 13.8 million): its average market share of 55 per cent shows how drama had lost its pulling power during this period.[9] For all the criticism of the docu-soap as 'documentary-lite', Winston is right to point out that 'the shows received an unexpectedly large audience, largely without crime or (much) sexual exploitation' and managed to 'escape from documentary's traditional small-audience elite demographic ghetto [which was] no mean feat' (2000: 55).

As the docu-soap reached its peak, the general audience began to switch off: 'in 1997, nine of 11 soap-doc runs beat their network's nightly [market share] averages; in 1998 it was 13 out of 22; and between January to May 1999 … 4 out of 21' (Phillips 1999b: 23). In addition, the docu-soap did not fare well abroad. American documentary producer Nancy Walzog commented, 'someone here has to take a risk in scheduling if this genre is to become anything like the commercial craze it is in Britain' (Biddiscomb 1998: 16). Whilst American reality TV championed the ordinary person doing extraordinary things, in Britain the opposite was the case, as 'over 12 million viewers regularly watched a fiftysomething housewife try to pass her driving test in *The Driving School'* (ibid.). Some Northern European countries have produced their own versions of docu-soaps, for example the German series *Wunschkinder (Planned Families)* (ZDF, 2001–), and some British docu-soaps have been screened abroad, e.g. *Airport* on PBS (USA), but the format seems to work best on home territory. Critics argue that the docu-soap is 'all washed out' (Phillips 1999a: 22). Docu-soaps may not be the 'motor of primetime', but stalwarts such as *Airline/Airport* still rank number one in the top 10 factual programmes, with audiences of between 6 and 10 million preferring everyday stories about airports to the cut and thrust of reality gameshows such as *Survivor*.[10] In the top 100 factual entertainment programmes in the UK for 2003, two of the programmes were docu-soaps about airports – *Airline* (7.95 million viewers, and a 31 per cent share), and *Holiday Airport: Lanzarote* (7.65 million viewers, 31 per cent share).[11]

Another strand of reality programming that dominated the peaktime schedules in the UK during the latter half of the 1990s is that of lifestyle programming, in particular makeover shows. Not content with the range of popular factual programming already on offer, the BBC actively developed its range of daytime leisure programmes, building on existing formats in leisure and instructional shows. In order to create peaktime fare about home improvement, fashion, and cookery, British lifestyle programming borrowed ideas from women's magazines, and daytime magazine format series A precursor to peaktime leisure programming was the daytime series *Style Challenge* (BBC, 1996–), with its focus on image transformation, or the daytime series *This Morning* (ITV, 1988–2002), with its focus on human interest stories.

Lifestyle programming, exemplified by *Changing Rooms* (BBC, 1996–), took its place alongside infotainment and docu-soaps, as popular factual for general audiences. The essence of lifestyle programming is the involvement of ordinary people and their ordinary leisure interests (gardening, cookery, fashion, home improvement) with experts who transform the ordinary into the extraordinary. Usually, the transformation of people or homes is linked to a competition, but it isn't the winning that counts, but rather the moment of surprise, or 'the reveal', when ordinary people respond to the end results. *Changing Rooms*, *Ground Force* (BBC, 1997–), and *Carol Vorderman's Better Homes* (ITV, 1999–) all draw on the makeover, along with elements from the gameshow, to heighten drama. Brunsdon *et al.* comment:

Contemporary lifestyle programmes in many cases introduce the possibility of humiliation and embarrassment for participants, through devices such as having neighbours decorate each other's room, or partners buy each other outfits. While the programmes do show what has been done to the room or the new outfit, it is the expression flitting across the participant's face in the attempt to organise their response in the public place of a close-up that is significant. It is the reaction, not the action that matters.

(2001: 56)

Most lifestyle programming in the 1990s adopted this format, subsuming an informative address (the instructional part of the programme) within the spectacle of 'the reveal' (the makeover part of the programme). The producer of *Changing Rooms*, Peter Bazalgette, summed up the success of the series: 'the key is the resolution, whether they like it or hate it … the show is really about watching other people in the raw' (cited in Moseley 2000: 312). *Changing Rooms* has proved a consistent ratings winner, with regular audiences of 10 million in the UK. Unlike the docu-soap, lifestyle programming has proved successful in the world market. For example, local versions of *Changing Rooms* have been produced in Australia and the USA.

The success of lifestyle programming has ensured many variations of the makeover format. There are lifestyle series involving food (*Ready Steady Cook*, BBC, 1997–), fashion (*What Not to Wear*, BBC, 2001–), and even scrap metal (*Scrapheap Challenge*, Channel 4, 2000–). There is now a makeover series that combines advice on style, psychology and body language in order to transform an ordinary person from dating disaster to success (*Would Like to Meet*, BBC, 2001–). There is also gay lifestyle programming, with the makeover fashion series *Queer Eye for the Straight Guy* (Bravo, 2003–), where straight guys are transformed into style-conscious males, or makeover dating series *Queer Dates for Straight Mates* (Living, 2003–), where heterosexual singles date gay men and women. There has also been a rise in property lifestyle series during the 2000s. In the UK, there are various series about how to make a property fortune, such as *How I Made My Property Fortune* (BBC2, 2003–). In Australia, the lifestyle series *The Block* is based on the idea that the home owners compete to renovate their homes and sell them to the highest bidder. In the USA, the makeover is taken to another extreme as ordinary people are given a new look courtesy of plastic surgery (*Ultimate Makeover*, ABC, 2003–). In the UK, another idea for the 'ultimate makeover' involves the use of a terminally ill patient in their transformation from life to death, and in death from 'ordinary' corpse to 'extraordinary' science exhibit.[12] With so many variations on a theme, lifestyle programming is able to transform itself over and over again. The ability to makeover itself means lifestyle programming continues to perform well in the ratings.

Reality gameshows

The reality gameshow has become an international bestseller since its arrival in 2000. The birth of the reality gameshow format can be traced to British producer Charlie Parsons, who developed the idea for *Survivor* in the early 1990s, and sold an option on the rights to Endemol, before a Swedish company bought the format and renamed it *Expedition Robinson*. In the meantime, Endemol had been working on a similar idea, *Big Brother*, the brainchild of Dutch TV producer John de Mol, who described the format as

> the voluntary locking up of nine people during a hundred days in a house, watched continuously by 24 television cameras, to which the viewers, at the intercession of the inmates, once in two weeks vote against one of the inmates who has to leave the house, until the last person to stay in can be called a winner.
>
> (Costera Meijer and Reesink 2000: 10)[13]

Surprisingly, *Big Brother* was a hit. More than 3 million people watched the finale in the Netherlands (RTL, 1999) and voted by telephone for the winner. The fact that the format worked well with converging media, such as websites and telephones, only added to its strong economic performance in the television marketplace.

Endemol sold the format for *Big Brother* around the world, at the same time that *Survivor* was also making the rounds. Parsons took Endemol to court for allegedly copying the *Survivor* format.[14] Although there are similarities in terms of the hybridisation of the gameshow and observational documentary, the formats are different in tone and style. *Survivor* uses an exotic location as a backdrop to the emotional tensions and psychological machinations of the contestants who compete to win a million. The size of the prize money is a clue as to the scale of the show: there are big tasks, big fights, big tears, and big production values. *Big Brother* uses an ordinary location as a backdrop to the emotional tensions and psychological machinations of the contestants who compete to win much less than a million. Again, the size of the prize money – a mere £70,000 in the UK – points to the nature of the show which is about small-scale, everyday activities, which are then magnified in the house and on TV because there is little else to focus on (the main activity is sleeping).

Although *Survivor* was the number one hit of the summer schedules in America (CBS, 2001), it was *Big Brother* that made its mark internationally. The first series of *Big Brother* in Germany (RTL2 and RTL, 2000) was so successful that a second was commissioned immediately for the autumn schedule. In Spain, *Big Brother* is broadcast on Tele 5 (2000), whose average market share is 21 per cent. For the final show more people tuned in to watch *Big Brother* than the Champions League semi-final match between Real Madrid and Bayern Munich, giving Tele 5 a 70 per cent market share. Belgium's television channel, Kanaal 2, has an average 9 per cent market share; after it had broadcast *Big Brother* the audience share increased to nearly 50 per cent.[15] In Australia, *Big Brother* was shown on Channel Ten (2001), which attracted over 50 per cent of its target audience (19–39 year olds), and became 'the most expensive 12-week shoot to hit Australia', with an estimated cost of A$13–16 million (Roscoe 2001: 475).

A more detailed breakdown for *Big Brother* in the UK (Channel 4) reveals the extent of the success of *Big Brother* across converging media. Channel 4 had the best Friday night ratings in its history, with 9 million viewers (46 per cent share) tuning in to watch the first series finale of *Big Brother*. Sixty-seven per cent of the UK population watched *Big Brother* at least once. Over 7 million viewers telephoned Channel 4's hotline to vote for the winner, which broke the record for viewer participation in a UK TV programme. As for the website, it received 3 million page impressions each day, which made it Europe's top website during the summer of 2000. The second series averaged more than 4 million viewers, giving Channel 4 more than a 70 per cent increase on their average broadcast share. Channel 4's digital youth channel, E4, screened *Big Brother 2* continuously during the second series, and at peak moments in the house (e.g. Paul and Helen's candlelit tryst) attracted record figures, propelling the digital channel ahead of terrestrial minority channels.[16] More than 15 million viewers voted to evict contestants, either using interactive TV handsets, or phonelines. The website received a total of 159 million page impressions and 16.4 million video streams were requested.[17] The third series of *Big Brother* averaged 4 million viewers, with the live final attracting 10 million in the summer of 2002. The fourth series of *Big Brother* under performed from the previous year, but was still in fifth place in the top ten programmes for viewers aged 16–25.[18] Table 2.1 illustrates the ratings for all series of *Big Brother* at the time of writing.

Table 2.1 Ratings for *Big Brother*

Series	Average (weekdays)	First show	Final show
BB1	4.6m (25%)	3.3m (17%)	9m (46.5%)
BB2	4.5m (25%)	3.3m (16.5%)	7.5m (46%)
BB3	5.9m (28%)	5.9m (25.9%)	10m (50.6%)
BB4	4.9m (24%)	6.9m (29.3%)	6.6m (34%)

Source: *Broadcast*, 1 August 2003

There have been many spin-offs from the success of *Big Brother*, most of them originating from Endemol. These include *The Bus*, *Big Brother* on a bus, *Chained*, a reality dating show where contestants were chained to their prospective date, and *The Mole*, where contestants completed various challenges whilst trying to eliminate the suspected 'mole'. *The Big Diet* was a *Big Brother* for weightwatchers, where contestants competed to lose the greatest amount of weight, whilst locked in a castle where they took regular exercise, and tried to avoid the 'temptation fridge'. Although the producer of *The Big Diet* promised 'it won't be like a freak show with sausages falling out of every drawer', criticism of the series suggested otherwise.[19]

Another successful international format was *Popstars*, a combination of reality gameshow and variety show that originated in New Zealand. Contestants auditioned for a place in a pop band, or in the case of *Soapstars* (ITV, 2001), a soap opera. The format usually involved a series of open auditions for thousands of 'wannabes', followed by a knockout competition where the final contestants performed in front of a panel of judges, who, along with the viewers, voted for the winners. Viewers got to see behind the scenes at the auditions, as well as the more polished performances of the final contestants who took part in variety shows. Thus, viewers observed 'talent in the making' and also acted as external judges in a national talent contest. In the UK, *Popstars* was a huge success, but the formula did not work so well for *Soapstars*, which only managed to attract 6 million viewers.[20] *Popstars* was so successful that it led to the creation of *Pop Idol* (ITV, 2002–), and *Fame Academy* (BBC, 2003–), which went on to do battle in the Saturday night ratings war. In 2003, *Pop Idol* attracted a 45 per cent market share (11 million viewers), and *Fame Academy* a 34 per cent market share (8 million viewers).[21] The success of *Pop Idol* led to the creation of *World Idol* (19TV, 2003), a spin-off show that 'pitched eleven international *Pop Idol* winners against each other'.[22] *World Idol* was shown in twenty-two different countries, with varying degrees of success – in Australia it was the highest rated show on Christmas Day (Network Ten), in Norway 'a third of the population watched the results, making it the highest rated show in broadcaster TV2's history', whilst the show 'proved to be a turkey' for ITV1 in Britain, and produced disappointing ratings for the Fox network in America.[23]

Another popular reality gameshow format is that of *I'm a Celebrity ... Get Me Out of Here!* The first series of *I'm a Celebrity ...* attracted 7.7 million viewers (34 per cent share). The second series increased its average ratings to 9.4 million viewers (38 per cent share), and the finale attracted 12 million viewers (50 per cent market share), making it the seventh most popular programme on television in 2003.[24] The third series did even better, with an average audience of 10.4 million viewers (42 per cent share), [25] and the finale attracted 15.7 million viewers, with a staggering 61 per cent share.[26] The format involved a group of celebrities, who lived together for several weeks in a purpose-built camp in the Australian rain forest. The celebrities underwent various 'bushtucker trials', such as crawling through confined spaces with hundreds of rats, in order to win food for the camp. Viewers voted celebrities out of the camp until there was only one king or queen of the jungle. The use of celebrities was central to the format's success. The highest rated episodes of the series were always when certain celebrities were faced with emotionally difficult situations, and/or became romantically involved with one another. Thus, in the third series (2004), the arguments between the glamour model Jordan and the punk rock musician Johnny Rotton were especially popular with viewers (11 million, 46 per cent share); likewise the flirtations between pop musician Peter André and Jordan were also popular with viewers (10 million, 42 per cent share).[27] The format is similar to *Survivor*, but it is also different in that it places celebrities under pressure, rather than ordinary people. Castaway TV threatened court proceedings, which were later withdrawn in 2003, precisely because the company that owned the rights to *Survivor* felt that Granada (the makers of *I'm a Celebrity* ...) had copied the *Survivor* format. CBS (the makers of the American version of *Survivor*) also issued court proceedings against Granada. The CBS courtcase against Granada was unsuccessful, and Castaway TV withdrew its allegations. In the case of CBS, the judge said that *I'm a Celebrity* ... did not borrow more substantially from *Survivor* than other types of US reality gameshows. One of the reasons why the case was unsuccessful was because the judge thought that programme making was a 'continual evolutionary process involving borrowing frequently from what has gone before'.[28] The *I'm a Celebrity* ... and *Survivor* copycat case, along with the *Survivor* and *Big Brother* copycat case, illustrate how reality gameshows freely borrow elements from existing formats in the television marketplace.

The successful export of reality gameshows from Europe to the USA occurred at the same time as gameshows experienced a resurgence in international trade – *Who Wants to be a Millionaire?* was described by the *New York Times*, as 'England's most successful cultural export in the last 30 years' (cited in Boddy 2001: 81). *Survivor* rated number one in network peaktime (27 million viewers) and earned CBS during the final three episodes an estimated $50 million in advertising revenue. After the 'smash hit' of *Survivor*, the networks scrambled to glut the market with a winning formula of gameshow, observational documentary and high drama. *Temptation Island*, Fox's answer to *Survivor*, involved four unmarried couples on a 'paradise island'. The couples were separated from their partners, and forced to fraternise with eligible singles on 'dream dates', before being reunited in a final showdown. The heady mixture of passion and betrayal, island location, attractive contestants, staged flirtations and surveillance footage all made for a fascinating, morally dubious reality gameshow – as one contestant explained, 'it's like being able to go down and take part in the Pepsi Challenge but have the ladies be the actual soft drink'. *Temptation Island* attracted more than 16 million viewers, mainly in the 18–49 demographic, and gave NBC drama *The West Wing* a run for its money. However, after two series it was axed, although ABC's anti-*Temptation Island*, *The Last Resort* (2001–), where couples in distress tried to patch things up in Hawaii, suggests the series might be due for a revival. Other reality shows include Japanese-style extreme gameshow *Fear Factor* (Fox, 2001–), dating reality gameshow *Joe Millionaire* (Fox, 2002–), and the US version of *Pop Idol*, *American Idol* (Fox, 2002–).

Big Brother was not a hit in its first season on NBC (the finale ranked 18 in the network primetime top 20). The reasons for its lack of success were partly because *Big Brother* ran alongside *Survivor*, and partly because the mundanity of the *Big Brother* house, which European audiences found so enthralling, failed to enliven American viewers. According to Ellis (2001), the failure of *Big Brother* was related to poor casting, and the fact that it was live and hastily edited for nightly review, whereas *Survivor* was well cast, edited after filming had finished, and carefully put together to maximise drama. Conversely, *Survivor* (ITV, 2000–) did not fare well in the UK, with ratings lower than 5 million, precisely because it did not involve interaction with viewers, and was pre-packaged for them, rather than filmed live (Ellis 2001). Although Neilson ratings for the first series of *Big Brother* suggest it was the live eviction shows that attracted most viewers (just as in Europe), later series sought to minimise the risks of live TV by introducing a longer time delay between actual events and the nightly reviews of the *Big Brother* house.[29] A similar strategy was adopted for Channel 4's *Teen Big Brother* (2003) in the UK, although in this instance the mini-series was pre-recorded and transmitted over one week.

As with docu-soaps, reality gameshows are reliant on peaktime scheduling for their success. Most reality gameshows are scheduled between 7pm and 10pm on American network and cable TV. And, like docu-soaps, reality gameshows go head-to-head in the schedules. For example, during the summer of 2002, first-run reality TV dominated primetime schedules, with seven of the top ten shows in the 18–49-year-old demographic group belonging to reality gameshows. During midweek, viewers could choose from *The Bachelor* (Family Channel), *Dog Eat Dog* (NBC), *Meet My Folks* (NBC), *American Idol* (Fox), *Mole II: the Next Betrayal* (ABC) and *Big Brother 3* (NBC), with *Big Brother*, *The Bachelor* and *American Idol* competing against each other during the same timeslot on the same night. Although Jeff Zucker, president of NBC Entertainment, claims that 'you have to program everything from *The West Wing* to *Fear Factor*', schedulers are clearly using reality gameshows in a ratings war.[30]

The fierce competition between reality gameshows in peak time is partly to do with increased costs in the production of reality shows like *American Idol* (approximately $800,000 per hour), which places pressure on producers and schedulers to recoup revenue during high-profile first-runs.

The scheduling of reality gameshows in the UK is not quite as competitive, primarily because British schedulers have continued to position docu-soaps, lifestyle programming and infotainment at peak time, and so reality gameshows are part of the mix of popular factual television on offer from 7pm to 11pm. Event reality gameshows such as *I'm a Celebrity ... Get Me Out of Here!* are often scheduled before the late evening news bulletin, and can increase audiences of news bulletins. For example, the third series of *I'm a Celebrity ...* was scheduled before ITV news at 10.30pm; the ratings for ITV news were as high as 4.4 million (24 per cent share) during the showing of *I'm a Celebrity ...* , but dropped by almost half to 2.4 million (16 per cent share) after the reality gameshow had finished.[31] During midweek in the summer of 2002, viewers could choose from docu-soaps *Vets in the Wild West*, and *Airport*, and makeover show *DIY SOS* on BBC1 (7–9pm), tabloid TV *Soap Star Lives*, makeover show *Carol Vorderman's Better Homes*, and dating gameshow *Elimidate* on ITV (7–11pm), lifestyle/heritage series *The Real Country House* and *Big Brother 3* on Channel 4 (8.30–10.30pm), and lifestyle series *Hot Property* and *House Doctor* on Channel 5 (8–9pm). Although this was a packed itinerary for any die-hard fan of reality programming, *Big Brother* and *Elimidate* were the only reality gameshows on offer (overlapping from 10pm to 11pm), whilst it was lifestyle programming and docu-soaps that competed for family viewers. This is not to say that reality gameshows never go head-to-head in the schedules; the BBC took on ITV in the fight for the Saturday night light entertainment slot by scheduling the second series of *Fame Academy* against the second series of *Pop Idol* and lost the ratings battle. But infotainment and docu-soaps have secured a strong place in British midweek evening schedules. The top five British popular factual programmes of 2003 included reality gameshows (*I'm a Celebrity ...*), infotainment (*Neighbours from Hell*), docu-soaps (*Airport*), lifestyle (*DIY SOS*), and life experiment programmes (*Holiday Showdown*).[32]

Life experiment programmes are a recent development in the reality genre. Part social experiment, part makeover, and part gameshow, life experiment programmes usually involve ordinary people experimenting with their lives in various different ways. For example, there are life experiment reality programmes where the experiment involves living with another family (*Wife Swap*, Channel 4, 2003–), living with your family (*Take My Mother-in-law*, ITV1, 2003–), going on holiday with another family (*Holiday Showdown*, ITV1, 2003–), learning another profession (*Faking It*, Channel 4, 2001–), masquerading as a man/woman (*Gender Swap*, Five, 2003–), living without an 'essential' item (*You Can Live Without* … , Channel 4, 2003–), living by domestic rules imposed by other people (*Trust Me, I'm a Teenager*, BBC2, 2003–), managing another business (*Boss Swap*, Channel 4, 2003–), being a master of servants, and being a servant to masters (*Masters and Servants*, Channel 4, 2003–). In all of these examples, the ordinary people are filmed as they experience the trials and tribulations of living/working in an alternative manner to that which they are used to in their everyday lives. Life experiment programmes are about transformation, as ordinary people experiment with different lifestyles, values, and work and domestic arrangements. Sometimes the experiment ends with a life-affirmative message – the participants want to change their lives for the better; more often the experiment ends with a negative message – the participants are judgemental of other people and their different life experiences.

Wife Swap is an example of a popular life experiment format. The series idea originated from a series of discussions with the Channel 4 commissioning editor, documentaries (Hilary Bell), and the director of programmes for RDF Media (Stephen Lambert). Lambert proposed a series called *Wife Swap*, and Bell responded: 'it was such a great title, it just made me laugh and you can imagine it in the listing mags and, on that basis, I said "Oh fuck it, let's commission it" '.[33] The first series of *Wife Swap* (Channel 4, 2003) attracted an audience of 6 million. The series won the *Broadcast* international programme sales award in 2004. The series has been acquired by France (M6), Denmark (TV3), the Netherlands (RTL4), Australia (Network Nine) and New Zealand (TVNZ), and the format has been bought by America (ABC), Norway (TV3), Germany (RTL), Belgium (VTM), Spain (Zeppelin), and Greece (Freemantle).[34] Typically, *Wife Swap* involves experimentation with different lifestyles, values and personal circumstances, for example a single mother with six children will swap with a working mother of two, or the mother of a white British family will swap with the mother of a black British family. Although all of the families profess to learn from the experiment, it is rarely the case that personal circumstances change dramatically upon the return of the wife/mother to her own family. More often than not the wives/mothers criticise each other regarding their domestic arrangements, the cleanliness of their homes, or their parenting skills. There has also been a *Celebrity Wife Swap*, involving a contestant in *Big Brother 3* known for her outspokenness, and a contestant of *Who Wants to be a Millionaire?* known for his deception.

And what of the future of reality TV? Television's ability to endlessly reinvent itself means that hybrid reality formats continue to be a popular choice for producers and executives (Kilborn 2003). The formats for reality TV – infotainment, docu-soaps, lifestyle programming, reality gameshows, and others – do not lend themselves to repeat viewing. Indeed, they quickly become yesterday's news. Reality formats provide a never-ending fresh supply of non-professional actors in new series of existing formats. *Big Brother*, *Survivor* and *Popstars* are cases in point, as minor changes to the formats, such as a new house/island/panel of judges, allow television producers to create new series out of essentially the same shows. And, of course, no series of *Survivor* is exactly the same, as the contestants are new to television. The problem is that contestants in reality gameshows learn how to behave from previous series, and there can be an element of parody to their performances. Thus, in *Big Brother 3/4* in the UK, contestants talked endlessly about how they would be perceived by the public and the media, knowing that once out of the house they would be media stars, even if only for a day. Indeed, some contestants have already appeared on other reality TV shows, and there is a danger of repeat performers flooding auditions for reality gameshows (Kilborn and Hibbard 2000). It is no surprise, therefore, that one development within the reality gameshow is to include media celebrities as contestants. *Celebrity Big Brother* (Channel 4) takes celebrities and turns them into 'ordinary people', before releasing them back into the world of the media. Another example is of a reality programme that uses celebrities rather than ordinary people is *I'm a Celebrity … Get Me Out of Here!* The trend in America for celebrity docu-soaps, such as *The Osbournes* (MTV, 2001–) or *The Anna Nicole Show* (E!, 2002–), rely on just this premise. It is inevitable that the participants of reality programmes will be invited as celebrities on other celebrity-based reality programmes. *Back to Reality* (Five, 2004–) is a case in point, where celebrities from a variety of popular factual programmes are invited to participate in a reality gameshow that involves living in a purpose-built mansion, undertaking various tasks, and being eliminated by viewers. We can also see the rise of docu-drama, or drama documentaries, as directly related to the success of popular factual television in peaktime schedules. Popular docu-dramas such as *Pornography: the Musical* (Channel 4, 2003) or films such as *The Day Britain Stopped* (BBC, 2003) indicate the crossovers between reality programmes and docu-drama. The BBC have created a new role within their Factual and Learning division for a producer of current affairs docu-drama, in order to tap into new audiences for current affairs.[35] Finally, let us not forget the significance of surveillance footage; as reality gameshows move into the realm of popular entertainment and performance becomes even more central to the success of contestants, raw footage of people going about their business with no knowledge they are being filmed will inevitably reappear on our television screens. The success of *The Secret Policeman*, an undercover investigative documentary about racism in the British police force, indicates audience attraction to surveillance footage, as 5 million people watched the one-off documentary. It won a Royal

Television Society award, and the BBC have commissioned a series of similar undercover investigations into public sector institutions.[36]

CONCLUSION

The rise of reality TV came at a time when networks were looking for a quick fix solution to economic problems within the cultural industries. Increased costs in the production of drama, sitcom and comedy ensured unscripted, popular factual programming became a viable economic option during the 1990s. The deregulation and marketisation of media industries, especially in America and Western Europe, also contributed to the rise of reality TV, as it performed well in a competitive, multichannel environment. Reality TV has its roots in tabloid journalism and popular entertainment, but it owes its greatest debt to documentary television, which has almost disappeared from television screens in the wake of popular factual programming. Documentary television, a 'duty genre', has withered on the vine during a decade of the commercialisation of public service channels. Although the popularity of reality TV comes at a cost, there is hope that its very success in peak time is the 'price of survival' for documentary (Winston 2000).

As for reality programming, the main formats – infotainment, docu-soap, lifestyle and reality gameshow – were successful in the 1990s and early 2000s because they drew on existing popular genres, such as soap opera or gameshows, to create hybrid programmes. In addition, these hybrid formats focused on telling stories about real people and real events in an entertaining style, usually foregrounding visuals, characterisation and narrative above all else. It is the 'see it happen' style of reality programming that makes it appealing to audiences, and the ratings success of infotainment, docu-soaps, lifestyle and reality gameshows is testament to the mass appeal of entertainment stories about real people caught on camera. Popular factual television has been the motor of peak time throughout the 1990s, drawing at times unprecedented market shares of over 50 per cent, and regularly appearing in the top 20 shows on network TV. With such high ratings, its place in peaktime schedules is assured for some time to come. In addition, popular factual formats are international bestsellers, with local versions of *Rescue 911*, *Changing Rooms*, *Big Brother*, and *Wife Swap* appearing all over the world. Only the docu-soap, a uniquely British format, has failed to travel well, although it has emerged in somewhat altered form as the celebrity docu-soap. All in all, reality programming is an extraordinary success story, an example of television's ability to cannibalise itself in order to survive in a commercially uncertain media environment. However, the costs incurred as a result of its success have been felt most by public service broadcasting, in particular news, current affairs and documentary. It remains to be seen whether public service and commercial networks can continue to popularise factual programming without doing away with traditional factual programming altogether.

Chapter 3

The reality genre

The category of reality TV is commonly used to describe a range of popular factual programming. There are a variety of styles and techniques associated with reality TV, such as non-professional actors, unscripted dialogue, surveillance footage, hand-held cameras, seeing events unfold as they are happening in front of the camera. However, the treatment of 'reality' in reality programming has changed as the genre has developed over the past decade. In the early stages of the genre, reality TV was associated with on-scene footage of law and order, or emergency services. More recently, reality TV is associated with anything and everything, from people to pets, from birth to death. So, how do we categorise this diverse genre? In this chapter, I outline the contradictory and at times confusing terms used by the television industry, scholars and audiences to describe a genre in transition. Jason Mittell (2001: 19–20) argues for an examination of television genres as 'cultural categories, unpacking the processes of definition, interpretation, and evaluation that constitute these categories' in order to better understand 'how genres work to shape our media experiences'.

The process of categorising reality TV highlights the inherent problems for the television industry, scholars and audiences in defining a genre that by its very nature is concerned with multiple generic participation, and constant regeneration. Robert Allen (1989), in his discussion of soap opera, talked about the limits of a genre in relation to the blurred boundaries between fact and fiction in television soap operas. Similarly, Bill Nichols (1994), in his book on documentary, *Blurred Boundaries*, discussed the limits of the genre reality TV. In the following sections, discussion by the television industry, scholars and audiences highlights the border crossing of factual/fictional television, and the limits of the 'reality' genre.

TELEVISION INDUSTRY

The television industry is a good place to chart the changing genre of reality TV. Television thrives on new formats, and, as the previous chapter shows, television often cannabilises itself, feeding off successful genres and formats in order to create new hybrid programmes. As Brunsdon *et al.* (2001) note, it is the hybridisation of successful genres that gives reality TV such strong market value. The soap opera and observational documentary came together in the creation of docu-soaps that in turn dominated peaktime schedules in the UK (e.g. *Airport*); the gameshow and observational documentary came together in the creation of reality gameshows that in turn dominated primetime schedules in the USA (e.g. *Survivor*). Perhaps the most traditional industry term for reality TV is factual entertainment. The term usefully merges factual programming with entertainment-based television, and highlights hybridisation, a common generic feature of most reality programmes. Another traditional industry term is that of popular factual, a term that links popular audiences with a variety of factual television genres and formats.

The industry terms of factual entertainment and popular factual television are umbrella categories for a range of formatted as well as non-formatted programmes and series. Previously, the BBC used a television genre structure that differentiated general from specialist (history, religion, etc.) factual programming. Under general factual programming, the genre of popular factual television included celebrity profiles, biographies, archives and formats, and sports factual. Other genres within general factual included documentaries, leisure, and daytime factual programmes. However, in 2003, the BBC changed the structure of factual genres to reflect the changing nature of factual television, and to create a 'more flexible and fast moving system'.[1] The new genre structure contains six categories: documentaries and contemporary factual; specialist factual; current affairs and investigations; arts and culture; lifeskills; and new media.[2] Under Documentaries and Contemporary Factual sits Popular Factual Television, with its own director and creative head of programming. The department of Popular Factual Television commissions formats, celebrity profiles and entertaining documentaries. The department of Leisure, also subsumed under Documentaries and Contemporary Factual, commissions lifestyle, history, relationships and popular documentaries. Documentaries and Contemporary Factual also includes a Features department that commissions popular crime, and consumer affairs programmes. Even Current Affairs and Investigations commissions popular formatted series, and also docu-dramas. Thus, popular factual can in theory come from any category within factual and learning. For example, *The Ship*, a history experiment that recreated the epic 1768 journey of Captain Cook around the north-east coast of Australia, was commissioned by BBC history and education, but its use of ordinary people as part of the experiment, and fly-on-the-wall filming techniques, made it difficult to categorise as specialist documentary –

indeed industry insiders dubbed it 'extreme history'.[3] The BBC factual commissioning system is designed to deal with exactly this type of hybrid factual programming.

Other British terrestrial, satellite, cable and digital channels categorise reality TV under a variety of headings. ITV categorises reality gameshows as Entertainment (*The Club*), lifestyle programmes appropriately come under Lifestyle (*I Want That Home*), but factual does not feature as part of its genre structure, as outlined on its website for viewers. This is perhaps because the number of companies working under the ITV umbrella means the output of factual programming comes from different departments. For example, Granada Features is a key supplier of popular factual television programmes for ITV. Granada Factual supplies popular observational documentaries such as *Airline*, and also reality gameshows such as *I'm a Celebrity* .... Granada Entertainment makes reality talent shows such as *Popstars*. Thus, classification for the reality genre is dependent on the companies working within ITV, and other independent suppliers of reality programming.

Similarly, Channel 4 categorises reality TV under several headings on its website. For example, reality gameshows and/or talentshows come under Entertainment (*Big Brother*) and also Culture (*Operatunity*), reality history shows come under History (*The Edwardian Country House*), docu-soaps come under any category (*The Clinic* is Health), and lifestyle comes under Life (*House Hunting*). In 2002, Channel 4 restructured its factual output in order to clarify responsibilities for specific genres. There is a Contemporary Factual group, and within it sits the Popular Factual Television department, and the Documentaries department. The Popular Factual Television department houses several subgroups: Features, Daytime, and Cross Platform Events. The Documentaries department commissions popular observational series and formatted factual series, as well as different types of documentaries.

This brief overview of factual commissioning suggests that UK terrestrial channels are positioning popular factual programming closer to documentary, and, in some cases, current affairs and investigative journalism. The merging of different types of factual programming under one roof – documentary and contemporary factual – speaks volumes about the way British television has come to rely on the variety of subgenres within popular factual television to make up a high quota of contemporary factual output. The commercial channel Five explicitly addresses the merger between contemporary factual and reality programming in its composite genre structure for popular factual television that includes Contemporary Biography, Popular Documentaries, Popular Factual Television Series, Formatted Manipulated Documentaries, Reality Formats, Experiments/Stunts/Events, and Features.

In terms of non-terrestrial channels, Sky One produces many in-house reality formats, such as the *Ibiza Uncovered* series, that feature as factual on Sky One, and travel on Sky Travel, and will soon feature as reality TV in its own right, owing to BSkyB's plans to stream reality programmes on dedicated channels. The creation of reality TV niche channels, such as the proposed Sky One Real, or US-based Reality TV, and the proposed Reality Central, illustrate how the television industry can capitalise on the generic branding of various types of popular factual programming under the heading of reality TV. The Reality TV channel focuses primarily on crime and emergency services reality programming, and clip shows of near-death experiences. Reality Central proposed to focus on documentary gameshows and talentshows. If the niche reality channels were to incorporate the type of flexible system of popular factual programming operated by terrestrial channels in the UK, then the channels could schedule daytime, evening and late night programming according to different types of reality shows – lifestyle (*Changing Rooms*) and infotainment (*Rescue 911*) during the daytime, observational popular factual (*Airport*) and formatted popular factual (*Survivor*) during the evening, and adult oriented reality programming (*Sex on the Beach*) for late night schedules.

In the USA, contemporary reality gameshows and talentshows are classified as reality TV, whilst older formats, such as *Cops*, are also classified as reality TV. This use of the same genre category for quite different formats can be explained by the history of the definition of reality TV. The term originally appeared in the US television industry in the 1980s, and was useful in defining 'the appeal of the "raw" amidst so many inventive as well as traditional varieties of "cooking"' (Corner 2003: 290). As reality TV took off, other reality formats were produced, taking the 'raw' ingredients of on-scene emergency services reality TV and processing them into more 'cooked' reality formats such as reality gameshows. These two types of reality programming are reflected in the content of the two US-based reality channels. As mentioned above, Reality TV favours reruns of more traditional reality programming. Reality Central favours reruns of reality gameshows. Reality Central's Larry Namer claims that 'reality is now a genre, just like any other'.[4] But the line-up for Reality Central suggests the channel is primarily interested in defining reality TV in relation to contemporary ratings successes, with reality 'stars' from popular series such as Richard Hatch from *Survivor*, or Tristan Rehn and Ryan Slutter from *The Bachelorette*, promoting the channel. Thus, reality TV in the USA primarily refers to the type of formatted popular factual that has dominated primetime network schedules since 2000. The 43rd Monte-Carlo Television Festival called it a 'reality explosion', with reality TV headlining the Formats Forum in 2003. The term reality TV is so flexible that it can be applied to any type of popular factual programming the industry wants to sell to channels and viewers at home or abroad.

Industry awards for television programming categorise reality TV under various headings. At BAFTA 2002, *Faking It*, a series about real people who try to fake it in another profession, was given the Features Award; and *Pop Idol*, a reality talentshow, was given the Entertainment Award. At the Indie Awards 2003, *Faking It* was given the Factual Award; *Jamie's Kitchen*, a fly-on-the-wall series about the celebrity chef Jamie Oliver, was given the Documentary Award; and *Pop Idol* was given the Indie Award, as the best independent production of 2002. The variety of categories reflects the somewhat complicated categorisation of popular factual television in the UK. In the USA, industry award categories reflect a two-tier system of old and new reality programming. The Academy of Television, Arts and Sciences created two Emmy award categories for reality TV: formats that include a gameshow element, and formats that seek to entertain by showing dramatic incidents in real life (a genre has to be represented by at least fourteen on-air series to become a category).

The people behind reality TV also define the genre in different ways. Peter Bazalgette was described by the Royal Television Society as a man who 'changed the terms of factual television'.[5] Bazalgette is an independent television producer, and responsible for leisure formats such as *Changing Rooms* and reality formats such as *Big Brother*, or *Fame Academy*. As head of the largest UK independent production company, Endemol UK, he is at the forefront of popular factual programming:

> There's a huge future – just as there's been a huge past – in British TV for so-called real people on TV … Some of these so-called reality shows are more factual, some are more formatted, like *Pop Idol*. A lot of them used to be called documentaries, but people are now just more inventive with them.[6]

For Bazalgette, it is human interest, rather than 'reality', that defines popular factual programmes, and he is therefore resistant to using the 'so-called' category of reality TV. Gary Carter, international director of licensing at Endemol, prefers to describe the genre as 'reality entertainment'. In fact, for Carter, what is more important is intellectual property rather than content. Carter and Bazalgette are primarily interested in 'an entertainment idea' that can be instantly accessed by audiences/users across different types of media – TV, radio, telephone, and the internet.[7]

As we have seen, the television industry is flexible in its categorisation of reality TV. Popular factual programming can fit under a range of traditional categories, such as entertainment, and/or topics, such as health, but it can also be labelled as reality TV when beneficial to the industry. Popular and broadsheet press discussion of reality TV suggests similar use of the category. The success of reality gameshows has led to more frequent use of 'reality TV' to describe popular factual, as the term is instantly recognisable and instantly categorises programmes as a particular type of television, usually cheap, tasteless, and compelling. Bonner (2003: 23) charts the use of the term infotainment, an early precursor of reality TV, in her book *Ordinary Television*. The term was first used in the USA in the early 1980s in order to describe types of programming that blurred boundaries between fact and fiction. But it was not until the early 1990s, when infotainment shows such as *Rescue 911* performed strongly in the television market at home and abroad, that the category began to be used on a more regular basis. Journalists reporting on the rise of the reality genre struggled to describe the programmes, using terms such as popular factual television, real people shows, infotainment, topical features, on-scene reality shows, tabloid TV, etc., before settling for the interchangeable terms, reality TV, reality genre, or reality shows (see Holmes and Jermyn 2003). Corner reflects on the use of the term 'reality TV' to describe what was perceived by the British press as an American import pretending to be documentary when it was really entertainment (2003: 291).

In 1997, an article in *The Journal of the Royal Television Society* bemoaned 'real people TV', whilst the broadsheet UK newspaper the *Guardian* criticised 'Victim TV'.[8] In 1999, the London listings magazine *Time Out* published a polemic on 'edutainment', asking why 'documentaries that merely inform are so passé?', whilst the broadsheet newspaper the *Observer* published a polemic on 'conflict TV'.[9] In 2000, the *Independent* interviewed John de Mol, the creator of *Big Brother*, calling the genre 'reality programming', 'psycho TV', and 'deprivational voyeurism'.[10] Since the success of *Big Brother*, the various terms used to describe popular factual programming have mainly disappeared, to be replaced by 'reality' TV/genre/show. The *Guardian* website has a special section devoted to archive articles about reality TV. The *Guardian* also ran an article in 2003 stating 'Reality TV is Here to Stay', an indication of the strength of the category of 'reality TV' as much as the ratings success of the genre as a whole.[11]

TELEVISION SCHOLARS

Since the early 1990s television scholars have defined reality TV in a variety of different ways. Steve Neale (2001: 3) points out that 'there is a generic aspect to all instances of cultural production, and that these instances are usually multiple, not single, in kind'. In terms of reality TV, there are 'numerous aspects', 'numerous meanings', and 'numerous analytical uses' of the genre within the academic community (ibid.).

One of the earliest discussions of the genre is by Richard Kilborn who points out that 'reality programming, or reality television as it is sometimes called, is … a term [that] has become something of a catch-all phrase' (1994: 423). As Kilborn suggests, reality TV can include 'slice-of-life observational modes of documentary film making', 'fictional drama rooted in real-life situations', and also infotainment, or what Kilborn calls reality programming: 'the recording on the wing … of events in the lives of individuals or groups, the attempt to simulate such real-life events through various forms of dramatised reconstruction and the incorporation of this material … into an attractively packaged television programme' (ibid.). In a more recent account of reality TV (2003) Kilborn argues that the terms 'reality TV' or 'reality programming' have 'been used to cover a broad range of popular factual formats and have, for this reason probably outlived their critical usefulness' (2003: 55). Kilborn suggests it would be more useful to refer to reality programmes as 'reality formats' because 'the term "format" both underscores the commercially driven need of broadcasters to produce work according to established formulae and draws attention to the crucial importance of packaging in the development of a programme concept' (ibid.). Kilborn's categorisation of reality programmes as reality formats indicates the significance of the production context to his understanding of the reality genre.

Kilborn's earlier definition of the reality genre was echoed by Chad Raphael, who opted for the term 'reali-TV' as 'an umbrella term for a number of programming trends' on US television since the late 1980s (1997: 102). Another early discussion of the genre is by Bill Nichols (1994) in *Blurred Boundaries*, a book on documentary that includes a chapter titled 'At the Limits of Reality (TV)'. For Nichols, reality TV 'includes all those shows that present dangerous events, unusual situations, or actual police cases, often re-enacting aspects of them and sometimes enlisting our assistance in apprehending criminals still at large' (1994: 45). Thus, tabloid news programmes and infotainment sit within his definition of the genre. He also refers to soap opera as an influential genre within reality TV, something that would be picked up later by scholars in discussion of the docu-soap.

In a similar vein, Ib Bondebjerg (1996) highlights the blurred boundaries between fact and fiction in his article on 'true-life-story' genres. Here, tabloid journalism becomes a key influence on a range of genres that incorporate true-life-stories, including infotainment and human interest documentaries. In a more recent article, Bondebjerg (2002: 171–2) identifies 'three basic sub-forms of reality TV': the docu-soap ('characterised by a link to reality through its characters and settings'); the reality-magazine ('presenting cases from real life, mostly about crime and accidents, or other spectacular human interest stories'); and the reality-show ('a serialized form of game show where ordinary people are put in extraordinary situations in order to cooperate with and compete against one another').

John Corner has consistently addressed developments within news and documentary, and reality TV. In his book *Television Form and Public Address* Corner discussed early examples of 'real-life' programming that contained a 'mix of entertaining drama and documentary/current affairs exposition' (1995: 20). Corner's interest in the 'capacity which television has to let people "see for themselves" ' (1995: 30) ensured a watchful eye among media scholars on the development of reality TV over the next few years. In a review of documentary studies in 2000 Corner outlined several phases in popular factual television:

> A huge expansion of actuality-based programming ... has appropriated documentary's fundamental dynamics for a very wide range of more sensational and also more casual uses. In the first phase, popular factual television was 'reality television', with a focus on the work of police and emergency services ... In its second phase, in Britain and elsewhere, there emerged the 'docu-soap', a form of nosey sociability which has to be seen not only in relation to the soap opera but to the appeal of the new daytime talkshows ... In the last few years, it is possible to see a third phase of development, what we might call the 'docushow' phase ... (eg those about cookery, DIY ...). Together with those shows which have adopted the framing and participant roles of a game, perhaps with time-limits as part of the rules (gamedocs?), these have provided innovative kinds of infotainment mix by drawing extensively on the documentary mode.
>
> (2000: 687)

Corner deliberately locates reality TV within the framework of documentary, summarising different types of reality TV as 'documentary-lite'. However, he is also careful to situate reality TV in relation to other popular genres, such as soap operas, talkshows, gameshows, all genres that have influenced formats within the reality genre. Indeed, Corner goes so far as to suggest that reality TV, in all its various guises, has pushed the limits of the reality genre, and in turn has pushed the limits of documentary. He suggests that 'thinking outside and beyond the documentary category' can help us to understand the 'realities' in factual and fictional television (2002b: 155). In Corner's 'post documentary culture', reality television is less about genre and more about the treatment of 'realities' in the 'border crossing' between fact and fiction (2002b: 156).

Most television scholars who discuss reality TV tend to include a variety of television genres in their definitions of the 'reality genre' precisely because reality TV borrows from so many different existing genres. Dovey (2000), for example, in his book *Freakshow: First Person Media and Factual Television*, considers the proliferation of 'subjective, autobiographical and confessional modes of expression' (first-person media) within infotainment, docu-soaps and talkshows. Humm (1998) is also interested in first-person media, but charts the trend in 'real people shows' to light entertainment, lifestyle and gameshows, as well as documentary. Brunsdon *et al.* (2001) discuss popular factual television in relation to two main strands – docu-soap and lifestyle programmes. For some scholars, even the subgenres within reality TV are the result of a complex borrowing from other television genres. Turner (2001: 7) describes lifestyle programmes as containing 'the following television genres: gameshows, soap opera, reality-TV or "fly-on-the-wall documentary", confessional talkshows, daytime product-based talkshows, and gardening advice programmes'. Hartley defines infotainment as a combination of lifestyle, reality TV, tabloid news, investigative journalism, talkshows and animal series (Hartley 2001b).

Scholars of popular factual television can be in danger of genre overload when defining the reality genre. It is all too easy to stray into the outer limits of the reality genre. As we saw with the discussion of 'so-called reality TV' in the previous section, the television industry pushes the boundaries of popular factual television to create new hybrid formats. Corner touched on one of the core issues in the definition of reality TV: by its very nature popular factual entertainment sits in the spaces between fact and fiction. Jane Roscoe and Craig Hight (2001), in their book *Faking It*, have identified the flexible, self-reflexive, and limitless appeal of fact/fiction formats. Roscoe and Hight assert that rather than thinking about a 'fact/fiction dichotomy', they 'prefer to think about documentary as existing along a fact–fictional continuum, each text constructing relationships with both factual and fictional discourses' (2001: 7). Their perspective on documentary draws on existing arguments within documentary studies about the evidential status of documentary as a record of reality, and/or a creative treatment of reality:

> Documentary does not provide an unmediated view of the world, nor can it live up to its claims to be a mirror on society. Rather, like any fictional text, it is constructed with a view to producing certain versions of the social world … Even though we may agree that documentary representations are as constructed as fictional ones, the stance that documentary takes toward the social world is one that is grounded on a belief that it can access the real.
>
> (2001: 8)

The continuum between fact and fiction is a useful way to think of the relationship between contemporary factual programming and the various types of popular factual television that make up the reality genre. There is a fact/fiction continuum between contemporary documentaries and popular factual television. There is also a sliding scale of factuality in reality programming. At the far end of the continuum are more informative based programmes such as *Animal Hospital*, and at the other end are documentary gameshows such as *Survivor*. In the next section, television audiences talk about the status of reality TV in contemporary factual television.

TELEVISION AUDIENCES

Given the variety of categories for reality TV used within the television industry, and by television scholars, it is no surprise that television audiences have several definitions for reality programming. In focus group discussions with British television viewers, I encountered the following unprompted definitions of reality programmes: 'people programmes'; 'documentaries of the real life'; 'public, real life sort of thing'; 'fly-on-the-wall stuff'; 'sort of almost reality programmes'. The following comment by a 26-year-old estate agent summed up the way viewers perceived the general content of popular factual programmes as 'real life documentaries, like things which have happened to people, people getting evicted, you know, cameras following people around'. Thus, viewers equated reality TV with 'cameras following people around'. When conducting audience research with viewers of reality TV, one of the first issues to overcome was to find a neutral category for reality programmes. I chose to use the phrase 'entertainment programmes about real people', and the names of individual programmes to prompt discussion (see Appendix 2). However, participants quickly picked up on the lack of clarity in my definition – one participant asked 'have you got a name for them all?' (31-year-old-housewife), and when I shook my head she laughed. As viewers were left to their own devices as to how to define reality programming, discussion often focused on when the programmes were on, and the differences between reality programmes. In the final section of this chapter, I want to illustrate the significance of scheduling and subgenres within reality programming to audience awareness and evaluation of popular factual television.

In the previous chapter, I discussed the significance of scheduling to the viewing experience of popular factual television. Following John Ellis' account of scheduling as indicative of the power of television to attract and maintain viewers (2000), the scheduling for British popular factual programming is primarily from 6pm to 11pm, the most competitive and most coveted slot in the schedule.[12] Thus, viewers are most likely to watch popular factual after the six o'clock news, in between soap operas, drama, and occasional light entertainment, and before the ten o'clock news on the terrestrial channels. This viewing experience is one that is most conducive to watching a range of popular factual output. Reality programmes are part of the landscape of the evening schedule, bridging the divide between traditional factual television (news) and traditional fictional television (soaps, drama, and light entertainment). In later chapters, I consider the viewing experience for popular factual television in relation to viewing strategies for factual and fictional programming, but here I want to comment on how the schedule is a key factor in the way audiences define the reality genre.

Perhaps one of the key reasons why the different subgenres within popular factual programming are so successful in the ratings is because they appeal to a broad range of occasional viewers. Regular viewers of reality TV are often in the minority, or located around an event show such as *I'm a Celebrity ... Get Me Out of Here!* The types of popular factual television programmes watched most often across a range of British viewers in 2000 were: police/crime programmes (e.g. *Police Camera Action!*) watched either regularly or occasionally by 72 per cent of adults and 71 per cent of children; 'places' programmes (e.g. *Airport*) – 71 per cent of adults and 75 per cent of children; home/garden shows (e.g. *Changing Rooms*) – 67 per cent of adults and 84 per cent of children (Hill/ITC 2000). If we break these figures down according to regular and occasional viewers we find these programmes are more likely to attract occasional adult viewers. Police/crime programmes were watched regularly by 24 per cent of adults, and occasionally by 48 per cent of adults; 'places' programmes 31 per cent (regular) and 40 per cent (occasional) of adults; home/garden shows 26 per cent (regular) and 41 per cent (occasional) of adults. The picture was the same for children, except regarding programmes about pets, and home/garden shows which attracted an even mix of regular and occasional young viewers – e.g. home/garden shows were watched by 44 per cent (regular) and 40 per cent (occasional) of young viewers (see Chapter 6 for further discussion).

Why does popular factual programming attract so many occasional viewers? These 12–13 year old boys commented on scheduling in relation to their viewing habits:

Michael: Yeah, *Changing Rooms* is after *EastEnders*.
Garry: Which is probably why I watch it.
Ed: I can find better things to watch 'cos I don't really like watching about normal life stuff.
Michael: Yeah, but we're talking about that here.

Ed: Yeah, I know, I'm just saying I can find better things to watch but I have watched quite a lot of them.

There is a lack of interest in programmes about 'normal life stuff', but also an acknowledgement that they are familiar with 'quite a lot of them'. Of course, there are reality TV shows that do excite this age group, *Big Brother* being one example I discuss in the next chapter. But there is something about many popular factual programmes that causes young viewers to categorise them as 'boring programmes on about eight o'clock when there's nothing else to do' (14-year-old schoolgirl).

Another reason why popular factual programmes appeal to occasional viewers relates to the accessible format of much popular factual television, such as self-contained, short segments, and/or serialised stories with strong, identifiable characters. The self-contained stories in programmes such as *Police Camera Action!* attract occasional viewers who dip in and out of the series. As these two viewers (42-year-old female childminder, and 26-year-old male professional golfer) explained:

Yolanda: I think 'cos ... most of these programmes are on, sometimes for just half an hour ... you know, so you don't have to get too into it, it's not a series.
Michael: It's easy watching, isn't it?
Yolanda: Yeah.
Michael: You can miss it for a few weeks and you can watch it.
Yolanda: Yeah, it doesn't matter.

Of course, many popular factual formats also contain other storytelling techniques, such as strong characterisation, and/or serial narratives, in order to attract repeat viewers. But the way these viewers talk about the everyday, almost throw-away nature of certain types of popular factual programming suggests the appeal of these programmes is partly explained by viewers looking for undemanding factual television.

Within the genre of reality TV, viewers make distinctions between different types of programmes. In 2000, I examined preferences for three core types of programming in a national survey (Hill/ITC 2000). These types of reality programming included 'observation' programmes (often about watching people in everyday places, e.g. *Airport*); 'information' programmes (often using true stories to tell us about something, like driving, first aid, or pets, e.g. *999*); and 'created for TV' programmes (often about putting real people in a manufactured situation, like a house or an island, and filming what happens, e.g. *Big Brother*). The types of popular factual television liked most by the British public were observation (67 per cent), information (64 per cent), and created for TV (28 per cent).

Viewers adopted a sliding scale between more informative, 'real' programmes, like *999*, and more entertaining, less 'real' programmes, like *Big Brother*: '*Big Brother* [is] kind of light-hearted, you know, easy to watch and ... I like *Police Camera Action!* 'cos it's like real life, what happens and stuff' (16-year-old female student). It is not the case that viewers prefer to watch informative programmes instead of entertaining ones. The target viewers of reality TV are the type of viewers who choose popular rather than traditional or specialist factual programming precisely because it is factual and entertaining. However, it is the case that viewers make distinctions between different types of reality TV based on older, more familiar formats such as infotainment, or docu-soaps, and newer formats, such as reality gameshows. In the same way that the niche channels Reality TV and Reality Central differentiate themselves in the reality TV market by programming *Cops* on one channel and *Survivor* on another, audiences of popular factual television differentiate themselves by showing awareness of the assorted formats on offer. Thus, viewers of reality TV are not a mass of undifferentiated people who like the same programmes, but groups of viewers who make distinctions about different types of reality programming, and different ways of watching these programmes.

Reality TV viewers classify programmes according to fact/fiction criteria. Corner (1995) argues that a key characteristic of television is to let people see for themselves. Popular factual television's core attraction for viewers is its capacity to let viewers see for themselves. Almost 70 per cent of the British public like to see stories about real people caught on camera in popular factual television (Hill/ITC 2000). A fundamental characteristic of reality TV is its 'see it happen' style of factual footage. The 'see it happen' style of the reality genre ensures that viewers often classify programmes within the genre according to how real they appear to be. The following comment by a viewer is typical of the way audiences distinguish between assorted formats within the reality genre according to their assessment of the truth claims of the programmes:

'Well, like *Children's Hospital* is factual isn't it? It's not, it's not glossing over anything, you're seeing what is actually happening so that's the good point of it. If you're into real TV, you can't get more real than that ... I mean, that's a real factual programme and *999* reconstructions, they're not made up are they, they're actual accidents ... I find a lot of these so called documentaries are not true to life and that's annoying 'cos I think people are easily taken in, you know. I just think it's a set-up ... d'you know what I mean? I just can't hack it, it's so false to me and they play up, I'm sure they play up to the camera and it's nothing like real-life documentaries and that.'

(39-year-old groundsman)

For this viewer, infotainment and docu-soaps are reality TV because they are 'not made up', we can see 'what is actually happening'. But new formats, 'these so-called documentaries', make false claims about the visual evidence in the programmes.

Similarly, the following extract from a group discussion illustrates the way viewers apply a fact/fiction continuum to different degrees of 'reality' in popular factual formats:

Interviewer: What about something like *Big Brother*?

Eleanor: It's not as real as a hospital programme I don't think because they knew cameras were on them.

Charlotte: And they had actually gone there for that reason, to be filmed, so everything they do is for the cameras, isn't it?

Eleanor: I think there was a lot of playing up to the cameras.

General: Yeah.

Mary: But after a while they might have been themselves, I think.

Chris: *Children's Hospital* is so true to life, it just happens, there's nothing you can do about it but with that it was more contrived.

In another discussion, a viewer compares particular popular factual formats with the experience of fictional television: 'Well, *Big Brother* is entertainment ... you'd just watch it like you'd watch *EastEnders* or *Coronation Street*, really ... sort of along that line more than watching *Airport* or *Animal Hospital*' (40-year-old female part-time secretary).

This way of classifying reality TV according to the actuality of individual programmes, and/or formats, is complex and deserves more discussion. In many ways, the classification of reality TV in relation to 'reality' is connected with audience understanding of the performance of non-professional actors in the programmes, and the ways 'real people' play up to the cameras. Clearly, reality gameshows such as *Big Brother* invite ordinary people to perform for the cameras, and viewers are more than aware of the impact of the genre of light entertainment on the more observational factual genre adopted within such formats. Viewers refer to *Big Brother* as 'entertaining' because the hybrid format prioritises the gameshow over observational documentary. The fact/fiction continuum is a useful way for viewers to categorise the different types of hybrid formats within the reality genre – infotainment or docu-soaps are 'more true to life', the events they record 'just happen', whereas reality gameshows are 'contrived' and therefore less true to life. The fact/fiction continuum is also an opportunity to evaluate the genre according to its truth claims. As we have seen, audiences of reality TV classify programmes in a manner that invites criticism. In part this reflects a common way of talking about reality TV as 'trash TV', something I addressed earlier. But it also reflects audience expectations of the genre, expectations that are based on a traditional understanding of factual television. These expectations are connected to the television schedule, where news frames popular factual programming in the evening schedule on UK terrestrial television. Although reality TV is not news, nevertheless the viewing expectations for popular factual television are framed by audience understanding of factual programming as 'true to life', recording events that 'just happen'. These expectations can create a critical approach to the reality genre. But this doesn't mean to say that viewers do not enjoy the more entertaining formats such as *Big Brother*. They just classify them differently. In the next chapter, I consider how performance and social drama in popular factual formats such as *Big Brother* can lead to complex and often contradictory viewing experiences.

CONCLUSION

This chapter has provided an overview of the various ways the television industry, scholars and audiences classify reality TV. There is no one definition of reality programming, but many, competing definitions of what has come to be called the reality genre. This is because the reality genre is made of a number of distinctive and historically based television genres, such as lifestyle, or documentary. These television genres have merged with each other to create a number of hybrid genres that we now call reality TV, or popular factual television. The term reality TV neatly sums up the type of programming the television industry, scholars and audiences refer to in their discussion of the genre, but it fails to differentiate between the different styles and formats within the reality genre. As we have seen in discussion by members of the television industry about commissioning reality programming, by scholars about the development of reality programming, and by audiences about their viewing experience of reality programming, the one thing in common amongst these groups of people is their desire to differentiate between the rapidly expanding and somewhat bewildering range of programming that comes under the category of reality TV. The way in which the UK television industry has redefined its generic structure for documentary and contemporary factual programming due to developments within the reality genre is also reflected in the way scholars and audiences locate the 'so-called' reality genre within a broader understanding of general factual, and indeed fictional, television.

If there is one defining characteristic that unites the disparate group of programmes that make up the reality genre it is the capacity to let viewers see for themselves. This unique function of factual television has become a key attraction for audiences of reality TV. However, the capacity of reality TV to let viewers see for themselves has ensured a predominantly critical viewing position. Audiences judge the 'reality' of reality programmes according to a fact/fiction continuum, with at the far end of the continuum infotainment or docu-soaps, and at the other end formatted reality gameshows. As the genre continues to develop, perhaps it is only a matter of time before the television industry, scholars and audiences begin to include other types of factual television within the category of 'reality'.

Chapter 4

Performance and authenticity

The debate about what is real and what is not is the million-dollar question for popular factual television. In this chapter, I explore the twin issues of performance and authenticity, as the performance of non-professional actors often frames discussion about the authenticity of visual evidence in popular factual television. The way real people and their stories are represented on television is closely connected to how we judge the truthfulness of visual evidence. To invoke the work of Brian Winston (1995), 'claiming the real' is a common practice of reality programming, but there is little interrogation of these truth claims in the programmes themselves. Television audiences are certainly aware of the ways television 'puts reality together' (Schlesinger 1978), and talk about how various formats, or editing techniques, can create different degrees of 'reality' in popular factual television. However, viewers of reality programming are most likely to talk about the truth of what they are seeing in relation to the way real people act in front of television cameras. The more ordinary people are perceived to perform for the cameras, the less real the programme appears to be to viewers. Thus, performance becomes a powerful framing device for judging reality TV's claims to the real. And television audiences are highly sceptical of the truth claims of much reality programming precisely because they expect people to 'act up' in order to make entertaining factual television.

PARADOX

At the heart of the debate about the reality of reality TV is a paradox: the more entertaining a factual programme is, the less real it appears to viewers. Corner notes 'the legacy of documentary is still at work' in popular factual television, but in 'partial and revised' form (2002a: 260). The partial and revised factual elements of reality TV are borrowed from documentary genres, such as observational documentary, and serve to put the factual into popular factual television. As Corner explains: the 'documentary imperative' is used as a 'vehicle variously for the high-intensity incident (the reconstructed accident, the police raid), for anecdotal knowledge (gossipy first-person accounts), and for snoopy sociability (as an amused bystander to the mixture of mess and routine in other people's working lives)' (2002a: 260). Kilborn (2003: 119) notes the influence of fictional genres, in particular 'character-and speech-focused entertainments', within reality programming. These entertaining elements of reality TV are borrowed from fictional genres, such as soap opera, and serve to put the popular into popular factual television. For example, 'all docu-soaps – to a greater or lesser degree – make use of structuring devices inherited from fictional serial drama' (2003: 114). With regard to *Big Brother*, 'techniques appropriated from narrative fiction were used to ensure that sufficient pace and variety were introduced into what would otherwise have been a highly pedestrian sequence of events' (2003: 83). Viewers of reality programming are attracted to various formats because they feature real people's stories in an entertaining manner. However, they are also distrustful of the authenticity of various reality formats *precisely because* these real people's stories are presented in an entertaining manner.

In his article 'Reality TV in the Digital Era: A Paradox in Visual Culture', Arild Fetveit argues:

> The advent of digital manipulation and image generation techniques has seriously challenged the credibility of photographic discourses. At the same time, however, we are experiencing a growing use of surveillance cameras, and a form of factual television that seems to depend more heavily on the evidential force of the photographic image than any previous form: *reality* TV.
>
> (2002: 119)

Fetveit's argument draws on the development of photographic practices to understand the growth of reality programming in the 1990s. The history of photography suggests that the way we look at photographic images has changed over time, from viewing images as illustrative of real objects or people, to viewing images as evidence of real objects or people. The introduction of digital manipulation as a photographic technique during the 1990s has ensured that we are more likely to look at digitally enhanced photographic images as illustrations of real objects or people. Take, for example, the playful photographs of famous people that regularly feature on the front pages of tabloid newspapers; readers are likely to view a photograph of President George W. Bush and Prime Minister Tony Blair kissing as illustrative of their close relationship as political leaders of the USA and UK, rather than as actual evidence of a romantic relationship. Fetveit argues that it is precisely at this moment of change in our 'belief in the evidential powers of photographic images'

(2002: 123) that reality TV has flourished. For Fetveit, it is no coincidence that reality programming directs viewers to its television images of reality, showing caught on camera footage of car crashes, or rescue operations, again and again in order to draw attention to the evidential powers of on-scene reality footage. With one eye on photography and another on reality TV, Fetveit suggests our loss of faith in the evidential nature of digitally enhanced photography has been replaced by our faith in the evidential nature of reality TV.

Fetveit's argument is useful in understanding why viewers may trust the type of on-scene footage, or surveillance footage, so common to reality programming such as *Cops* or *Neighbours from Hell*. Audiences place a great deal of trust in the ability of television cameras to capture real events as they happen. However, as I discussed in the previous chapter, audience trust in the authenticity of reality television is complex, and dependent on the ways in which each reality format is set up to capture the stories of everyday people. In fact, audiences are likely to distrust visual evidence in reality programming – 'I'm not quite sure I trust that what we're seeing is not being staged' (31-year-old housewife). Just as the development of photographic techniques is connected with the changing ways we look at photographic images, so too is the development of production techniques within reality programming connected with the changing ways we look at television images. In this section, I want to briefly discuss the significance of factual television, and academic research within documentary studies, as a means of understanding how viewers critically respond to hybrid formats within popular factual television.

Viewers expect particular types of factual television to offer them visual evidence of real life. News and documentary are the two most common genres within factual television where viewers place a great deal of trust in the truth claims of audio-visual documentation. If we look at research by the television regulatory bodies the Independent Television Commission (ITC) and the Broadcasting Standards Commission (BSC) in the UK in 2002, we can see that over 90 per cent of the UK population were interested in watching news, and nearly 90 per cent believed television news provided accurate information (ITC/BSC 2003: 60). In relation to documentary, almost 80 per cent of the public were interested in watching documentary television, and nearly 60 per cent believed documentaries provided accurate information. With regard to popular factual television, audience trust in the honesty of the situations portrayed was lower than news or documentary, and varied according to different types of reality programming. Less than half of the UK population (42 per cent) believed docu-soaps were accurate, and only 20 per cent believed reality gameshows were accurate. In fact, with regard to accuracy, infotainment programmes such as *999* scored higher than docu-soaps or reality gameshows, with 68 per cent of viewers claiming these programmes provided accurate information. These statistics not only suggest that traditional formats within reality programming are perceived as more authentic than other, newer types of reality formats, but also that infotainment shows are thought to be more accurate than television documentary.

The findings from the ITC/BSC research raise significant issues regarding authenticity within factual television. The accuracy and honesty of news, documentary and popular factual programming forms the basis of much debate within the media itself. Brian Winston, in his aptly titled book *Lies, Damn Lies and Documentaries*, summarises the intense debate in the British press concerning documentary practice during the infamous case of *The Connection*. *The Connection* was an investigative documentary about illegal drug trade that was exposed by the British press for fabricating certain events in the programme, and as a result Carlton was fined £2 million by the ITC for breach of the programme code related to accuracy and impartiality (Winston 2000: 9–39). With headlines such as 'Can We Believe Anything We See on TV?', the scandal 'acquired legs' and other documentaries were also subject to intense scrutiny (2000: 2). *The Connection* scandal had major consequences not just for documentary practitioners, but also for viewers. The degree of audience distrust in documentary, as outlined in the ITC/BSC research, is related to the frequency and force of the fakery debate in the British press during the late 1990s (see also Kilborn 2003). Audience distrust in the truth claims of documentary also relates to the way viewers carry over expectations about the accuracy of news into other factual genres, such as documentary. In the previous chapter, I discussed the fact/fiction continuum applied by viewers to different types of reality programming. We can see from the statistics above that viewers extend this continuum to other types of factual programming, rating news more factual, i.e. more accurate, than other types of factual television. On a sliding scale of factual programming, infotainment scores higher than documentary in terms of accuracy. The ITC/BSC audience data suggests how damaging fakery scandals can be to audience trust in the evidential status of documentary footage.

Given the dramatised nature of reconstructions and factual footage in reality programming, it is difficult to understand why audiences are more likely to trust the information they receive in dramatised reconstructions of real people's stories in reality programmes than documentaries. As I discussed in Chapter 2, infotainment, or what was originally called 'on-scene' reality programming, had its origins in tabloid journalism and American local news bulletins. Dramatised reconstructions of real people's stories primarily occur in crime and emergency services reality programmes, and audiences associate these reality programmes with news. Audiences also associate documentary with news. The dominance of two particular styles of documentary in British television, documentary journalism and observational documentary (see Chapter 2), has had an impact on audiences. Viewers commonly associate documentary with factual footage that claims to be accurate, impartial, and based on first-hand observation. In relation to the sliding scale of factual programming we could expect audiences to perceive documentary as more accurate than dramatised reconstructions of real people's stories in reality programmes. However, the damage caused by the documentary fakery scandals has been so detrimental that audiences are distrustful of the documentary genre as a whole.

John Ellis, in his book *Seeing Things*, talks about how television is 'a vast mechanism for processing the material of the witnessed world into more narrativised, explained forms' (2000: 78). Factual television is a primary vehicle for witnessing the world, and news bulletins, and crime and emergency services reality programming, offer an opportunity to witness events as they happen. The stories in crime and emergency services reality programming may be dramatised, they may be reconstructed, but they make direct claims to journalistic inquiry, even to the extent of using newsreaders as presenters of the programmes (see Hill 2000b). When factual television's ability to witness the world is challenged, as in the documentary fakery scandal in the UK, audiences come to question the genre, and judge it in relation to other factual genres.

It would be wrong to suggest that audiences never question the accuracy and impartiality of television news. We know from the research already conducted in news and its audience that news stories are constructed and framed according to personal/political/social interests, and that audiences can be critical of journalistic practices, especially regarding high-profile events such as war.[1] According to John Ellis, factual genres have communities of viewers who understand the 'protocols and ideas of appropriate behaviour which are sustained by concrete institutions and common practices' (2002: 206). For Ellis, television viewers are part of the critical evaluation of factual genres, and their ability to question and debate the truth claims of audio-visual documentation is vital to the continuation of factual programming. Thus, 'the documentary genre depends on a series of assertions of the truthfulness of its material, and the criteria of truthfulness differ between cultures and historical periods' (ibid.). A 'criterion of truthfulness' can be applied to news, as well as to documentary or reality programming.

But what is the basis for this criterion of truthfulness? For Winston, the criterion applied by television audiences and regulators to documentary is based upon an ignorance of the origins of documentary, and the 'established grammar and procedures' that are associated with a range of documentary practices (2000: 2). For television audiences, the criteria applied to documentary are closely connected with expectations about the accuracy and impartiality of television news. When viewers come to watch reality TV these expectations do not disappear. Viewers are most likely to trust in the evidential power of reality TV when the factual footage is closest to footage viewers associate with news, or investigative journalism. But it is important to point out that only a certain type of more traditional reality programming, especially crime and emergency services programming, meets this criterion. Most contemporary programmes classified as reality TV are far removed from traditional factual television genres such as news or documentary. Therefore, most contemporary reality programmes fail to live up to audience expectations about the evidential status of factual television. Thus, the common viewing position when watching reality TV is one that is critical of the evidential claims of the programmes. The audience discussion that features in the rest of this chapter is evidence of a critically astute reality viewer – a viewer often ignored in popular and academic debates about reality TV.

ACTING UP

ITC/BSC (2003) research in audience trust in the accuracy of factual genres reveals an interesting link between news and nature/wildlife programmes. Viewers of nature and wildlife thought such programmes were just as accurate as news (89 per cent). Audience trust in the presenters of natural history programmes and news bulletins must surely play a part in explaining these statistics. Television audiences often perceive news and natural history presenters as 'friends', and as such these television presenters are trusted to present facts in a truthful manner (Gauntlett and Hill 1999). The issue of performance is also notable, as these two genres are less likely to contain overt performances by humans or animals. Audiences are far more distrustful of factual genres that may appear to encourage non-professional actors to 'act up', such as docu-soaps or reality gameshows. The ITC/BSC research indicates that reality gameshows like *Big Brother* scored low (20 per cent) in audience assessment of the honesty of situations portrayed in these programmes. One of the reasons this is the case is that the format is designed to promote performance. Contestants are engaged in a popularity contest, where they are on display in the performance space of the *Big Brother* house (Corner 2002b: 257). As one viewer commented on a contestant in *Big Brother*: 'I don't think she ever forgot that the cameras were there ... she was plucking her ... pubic hairs with her tweezers! In the garden with everyone else watching!' (31-year-old housewife). In this section, I consider how the 'criteria of truthfulness' (Ellis 2002) applied by viewers to reality television are often associated with their belief that the more people act up in front of cameras, the less real a programme appears to be.

Research within documentary studies has addressed the issue of performance primarily in relation to the development of specific genres and their truth claims. Theatrical documentary films, such as *Night Mail* (Grierson, 1936), or *The Thin Blue Line* (Morris, 1988), reconstruct events using people originally involved. Despite the obvious construction of theatrical documentaries, according to Nichols (1991) we engage with such films as documentaries rather than fiction films. However, the fact that this mode of documentary is rarely used in television suggests that viewers are probably unfamiliar with this type of treatment of real events. Another type of documentary is the performative documentary, whereby texts are less about objective accounts of the world and more about subjective interpretations of reality (Nichols 1994). Performative documentaries blur boundaries between fact and fiction. Bruzzi suggests that the performative documentary is 'a mode which emphasises – and indeed constructs a film around – the often hidden aspect of performance, whether on the part of the documentary subjects or the filmmakers' (2000: 153). For Bruzzi, documentary filmmakers such as Nick Broomfield or Michael Moore draw attention to the inherent performance and artifice in any documentary film. All documentary is 'necessarily performative because it is given meaning by the interaction between performance and reality' (2000: 154). Although Bruzzi makes a suggestive link between performative documentary and reality programming in her reference to the performance of documentary subjects, her definition of this genre is more associated with the filmmakers themselves, or celebrities in the films, rather than the performance of ordinary people in popular factual television.

A more appropriate mode of documentary for understanding performance in reality TV is the drama-documentary. Derek Paget (1998: 82) defines drama-documentary as a 'sequence of events from a real historical occurrence or situation and the identities of the protagonists to underpin a film script intended to provoke debate'. When real people who have experienced an occurrence or situation are involved in a drama-documentary (usually as minor 'characters'), they are there to authenticate the dramatisation of the event. Even though their somewhat self-conscious acting style may differ from the naturalist/realist style of professional actors, their performance draws attention to the truth claims of the documentary. Another related example of the use of professional and non-professional actors in reality programming is that of dramatised reconstructions of accidents or crime. For example, *999* often tells the story of a rescue operation by including the emergency services personnel involved, along with actors representing other people involved in the rescue. Although technically the emergency services personnel are re-creating the rescue for the cameras, their performance is an indication of the authenticity of the story – this is how it happened, according to the people involved.

Thus, there are certain types of factual genres whereby real people perform for the cameras, and their performance is taken as evidence of the truthfulness of the programme itself. However, in terms of reality TV, many programmes are judged by viewers as unreal precisely because of the performance of non-professional actors.

Audiences have a high degree of cynicism regarding the portrayal of real people in popular factual television. In 2000, 73 per cent of the public thought stories in reality programming were sometimes made up or exaggerated for TV, and only 12 per cent thought stories about real people really actually happened as portrayed in the programmes (Hill/ITC 2000). The general public's lack of trust in the actuality of popular factual television is partly explained by the documentary fakery scandals discussed in the previous section, and partly by the use of formats associated with fictional genres in popular factual series. During the fakery scandal in the UK, several docu-soaps were accused of faking certain scenes for dramatic effect. According to Bruzzi (2000), *Driving School* (which attracted over 12 million viewers) reconstructed certain scenes and manipulated others in order to maximise the drama of Maureen's story as we saw her struggle to pass her driving test. The producers intervened in the outcome of the story: 'they were concerned that Maureen, the series "star" subject, would not pass her manual driving test, an event they felt would be the series' natural and desired conclusion, and so suggested that she learn instead in an automatic' (2000: 88). Despite, or perhaps because of, press discussion about the truthfulness of *Driving School*, Maureen became a celebrity in her own right. This example of the blurring of the boundaries between documentary and soap opera, and between non-professional actors and television celebrities, is only one example of the type of public discussion surrounding reality programmes. This public discussion fuels audience scepticism about the authenticity of reality TV, and leads to a high degree of anticipation that 'real' people perform in popular factual television. In 2000, 70 per cent of adult viewers thought that members of the public usually overacted in front of cameras in reality programmes (Hill/ITC 2000).

The way viewers talk about ordinary people in reality programmes illustrates their inherent distrust in particular types of reality formats. This 41-year-old male carpenter makes a clear distinction between hidden camera programmes, and other types of reality formats:

> 'I just think that they're two entirely different programmes – the ones with the hidden camera and the ones where, like *Big Brother*, where they're actually acting to the camera – to me, they're entirely different

categories, I don't even think they're in the same thing. I mean … it's the same with *Changing Rooms*, these people on there they're just playing to … I'd rather watch something where the camera's hidden and you actually see people … I mean just through the day, talking to people … that is something natural, you ain't acting, you know. That is actually what happens, that is a true to life thing.'

This viewer's perception of hidden camera formats as more 'true to life' than formats 'where they're actually acting to the camera' was common to all the respondents in my research. Even though hidden camera programmes involve a high degree of construction, where people are set up and filmed without their prior knowledge or consent, the very fact that they do not know they are being filmed is a clear indication for audiences that the programmes are authentic. Here are a group of adult viewers discussing a particular hidden camera series, *House of Horrors*, which attempts to shame dishonest builders by secretly filming them on the job:

Esther: This is a fairly real one 'cos nobody knows the camera's there, so they're just being natural and they're being caught out and if they knew the camera was there, they'd behave completely differently, I believe.

Eric: I think we'd all behave completely differently, wouldn't we, if there are cameras there.

Esther: But if you're being a crook, which is what these people are, then they're really being caught out then, it would be a completely different story if they knew the cameras were there.

Pantelis: They'd be completely honest if they knew the camera was there.

Their discussion of the naturalness of ordinary people on television encapsulates the way audiences make judgements about the 'honesty' of people and programmes, depending on whether there is prior knowledge of filming. The programme might be 'set up', as in the case of *House of Horrors*, where the builders work on a site pre-fitted with hidden cameras. But people's reactions are natural. In *House of Horrors* dishonesty is actually a sign of honesty because the programme is about crooked builders who pretend to be trustworthy.

Most viewers argue that the only way ordinary people will be themselves on television is if they don't know they're on television in the first place: 'I wouldn't be who I really am … trying to talk differently, talk posh and everything! [laughs] You know, I just wouldn't be myself' (40-year-old female part-time secretary). There is also a general assumption that if people could 'be themselves' twenty-four hours a day on TV, then this would not make for very exciting television: 'They could follow me all day but it would be boring [laughs]. They could follow me all day and night, somebody might jump in front of me, other than that totally boring' (38-year-old underground train driver). The repetition of the word 'boring' to describe this train driver's typical day illuminates the way many viewers assume stories in reality programmes are exaggerated or made up in order to make interesting television. There are exceptions to the rule. For example, emergency services programmes already contain dramatic stories, and few viewers believe these are made up, or indeed that the people involved are acting up for the cameras (even though some people are doing just that in order to re-create the event for television). But, overall, audiences categorise most reality TV as unreal because they believe ordinary people cannot help but perform once cameras are rolling.

Bill Nichols has argued that our assumptions about documentary frame our reception of it. We have 'a documentary mode of engagement' (1991: 25), whereby we watch documentary texts with knowledge of how these texts are put together, and with expectations that the portrayal of real events will be truthful and accurate. Roscoe and Hight explain that when we watch a documentary 'we expect that events we see on screen would have happened, as they happened, even if the filmmaker had not been present'. In addition, they argue:

> Although it is essential that we recognise and believe that documentary is concerned with the real world, it also sets up a position for viewers in which we are encouraged to interact with those representations, and not necessarily accept the arguments presented. Although documentary has been accorded its special position on the basis of its claims to truth, documentary also includes a contradictory position for viewers in which they can argue against its truth claims ... the expectations, assumptions and positions constructed by documentary for viewers are also ... complex and complicated.
>
> (2002: 21)

If we accept there is a documentary mode of engagement, then this engagement is characterised by a contradictory response that is based on trust in the truth claims of documentary, and criticism of these truth claims. This model has implications for a reality mode of engagement. A reality mode of engagement is characterised by a contradictory response that is based on audience assessment of the authenticity of real people's stories and situations within the performative environment of popular factual television. This mode of engagement involves criticism of the truth claims of reality programming, but also some degree of trust in the old adage 'truth will out'. The next section examines audience discussion of performance in order to illustrate how viewers judge the authenticity of ordinary people in reality programming.

PERFORMING THE REAL

A reality format like *Big Brother* can be understood in terms of the tensions and contradictions between the performance of non-professional actors, and their authentic behaviour in the *Big Brother* house. This is, of course, not the only way to understand *Big Brother*, and other researchers have commented on the significance of surveillance (Palmer 2002a), or media events (Scannell 2002; Couldry 2002), to our understanding of the popularity and impact of reality gameshows. In terms of television audiences, there is evidence to suggest that the improvised performances of ordinary people frame discussion of this format, and indeed other reality gameshows, such as *Survivor* or *Temptation Island*. In an article on *Big Brother* titled 'Performing the Real', John Corner (2002b: 263–4) comments on the 'degree of self-consciousness' and 'display' by the various personalities in the 'predefined stage' of the *Big Brother* house. As Corner notes, the performance of contestants gives television audiences the opportunity for 'thick judgemental and speculative discourse around participants' motives, actions and likely future behaviour' (2002b: 264). I want to focus on the way audiences speculate and judge moments when the performance of non-professional actors breaks down, and they are 'true to themselves'. Corner sums up this viewing process as follows:

> One might use the term 'selving' to describe the central process whereby 'true selves' are seen to emerge (and develop) from underneath and, indeed, through, the 'performed selves' projected for us, as a consequence of the applied pressures of objective circumstance and group dynamics. A certain amount of the humdrum and the routine may be a necessary element in giving this selving process, this unwitting disclosure of personal core, a measure of plausibility, aligning it with the mundane rhythms and naturalistic portrayals of docu soap, soap opera itself, and at times, the registers of game-show participation.
>
> (2002b: 263–4)

Other researchers have also discussed this notion of 'performed selves' and 'true selves' co-existing in hybrid formats within the reality genre. Roscoe and Hight (2001: 38) discuss the 'performed' nature of docu-soaps, and how this type of construction of documentary footage can open up space for debate about the documentary genre. Jane Roscoe comments on how *Big Brother* is 'constructed around performance' (2001: 482), with participants involved in different levels of performance, based on the roles of 'housemate', 'gameshow contestant' and 'television personality', and how audiences are invited to join in with these performances 'across the formats of the different shows'. Lothar Mikos *et al.* (2000), in their research of *Big Brother* in Germany, also suggest that audiences are engaged in an assessment of performance and authenticity. In my earlier research on *Big Brother*, I noted that the tension between performance and authenticity in the documentary gameshow format invites viewers to look for 'moments of truth' in a constructed television environment (Hill 2002).

Audiences frequently discuss the difference between performed selves and true selves in reality programming, speculating and judging the behaviour of ordinary people, comparing the motives and actions of people who choose to take part in a reality programme. And they discuss the behaviour of ordinary people in a reality programme on an everyday basis. Here is a typical example of the way viewers talk about acting in *Big Brother*:

> 'Sometimes, I think, can you really act like your true self when there's a camera there? You know. Maybe in *Big Brother* a little bit more you can act yourself because you're going to forget after a while, aren't you? But I'm a bit dubious about people acting themselves ... The way they were all acting, the way of their body movements and all that, it just looked too fake ... to me.'
>
> (21-year-old male dairy worker)

This viewer's tentative question about being able to 'act like your true self' in front of a television camera opens the door to speculation about levels of acting in the *Big Brother* house, and to judgement of individual contestants' 'true' or 'fake' behaviour. I want to highlight several examples of audience discussion about the improvised performances of contestants in *Big Brother* in order to explore how viewers engage with the inherent contradictions between fact and fiction in this type of hybrid genre.

There is a common mode of engagement when watching *Big Brother* and this is characterised by discussion that goes backwards and forwards between trust and suspicion of the behaviour of ordinary people in the house. In the following debate, a group of male and female adult viewers discuss the various 'selves' on display in the *Big Brother* house:

Rick: With *Big Brother* you don't know if they're playing up, yeah, it's just, it's a weird scenario for them to be in, you must just think ... well, you don't know what's going on inside their head.

Paul: Maybe you put yourself in that situation and, see, it's like I watch it and if, if I was on *Big Brother*, I'd want everyone to like

me or ... I think of myself as an alright person but then if I was
on there I'd, I'd be acting different, thinking 'I've got to do this
'cos people are going to like me', so maybe that's, that's why,
maybe, I think they're acting up.

Peter: They must have thought about everything they've done and
said before they actually said or done it. Not like real life, just
someone coming out with a comment, but, this could get me out
this week – I better not say that, I better just say 'does anyone
want a cup of tea?' Not 'cos I want to make it but I better ask
them to look good.

Pauline: 'Cos at the end of the day, it's a competition, isn't it? There was
seventy grand on the line, wasn't there? I'd act up for it! [laughs]

Their discussion is characterised by a cautious assessment of the abilities
of *Big Brother* contestants to 'act up'. A point to remember is that the *Big
Brother* contestants are strangers to themselves, and to viewers. Unlike
celebrity reality gameshows, such as *Celebrity Big Brother*, or *I'm a
Celebrity ...* , where we know the 'personality' of the contestants
beforehand, in the case of ordinary people shows the participants are
strangers to us. When audiences attempt to judge the difference between
the contestants' performing selves and true selves in *Big Brother*, they
cannot refer to past performances but must rely on their own judgement
of the contestants' behaviour and 'what's going on inside their head'.
Inevitably, viewers turn to their own experience, and speculate about how
they might behave in a similar situation. The discussion therefore
becomes one based on hypothetical situations – 'if I was on *Big Brother*' –
interspersed with knowledge of the format, and the effect of the game on
contestants' behaviour – 'they must have thought about everything
they've done and said before they actually said or done it'.

Audience assessment of the performance of non-professional actors in
reality gameshows can often be based on how well the contestants play
the game, and also how well contestants remain true to themselves. In the
above discussion, viewers were commenting on the contestants in *Big
Brother* 2000 in the UK, where the winner was someone who managed to
remain popular with his fellow contestants, and with viewers, by
carefully balancing his performing self with his true self – Craig was
likeable, and certainly made lots of cups of tea, but he didn't go out of his
way to grab attention. Even in the first season of *Survivor* (2000) in
America, where the winner constantly reminded contestants and viewers
of his ability to 'play the game', he managed to portray himself as himself
– a competitive, ruthless 'survivor'. Karen Lury (1996: 126) suggests that
television audiences may be anxious about watching ordinary people
perform because 'if real people convincingly "put on an act" where can
sincerity, authenticity and real emotion be located with any conviction?'.

In the case of reality gameshows, any 'claims to the real' are immediately undermined by the ability of contestants to 'put on an act'. As Lury explains:

> While acting may be pleasurable when we know we are watching a performance (it is after all a 'skillful' activity), when an ordinary performer acts, we may become uncomfortably aware of how appearance and reality (the behaviour and the feelings) of the performer may be no more matched in the everyday than they are on screen.
>
> (1996: 126)

Reality gameshows have capitalised on this tension between appearance and reality by ensuring that viewers have to judge for themselves which of the contestants are being genuine. In fact, audiences enjoy debating the appearance and reality of ordinary people in reality gameshows. The potential for gossip, opinion and conjecture is far greater when watching reality gameshows because this hybrid format openly invites viewers to decide not just who wins or loses, but who is true or false in the documentary/game environment.

Lury (1996: 126) also suggests that audiences may be uncomfortable watching ordinary people on television because the participants in the show have been 'coerced into making a fool of themselves, and that their presence or image on screen has been manipulated by technicians, producers and bullying presenters'. This type of 'uncomfortable' viewing position is applicable to certain forms of reality programming, such as health-based reality programmes (or, for me, *The Anna Nicole Show*), where people may be perceived as 'victims' of ratings-driven popular factual television (see Chapters 6 and 7 for further discussion). However, with regard to reality gameshows, the majority of audiences are not so much uncomfortable with the manipulation of contestants as sceptical that anything that goes on in the *Big Brother* house can be unscripted and natural. Thus, when contestants in the *Big Brother* house are given alcohol as a reward for completing various challenges, viewers are likely to not blame the producers for the drunken behaviour of contestants but to judge the housemates critically for making fools of themselves. Most viewers think the humiliation, or emotional trauma, experienced by housemates is generated by housemates, and therefore cannot be trusted as genuine emotional experiences, experiences that in other circumstances might be viewed more sympathetically (e.g., health-based reality programmes).

Most of the people involved in the making of *Big Brother* argue that ordinary people cannot act up twenty-four hours a day. For example, Dermot O'Leary, the presenter of *Big Brother's Little Brother*, which accompanies *Big Brother* on Channel 4 and E4 in the UK, claims 'no one can act for 24 hours a day, or indeed, for 24 minutes an hour, so we know that the housemates' reactions are genuine'.[2] It is not my intention to question the insider's perception of levels of acting in reality gameshows. The belief that people can't keep up an act forever is also common to discussion by observational documentary practitioners (see Bruzzi 2000), and echoed by this television presenter. It is my intention to question how audiences make sense of such truth claims from the makers of documentary gameshows. The behaviour of ordinary people in *Big Brother* allows audiences to assess the truth claims of the programme itself. In the following extract, a group of teenage girls discuss an infamous scene in UK *Big Brother* (2000). In the scene, 'Nasty Nick' was accused of attempting to influence the voting behaviour of other contestants, and after denying the charge, he retreated to the bedroom where he packed his suitcase, shed a few tears, and listened to advice from fellow housemate Mel. The girls begin their discussion with a prompt about the possible 'crocodile' tears of 'Nasty Nick':

Interviewer: Do you think in that scene when he was crying that was really coming from him?

Sharon: Erm, it could have been, 'cos in a way he was kicked out and he didn't have any way of winning now and … as you saw, the public was really negative towards him.

Nicola: I don't think that's as real life as it could have been, 'cos they know they're going to make quite a bit of money.

Angela: [shakes her head] *Big Brother*. I felt I knew the people in there, 'cos after a while, although there's cameras there, in the beginning they all did act up but you can't do it all the time. You know when you're upset and crying you can't act happy, you know what I mean. And you get really close to the people, 'cos you, like, get to know them. It's really weird, 'cos, like, we're talking about them now as if we know them and it's people we've never ever met in our lives who are on TV.

Interviewer: Are there moments when you're not sure? How do you tell if someone's acting up or not?

Nicola: I think if they're just, like, acting out of the normal, how you wouldn't expect someone to act and you just think they're acting up whether they are or not.

Interviewer: So, it's sort of based on what you think?

Nicola: Yeah, what you think they should act like, but if they're not acting like that.

Laura: No, but some people are extroverts though, you can't say that. Some people are very forward and open-minded and they don't care what people think. But I think you can always tell when people are showing off.

Angela: Yeah, but if you genuinely like them. Say, I liked Anna and if someone said 'Oh, Anna's this, oh, Anna's that', I wouldn't think she's acting up, do you know what I mean. I think it depends on your attitude towards the person. Do you know what I mean? 'Cos people genuinely didn't like Nick 'cos they'd seen that he was doing these kinds of things ... Yeah and I hated Mel so whatever anybody said that was good about her, I was, like, 'oh, I don't like her, whatever she does, she's a bitch'.

Sharon: I think the only people that could tell if these people are acting up are the people that knew them. We don't know them so we *couldn't really judge.*

Interviewer: Do you end up judging anyway?

Sharon: Yeah, well I do!

Laura: But they have to be acting up at the end of the day 'cos if they want to get our votes, they can't sit there and ... say, they're a really bitchy person, they're not going to sit there and literally be a bitch about everyone 'cos then they're going to be kicked out. They've got to put on an act, they've got to try and make the effort and they've got to try and sweeten us up so we won't kick them out.

Angela: But none of them know, that's the thing, none of them in the house would actually really know if, like, one of them was acting up or not.

Laura: That's what I'm saying.

There are several points raised in this discussion that are relevant to the twin issues of performance and authenticity. The first is that there is no clear agreement about the performing self and true self of the character of Nasty Nick. Even though he appeared to break down and reveal his true self in a moment of personal conflict, according to these viewers he needed sympathy from the public, and therefore his tears could be perceived as part of a performance. They are suspicious of Nick because they have witnessed his duplicitous behaviour prior to the housemates' intervention, and because he is a contestant in a gameshow. Another point is that the discussion has a backwards and forwards rhythm characteristic to talk about what is real and what is not in reality gameshows. *Big Brother* is not 'as real life as it could have been' because of the gameshow element to the format, but contestants in the house can't act all of the time, so parts of it are real. We 'get to know' the housemates intimately, as if they are people we have actually met in our everyday lives, but 'we don't know them' because we have never really met them. In many ways, their discussion about acting highlights a philosophical conundrum – how can we really know what we are seeing is real? These teenage viewers of *Big Brother* struggle to come to terms with the age-old question 'what is reality?'.

The sociologist Erving Goffman, in his book *The Presentation of the Self in Everyday Life* claims we are all performing all of the time on various different stages, such as work or home, to various different audiences, such as our boss or our family. For Goffman, our houses, cars, clothing, and other such everyday items are 'props' and 'scenery' required for the 'work of successfully staging a character' (1969: 203). In any social encounter, a performer will be aware of their audience and vice versa. The process of communication between the performer and audience is an 'information game', where performers will reveal and conceal their behaviour to others (1969: 20). On the *Big Brother* stage there are two types of audience, one that is inside and another that is outside the house. The inside audience has first-hand knowledge of the performance of individuals within the group, but this knowledge is only partial, as the contestants cannot witness all the actions, or performances, of the other members of the social group. The outside audience has second-hand knowledge, but is witness to, in Goffman's terms, the 'front' and 'backstage' behaviour of the housemates via the twenty-four-hour surveillance cameras. By front and backstage Goffman (1969: 34) refers to moments in social interaction when an individual ceases to play a part convincingly, when we see beyond a 'personal front' to the real person inside the performer. In the discussion by the teenage girls about the performance of housemates, they highlighted how 'none of them in the house would actually really know if, like, one of them was acting up or not'. This would suggest that viewers of *Big Brother* would have a privileged position in the 'information game', and be able to anticipate future incidents or behaviour based on prior knowledge of the front and backstage behaviour of housemates. Certainly, in the scene with Nasty Nick confrontation by the other housemates disrupted the natural harmony of the *Big Brother* house, literally 'creating a scene' which millions of viewers tuned in to watch. The housemates' intervention provided a backstage view of one particular performer and cast a shadow on the believability of his remaining performance in the house. Audiences were already suspicious of Nick's performance prior to the intervention, and remained suspicious at the point when he had lost everything and was most likely to reveal his 'true self'.

Although the above discussion suggests that viewers do feel they have a bird's eye view of events in the *Big Brother* house, there is a general questioning of how viewers can really get to know these performers at all. According to Goffman, when social interaction occurs there is a 'natural movement back and forth between cynicism and sincerity' (1969: 31) on behalf of performers and audiences. In the teenage girls' discussion of *Big Brother* there is a 'natural movement back and forth' in their talk of how viewers judge the sincerity of ordinary people in reality gameshows. I would argue it is in the act of trying to judge the scene change from performing self to true self that audiences draw on their own understanding of social behaviour in their everyday lives. As Goffman (1969: 241–2) indicates, when we do not have full information of a factual situation we 'rely on appearances ... and, paradoxically, the more the individual is concerned with the reality that is not available to perception, the more he must concentrate his attention on appearances'. Although when we watch a reality gameshow such as *Big Brother* we rely solely on representations of real people, we also rely on our knowledge of social interaction. In the final part of this chapter, I consider how we judge authentic performances – 'what you think they should act like, but if they're not acting like that' – in popular factual television.

AUTHENTICITY

According to Van Leeuwen (2001), authenticity can mean different things to different people. Authenticity can mean something is not an imitation, or copy, but the genuine article, as in an authentic Picasso painting. It can also mean something is reconstructed or represented just like the original, as in a translation of Homer's *The Iliad*. Authenticity can mean something is authorised, and has a seal of approval, as in ephemera sold as part of the Elvis Presley estate. And finally, authenticity can mean something is true. It is the final definition of authenticity that most concerns us here, as an ordinary person in a reality programme is often perceived as authentic if they are 'thought to be true to the essence of something, to a revealed truth, a deeply held sentiment' (Van Leeuwen 2001: 393).

Here is an example of the way audiences typically talk about authentic 'performances' in reality programming:

Peter: It's real life, innit, I mean.
Rick: I don't think it is though ... The ones on holiday are more real life than these people, I don't, I don't believe anything now, I think it's all an act but on holiday they might be acting a little bit more but because they're drunk as well it's real life, innit?
Nancy: It's not real life really, is it? 'Cos real life doesn't happen like that?
Rick: If it was real life you, you'd have to not know that the cameras were there and that's never the case in any of those programmes.
Paul: If it was real life I'd be watching someone sitting down watching telly all day.

This group of adult viewers were discussing travel reality series, such as *Ibiza Uncovered*, that often feature British tourists behaving badly abroad. Variations on the word 'reality' are echoed in each turn in the conversation ('real', 'real life'), and this points to a critical examination of the truth claims of these programmes. As with other examples of audience discussion I have used in this chapter, the authenticity of reality programming is examined in relation to the performances of the people featured in the programmes themselves. These viewers question how the talk and behaviour of the ordinary people being filmed on holiday in Ibiza can be judged as authentic given that they are under the influence of alcohol. For one viewer, the fact that British tourists are drunk is a good indication of the reality of their behaviour in the programme – the more drunk, the less control these tourists will have of their behaviour. But for other viewers in the group the fact that these tourists know they are being filmed for a reality programme is a good indication of the falseness of their behaviour. One viewer refers to the common-sense belief that in order to create entertaining television you need people to be entertaining – 'if it was real life I'd be watching someone sitting down watching telly all day'. The effect of the final statement is to end discussion – case closed.

Montgomery argues that there are three types of authentic talk in broadcasting:

> First there is talk that is deemed authentic because it does not sound contrived, simulated or performed but rather sounds natural, 'fresh', spontaneous. Second, there is talk that is deemed authentic because it seems truly to capture or present the experience of the speaker. Third, there is authentic talk that seems truly to project the core self of the speaker – talk that is true to the self of the speaker in an existential fashion.
>
> (2001: 403–4)

Although for Montgomery the second type of authentic talk is most common to television, in particular reality programming, audience talk about reality programming illustrates all three aspects of authenticity, not just in the way ordinary people talk, but also, perhaps more importantly, in how they behave on television. I'd like to return to the reality series *Ibiza Uncovered* in order to illustrate how audiences assess authentic performances of ordinary people according to what appears natural, what appears true to the situation portrayed, and what appears true to the self of the people portrayed.

The following discussion is based on a story in *Ibiza Uncovered* about two married men on holiday with their wives and children. The two men are 'Jack the lads', who are out on the town, looking for some action of the female persuasion. We follow them as they drink in bars, flirt with single girls, some of whom flash their breasts or bottoms at the men (and the cameras), and stagger home at the end of the night, somewhat the worse for wear. From the point of view of the programme itself, the authenticity of the talk and behaviour of these two guys is presented very much as true to their experience – 'this is what we are normally like on holiday in Ibiza.' From the point of view of the audience, the programme's truth claims are treated with suspicion, but not rejected outright. These male viewers (aged 18–44) draw on their own experience to assess the authenticity of the behaviour of the two men on holiday:

Max: You go to Southend, it's like filming Southend on a Friday or Saturday night, you see exactly the same thing.

Shaun: I think that's rubbish what they've put on there, if the camera's there, everybody's going to act up.

Max: Yeah, that's right, especially on holiday.

Shaun: They were in the bar, had a drink, turned around and that was it, straight away. It doesn't work, not so quick as that, but because the cameras are there, the girl sees the camera, thinks 'Oh, I want to be on TV'.

Max: And the thing is, it starts them off sober and 'we're going out clubbing', you can see them as they get … as they're getting a little bit tipsy but they're getting a little bit, they're getting tipsy a little too quick for my liking … and then it shows them being childish. …

Brian: I think they'd be worse if the cameras weren't there!

Shaun: They were in a different skin.

Max: In fact, I think it could have got naughtier … they were being a little bit the boys … people go out there and doing what they were doing to those girls, they wouldn't still be on that dance floor, I tell you that now. Not a chance, not a chance.

Terry: I've been to Spain and all that, with the boys and everything, and I've never seen anything like that.

Max: Let's face it, if you had two other guys who weren't two guys who were coming across Jack the lad. I mean, all us guys have been Jack the lad at some stage, most probably some of us still are, but, if they picked another two guys that were more, er, nervy, then how would it have gone? The entertainment might not have been there.

Brian: But they might have been actors, mightn't they?

Max: But you won't get … I don't think they were actors 'cos any guy that they says 'Right, there's a camera, we're making this, do you mind us filming you?' and they would have looked at these guys and said 'Well, like, they're a bit Jack the lad, they're game and we're in there'. Boom, that's what they got.

Barry: You've got to find someone whose wife, who'd let them go and film them anyway. I mean my wife wouldn't let me do that. I mean I'd love to go and do it. I mean it'd be great crack [laughs].

Terry: She'd know exactly what you were going to get up to!

There are several overlapping points being made by these male viewers about the authenticity of this scene from *Ibiza Uncovered*. Most of the viewers referred to their own experience of being out for a night on the town, being 'a bit Jack the lad', to make sense of the scene. They all agreed the scene was not authentic for different reasons. For Shaun, the two men attracted an unnatural (i.e. instantaneous) interest from girls precisely because there were cameras present. This meant the situation was unnatural, and the men weren't themselves – 'they were in a different skin'. For Max, the scenario seemed false because the men didn't act the way he imagined they would act – they were drunk too quickly, they didn't flirt enough, 'it could have got naughtier'. Thus, the scene wasn't true to this viewer's experience of similar situations (Southend on a Friday night), and the men weren't true to themselves, in the sense of being red-blooded males. There was certainly agreement that the men performed well, and provided entertainment – one viewer even suggested the men were actors. But the fact that the men gave such good performances drew attention to how the programme was constructed. The final reality check comes from one viewer who judges the scene untrue in relation to his own experience of being married – were those men really given permission by their wives to behave badly?

Van Leeuwen (2001: 397) argues that authenticity is in crisis because it can mean different things to different people. We have come to question the concept of authenticity, 'just as the idea of the reality of the photograph came into crisis earlier'. At the start of this chapter I discussed the relationship between photography and reality programming in the work of Fetveit (2002). Is the authenticity of visual evidence in reality programming in crisis, just like the authenticity of the digitally enhanced photograph? We have to take into account the various different types of reality programming in order to answer that question. As I discussed previously in this chapter, audiences are far more likely to question the authenticity of ordinary people and their behaviour in highly constructed reality programming, such as reality gameshows or docu-soaps, where the format is designed to encourage self-display. We can see from the way viewers talk about the characters in this type of reality programming that they are certainly sceptical of the authentic behaviour of ordinary people in televised situations. But, to quote Goffman again, there is a 'natural movement back and forth' between trust and suspicion (1969: 31) in audience understanding of authentic performances in formatted reality programming. Just as Van Leeuwen suggests that although authenticity may be in crisis it has not lost its validity, I would argue that television audiences may question the authenticity of people's performances in reality programming, but they have not stopped critically examining the concept of authenticity. In fact, the reverse is the case. As audiences question the authenticity of the behaviour of ordinary people in reality programming, they also question the meaning of authenticity itself.

CONCLUSION

I have argued that the twin issues of performance and authenticity are significant to our understanding of popular factual television. Much contemporary reality programming, especially documentary gameshows or docu-soaps, is concerned with self-display. The sites we associate with reality formats such as *Big Brother* are stages where ordinary people display their personalities to fellow performers and to audiences. The fact that reality gameshows are set up to encourage a variety of performances (as contestants, as TV personalities) ensures that such programmes are viewed as 'performative' popular factual television. The manner in which ordinary people perform in different types of reality programmes is subject to intense scrutiny by audiences. Discussion tends to focus on general home truths about 'acting up' in front of television cameras, and the unreality of television about real people. As one viewer put it: 'if it was real life I'd be watching someone sitting down watching telly all day'. Most viewers expect ordinary people to act for the cameras in the majority of reality programming. These expectations do not, however, stop audiences from assessing how true or false the behaviour of ordinary people can be in reality programming. Audiences gossip, speculate and judge how ordinary people perform themselves and stay true to themselves in the spectacle/performance environment of popular factual television. Audience discussion is characterised by a natural movement backwards and forwards between trust and suspicion of the truthfulness of ordinary people and their behaviour on TV. Inevitably, audiences draw on their own personal experience of social interaction to judge the authenticity of the way ordinary people talk, behave and respond to situations and other people in reality programmes. Whether people are authentic or not in the way they handle themselves in the *Big Brother* house, or on holiday in Ibiza, is a matter for audiences to debate and critically examine on an everyday basis. When audiences debate the authenticity of performances in reality programming they are also debating the truth claims of such programmes, and this can only be healthy for the development of the genre as a whole.

Chapter 5

The idea of learning

What can we learn from watching reality TV? In this chapter, I consider the role of information within our experience of popular factual television. In its early incarnation, reality programming was often categorised as infotainment precisely because programmes such as *Cops* or *999* blurred boundaries between information and entertainment. Contemporary reality formats such as *American Idol* or *Big Brother* are closely associated with light entertainment genres such as talentshows or gameshows, and therefore retain few links with traditional infotainment series. But there are other reality formats that contain informative elements within an entertainment frame. In particular, lifestyle programming offers advice and tips on how to makeover your home, relationship, business, health and personal well-being. Infotainment and lifestyle programmes, in different ways, contain an informative address to the viewer. These reality programmes encourage audiences to learn about first aid, or decorating, whilst at the same time entertaining audiences with dramatic stories of rescue operations, or revelatory stories of DIY makeovers. We can call the informative elements in such reality programmes 'learning opportunities', as viewers have the opportunity to learn from the advice given in the programmes, but may choose not to take up or act on such advice. What follows in the rest of this chapter is an exploration of different types of learning in reality programming, and the way audiences make sense of information in popular factual television.

INFORMATION

The suggestion that we can learn from watching reality TV is not common to discussion of the genre overall. The topics that dominate debate about reality TV in the media mainly refer to issues such as voyeurism, or quality standards (see Chapters 1 and 2). However, the first wave of reality programming in the late 1980s in America contained a range of programmes that were all, in one way or another, about information (see

Chapter 2). *America's Most Wanted* and *Crimewatch UK* offer information to the public about law and order, and invite the public to offer information about criminal activities to relevant authorities. *Animal Hospital* and *Children's Hospital* offer information to the public about healthcare, and encourage viewers to care for their own children and companion animals in an informed manner. Although certain types of reality formats (i.e. reality gameshows) have moved away from the origins of the genre, this does not mean to say all reality programming no longer informs viewers about a variety of issues.

A core feature of popular factual television is that it presents information in an entertaining manner. The origins of reality programming point towards a close association with tabloid news (see Chapter 2). Although the tabloid news connection is often used as evidence of the 'dumbing down' of factual television, the connection can also be used as evidence of the way reality TV attempts to present information to audiences who want to be entertained and informed at the same time. This is not to suggest that tabloid news is better than other types of news, or reality programming is better than other types of factual television simply because it attracts popular audiences. Traditional news bulletins and newspapers are primary providers of knowledge, and offer audiences and readers more 'accurate information or cogent analysis and argument' than other factual media (Corner 1999: 117). But the type of audience that chooses to regularly watch popular factual television is the type of audience that tends to tune in to television news bulletins, but to tune out of other traditional factual programming such as current affairs or documentary. The ratings for national news bulletins in the UK are similar to the ratings for popular factual, but far higher than ratings for documentary or current affairs (see Chapter 2). Therefore, popular factual serves an important function as a provider of 'entertainment and diversion, with its knowledge-providing role as a secondary function' (ibid.). Although other fictional genres can also provide knowledge as a secondary function (for example, health-based drama), the reality genre has its origins in television news, and therefore has strong associations with a factual genre the primary function of which is to provide knowledge.

The results of my research, in conjunction with the Independent Television Commission (ITC) and the Broadcasters' Audience Research Board (BARB), indicate just how important the issue of information is to general audiences of popular factual television (Hill/ITC 2000). In 2000, information was the programme element liked most by the UK population in all types of reality TV. Seventy-five per cent of all adults liked information more than any other programme characteristics, such as looking into other people's lives (46 per cent), or re-created accidents (33 per cent). This preference cut across social differences. For example, 72 per cent of men and 78 per cent of women preferred information to other programme elements in all types of reality TV. Seventy-five per cent of social category AB (upper middle class), and 74 per cent of social category DE (lower working class) preferred information to other programme elements in all types of reality TV. Similarly, 79 per cent of 16–34-year-olds and 71 per cent of 55-year-olds and over, and 78 per cent of people with secondary school education and 78 per cent with college education, preferred information to other programme elements in reality TV. In addition to information, the general public also liked other programme elements similar to the characteristics of news. Seventy-four per cent of all adults liked up-to-the-minute stories, and 68 per cent liked stories caught on camera in reality programmes, and again such preferences cut across all social differences. The picture was different for children, who preferred animals (83 per cent) and stories caught on camera (82 per cent) to other programme elements. This result is not surprising given children's natural aversion to 'learning programmes', something I discuss later in this chapter.

The importance of information cannot be overstressed in relation to understanding audience expectations of popular factual television. John Corner (1995: 11) argues that television is a 'message system' that is 'received "in private", but has a strong "public" character'. For television audiences, the public character of television is most commonly associated with news. As Corner notes, when television 'sees', it invites 'viewers into empathy and understanding; to create a "virtual community" of the commonly concerned, of vicarious witness; to cut through accommodating abstraction with the force and surprise of "things themselves"' (1995: 31). The informative elements of reality programming speak to the public character of television. The British public value the programme characteristics of information, up-to-the-minute stories, and stories caught on camera in reality programmes because these are characteristics associated with the news genre.

Corner's argument that the power of television lies in its ability to let people 'see for themselves' is useful in understanding the positioning of information within the entertainment frame of popular factual television. Corner acknowledges that the processes of production, and the necessary prior selection of televisual representations for public consumption, ensure that television can only provide 'second-hand seeing' that appears 'first-hand' to viewers (1995: 30). The conversion of second-hand seeing into first-hand seeing is a primary characteristic of reality programming and audiences are aware of the processes involved in producing a reality programme that packages second-hand experiences of ordinary people as first-hand experiences for viewers. Corner provides a concrete example of the 'seeing–knowing connection' in an extended analysis of an emergency services rescue operation in the infotainment series *999*: 'the multiple immediacies of the *999* story, its movement between tenses, between objective and subjective viewpoints, between instruction and dramatic entertainment and between particular incident and general truth, are illuminating' not only because the story sheds light on the particularities of reality television, but because it also sheds light on how television can convert second-hand seeing into powerful first-hand experiences (ibid.). The ability to see *through* television is fundamental to our understanding of the reality genre. Seeing through television involves television audiences witnessing real people's stories and experiences, as well as critiquing the process of selecting these stories and experiences for television.

Infotainment is the most obvious example of reality programming that allows viewers to 'see for themselves' and potentially learn from the experience. Lifestyle programming is another example. But there are other formats, such as reality gameshows, that appear to contain few characteristics that could be categorised as informative. The development of the reality genre from infotainment-type formats to formats within a strong entertainment frame directly relates to audience responses to traditional and contemporary reality programming. Although audiences place great value on the idea of information in all types of reality programming, in practice they perceive much contemporary reality programming as entertaining rather than informative. In 2000, only 50 per cent of the British public agreed with the statement 'I think these programmes are really useful as they give you all sorts of information about life' (Hill/ITC 2000). When we take into account the practice of watching a range of reality programming, there is a discrepancy between preferences for informative programme characteristics and attitudes towards information in reality programming. This would suggest that audience understanding of information in reality programming is complex and contradictory. However, just because audiences believe much reality programming to be entertaining rather than informative, does not mean that information is no longer important to viewers. In the same way that authenticity is essential to audience attraction to reality television, so too is information. Audiences may expect certain types of reality TV to be 'fake', but they still look for and critique 'moments of authenticity' in reality programmes (see Chapter 4). Similarly, audiences may expect certain types of reality TV to be entertaining rather than informative, but they still look for and critique information in reality programmes.

ENTERTAINMENT

In the previous section, I began with the statement 'the suggestion that we can learn from watching reality TV is not common to discussion of the genre overall'. Although I was referring to media discussion of reality TV, the statement is just as true of audience discussion of the genre. In fact, the two types of discussion, one public, one private, are connected. Television audiences are well aware of public discussion of reality TV, and take this discussion into account when they formulate their own attitudes towards the genre. In previous research I conducted on media violence, film audiences displayed a similar awareness of public attitudes towards the alleged negative effects of film violence (Hill 1997, 2001a, 2001b). Other researchers also discovered a connection between public attitudes towards media violence, and audience discussion of their viewing practices (see Buckingham 1996, and Barker and Petley 2001, amongst others). What viewers of horror films, or action movies, share with viewers of reality programmes are that these examples of popular culture are stigmatised by the media, and, to some degree, by society. To put it crudely, to say that you watch violent movies is to say you are violent; to say you watch reality TV is to say you are a voyeur. These crude statements are generalisations, and do not hold true when we look at actual reception practices. But it is the very fact that they are generalisations, that they are 'common truths', that makes such assertive statements a matter of public knowledge.

Since reality TV became popular primetime fare in the early 1990s, it has been under relentless attack from the press, and other social commentators. When the minister responsible for broadcasting in the UK told the BBC in 2003 to stop making 'mindless programmes' such as *Changing Rooms*, she echoed countless press articles on reality TV.[1] For example, Peter Paterson wrote: 'Roll up, roll up for *Big Brother*, the greatest show on earth – the greatest, that is, for peeping toms, voyeurs and nosy parkers.'[2] The comic effect of the circus barker, rounding up punters for a travelling freakshow encapsulates the general assumption of critics of reality TV that no 'normal' person would choose to watch such lowbrow entertainment. A quick overview of press articles on the reality genre highlights common topics of discussion. A popular topic is the issue of harm, with articles such as 'Danger: Reality TV Can Rot Your Brain' featuring regularly in the popular and broadsheet press.[3] Another related topic is the negative impact of reality TV on other types of factual television – lowest common denominator TV syndrome; and articles such as 'Ragbag of Cheap Thrills' sum up press discussion of reality programming as trash television.[4] Yet another topic is that of 'Voyeur Vision'. Voyeurism, or peeping tom syndrome, links with the other two topics of harm and 'dumbing down', as voyeurism implies watching reality TV is a form of socially deviant behaviour.[5]

Ernest Mathjis (2002: 311–12) has observed how reality formats such as *Big Brother* invite 'controversy and moral outrage', with journalists, psychologists, opinion leaders, and commentators 'condemning *Big Brother* as an "inhumane experiment", bordering on the bizarre and the unacceptable, exploiting voyeurism and invading personal privacy'. One German newspaper called *Big Brother* a 'cage full of shit' (2002: 312). Such criticism of reality gameshows extends to all types of reality programming. The psychologist Oliver James claims:

> The content of too much reality TV is values-rotting and depression-inducing. For a large slice of the population, watching it has largely replaced social life itself. When we are not at work, viewing other people living their lives on TV now constitutes a considerable part of our existence. Does anyone know how much harm this is doing to us?[6]

The connection between reality TV and negative effects is deliberate, as James implies a causal link between watching reality TV and the decline of society as a whole. Similarly, broadcaster Nick James thinks reality TV has 'destroyed Britain', by presenting false accounts of the world to viewers who can no longer tell the difference between reality and fantasy.[7]

Sociologist Erving Goffman notes how the term stigma refers 'to an attribute that is deeply discrediting' (1963: 13). Stigma is linked to the formation of our social identities. We stigmatise other people, or are stigmatised by other people, based on social expectations about what are normal and abnormal social attributes. Goffman calls people who stigmatise others 'the normals': 'the attitudes we normals have towards a person with a stigma, and the actions we take in regard to him are well known...we construct a stigma theory, an ideology to explain his inferiority and account for the danger he represents' (1963: 15). Goffman argues that people who are stigmatised by 'the normals' develop ways of managing information about themselves, and in turn develop ways of managing stigma (1963: 57). Although Goffman is referring to the stigmatisation of people, we can apply a similar concept of stigma to popular cultural reception practices. The brief account of press coverage of reality TV illustrates how journalists and social commentators who speak on behalf of 'the normals' construct a stigma theory that discredits reality TV. If watching reality TV is 'not normal', then it is a discredited activity. The metaphor of the circus freakshow creates an impression of reality TV that is wholly negative. The alleged 'risks' of watching reality

TV are so great that in extreme cases it can be a danger to people who watch such programmes, and to society as a whole.

The concept of stigma as applied to discussion of reality TV in the popular press provides some context to the way television audiences talk about information in reality programming. If viewers of reality TV claim certain programmes are informative, then this implies watching reality programmes can be beneficial. But viewers are hesitant to make such claims because of the common assumption that watching reality TV is bad for you. The stigma associated with watching reality TV is so great that the first response viewers commonly make when asked about informative elements in reality programming is to make a joke. The use of humour is a way of managing other people's responses ('the normals') to the stigma of watching reality TV. Here are some common responses to the idea of learning from reality programming:

> 'Is there something you can learn from *Big Brother*?' (interviewer)
> 'Yeah, turn it off!'
>
> > (39-year-old male groundsman)

> 'You learn not to turn up at an airport without your passport! [laughs] There's not a lot you can learn from *Airport*.'
>
> > (39-year-old male importer)

> 'It's entertainment [laughs]. It wasn't a learning thing, it was just entertainment.'
>
> > (32-year-old female nursery assistant)

> 'Is there anything you can learn from *Big Brother*?' (interviewer)
> 'Yeah, never live with ten people in a house!'
>
> > (26-year-old male estate agent)

> 'It's just mindless … entertainment.'
>
> > (31-year-old housewife and part-time nanny)

> 'Twaddle.'
>
> > (45-year-old unemployed male)

> 'It's embarrassing to say you enjoy it really … isn't it?'
>
> > (31-year-old housewife and part-time nanny)

This type of instant response to questions regarding learning in reality programming is typical of all the discussions. As viewers reject the idea of learning outright, they belittle reality programmes ('twaddle'), and in turn belittle their own viewing practices ('mindless'). The stigmatisation of reality TV as trash TV in the popular press impacts on viewers, who attempt to manage the impressions of other people (including academic researchers) by making light of the idea of learning from reality programming.

It is important to make a distinction between entertainment in factual rather than fictional programmes. In fictional programming, it is a sign of a good drama if television viewers find it entertaining. In factual programming, the reverse is true. If reality TV is mindless entertainment then this is a criticism of popular factual television and its role in the 'dumbing down' of television. Comments like those made by journalists, and viewers in the above extracts, relate to a wider critical debate about the way television hinders 'the formation and communication of knowledge' (Corner 1999: 108). 'Television's conventions of depiction and exposition are said to have led to a deterioration in the knowledge-processing capacities of the public' (Corner 1999: 110). According to critics such as Oliver James there is no better example of all that is wrong with society than the popularity of reality TV.

The commercialisation of reality formats such as *Popstars* or *American Idol* is also a factor in understanding why audiences categorise contemporary reality programming as 'mindless entertainment'. The popularity of reality talentshows, and accompanying merchandise to the series, increases the entertainment value of the programmes whilst at the same time decreasing the informative value of the programmes. For example, the Beech family were fans of *Popstars*, and talked about the series on a regular basis. The Beech children, three girls all in primary school, learnt some of the songs and dance routines performed by the budding 'popstars' (Hear'Say). In a discussion about *Popstars*, the mother and eldest daughter both made light of the potential learning elements of the series:

Interviewer: Is there anything to be learnt from *Popstars*?
Rachael: She's [her sister] got a Hear'Say top on.
Vivienne: That's what she learnt … how to spend money on the merchandise! [laughs] She got Harry Potter and she wanted Hear'Say.
Interviewer: Did you buy the album?
Sally: Yes, we got the album and the single.
Vivienne: Yes, joined everybody else.
Interviewer: Did you learn anything?
Sally: Well, about being famous … [laughs]
Vivienne: Absolutely nothing!
Sally: What it's like to be famous, that's about the only thing I learnt from it … and the things they write about you in the paper! [laughs]
Vivienne: How easy it is to get there! Thousands of people can sing … I don't think they learnt that much. They did enjoy that one

but, erm … there's nothing … well, perhaps there is something educational, I don't know, but if there is I can't see what it is [laughs].

The conversation is peppered with jokes about the merchandise and the marketing of celebrities in the series. When the daughter mentions *Popstars* in relation to learning about 'what it's like to be famous', her comment doesn't so much underscore potential learning elements in the series as negate there is anything really to learn in the first place. The final point made by the mother suggests that *Popstars* is so successful, and entertaining, that it is difficult to 'see' how it can be 'educational' at all.

There is another reason why audiences are so dismissive of the idea of learning in reality programming. And this relates to the stigmatisation of learning itself. In the above extracts from audience discussion, and from press criticism, we saw how reality TV was described as lowest common denominator TV. In terms of what the sociologist Pierre Bourdieu (1986) refers to as 'cultural capital', reality TV has low cultural capital, as it is commonly referred to as mindless entertainment ('twaddle'), and therefore has little value in the cultural marketplace. Of course, issues concerning quality come into play here, as reality TV is often used as a barometer of low versus high quality factual television (see Chapter 2). But there is another way of looking at the value of reality TV. For popular audiences, especially younger audiences, the value of reality TV is that it is entertaining. Davies, Buckingham and Kelley (2000) discuss the value children place on children's television. Citing Bourdieu's work on cultural capital, they argue that 'children's assertions of their own tastes necessarily entail a form of "identity work" – a positioning of the self in terms of publicly available discourses and categories' (2000: 21). For children, television is 'good' when it is engaging, action-packed, funny, and, above all, entertaining. The stigmatisation of reality programming as mere entertainment works in the reverse for young viewers, who are drawn to reality TV precisely because it promises to be entertaining.

The following extract from a discussion by a group of young female viewers (aged 12–14) illustrates the distinction between information and entertainment for young adults:

Rachael: No, but I think that's what I liked about *Big Brother*, 'cos you don't have to take anything in from it that much, just like watching it.

Kim: It was kind of interesting, though you don't have to learn about it. People our age aren't really interested in finding out information about how, like, stuff happens.

Clare: You learn that at school.

Kim: Like if they'd showed you, erm, like, learning stuff, I don't think
           it would be half as interesting.

These viewers associated learning with work, and work with school. They
made a distinction between *Big Brother* as engaging ('interesting') and as
non-engaging ('learning stuff'). Most importantly, they did not wish to
extract, or 'take', anything away from their viewing experience other than
the pleasure of 'just' watching *Big Brother*. Another extract, this time from
a group of young male viewers, serves to emphasise the stigmatisation of
learning for young adults:

Max: When I watch TV, I don't watch it to, like, learn something, I
            watch it to enjoy myself, unless it was something, like, really,
            really interesting.
Michael: Normally I watch TV when I'm either bored or ... well, then to
            entertain myself, but then I don't usually think about 'Oh, what
            have I learnt from this?' I just enjoy watching it.
Max: I think it's good ... I wouldn't watch a programme if it's called
            the Learning Programme but some programmes I think can be
            really good and at the same time you can, like, learn stuff but
            you don't actually realise it. But if the programme actually
            showed that it was a Learning Programme, I wouldn't watch it.

There is a distinction being made between informal and formal learning
in television programmes. Formal learning ('the Learning Programme') is
clearly associated with primary features of a programme, whereas
informal learning is more associated with secondary features. What
comes first is entertainment, and any secondary pleasures may include
the possibility of learning, but are optional extras. Compare the above
quote with the following from an adult viewer: 'I like learning
programmes, I think I do now, more than anything. Sadly, but I do, yeah'
(43-year-old self-employed builder). For young viewers, formal learning
is associated with school, and with being an adult, and if a television
programme advertises itself as 'a learning programme' then it loses its
attraction and becomes a teacher rather than an entertainer.

In relation to stigma, television audiences have a complicated
relationship with watching reality TV. When adult viewers claim reality
TV is entertaining they are discrediting an already discredited television
genre. When young viewers claim reality TV is entertaining they are
being complimentary towards the genre. In each scenario the idea of
learning is rejected. In the next section, I want to explore the idea of
learning, in particular informal learning in reality programming. It is my
contention that certain types of reality programming can offer learning
opportunities for viewers, but in order to illustrate this point I need to

explore further the complicated relationship between seeing and knowing for popular factual audiences.

PRACTICAL LEARNING

When audiences consider information in reality programmes they are likely to talk about information as learning, and learning as practical tips and advice for themselves and their loved ones. The term 'learning' suggests an informal, personal relationship with facts in popular factual television, compared to the more formal terms 'knowledge', 'information' or 'education' that we associate with more traditional types of factual television. A popular factual programme is judged as more informative than other programmes if it offers practical advice, and viewers can personally learn from it. Of all the UK reality programmes available to viewers, programmes such as *Changing Rooms* or *999* are thought to be the most informative. This suggests that viewers are likely to judge how informative reality programmes can be based on different types of reality formats, and the relationship these formats have to viewers' everyday lives.

The personalisation of information by viewers is significant because it highlights how viewers specifically relate to particular types of reality TV. As I argued in the previous section, reality TV can enable viewers to 'see for themselves', and this process of 'seeing' is connected with the informative elements in particular programmes. When audiences connect what they see with what they know, then reality TV 'elicits from viewers certain kinds of *investment of self* which other media cannot so easily generate, if at all' (Corner 1995: 31). The concept of the investment of the self is connected to reality programming in the way ordinary people are portrayed in certain types of formats. Makeover and infotainment programmes often take the specific experiences of ordinary people and make these stories generalisable, so that the stories are about Mr and Mrs X or Y and their health or home improvements, and about you and your health or home improvements. When we respond to individual stories in makeover or infotainment reality programmes we often draw on our own experiences to make sense of these stories.

Social theorist Anthony Giddens has explored the concept of the self in modern society. In his book *Modernity and Self Identity* (1991), Giddens argues that we live in a post-traditional (late modern) society that is characterised by a questioning of traditional values and ways of life: 'What to do? How to act? Who to be? These are focal questions for everyone living in circumstances of late modernity' (1991: 70). According to Giddens, our self-identities, or life biographies, are constructed on a daily basis. We are engaged in ongoing stories, creating a 'narrative of the self' that changes depending on our circumstances and our audience (1991: 20). There are similarities with Giddens' concept of 'narrative of the self' and Erving Goffman's idea of the presentation of the self in everyday life, discussed in the previous chapter. Both Goffman and Giddens claim that who we are at any given moment of the day is dependent on how we would like to appear to others. We therefore construct different narratives, or performances, for our work colleagues or family depending on whether we are at work or at home. The media contributes to the construction of narratives of the self. Shaun Moores argues that

> broadcasting provides viewers and listeners with a constant 'stream' of symbolic materials from which to fashion their senses of self ... this flow of images and sounds is creatively appropriated by social subjects as they seek to put together personal identities and lifestyles.
>
> (2000: 139)

Similarly, David Gauntlett (2002: 98) states that 'information and ideas from the media do not merely reflect the social world ... but contribute to its shape and are central to modern reflexivity'. Thus, when we watch television we can collect information and ideas that may help us to construct and maintain our own self-identities, or life biographies.

The concept of the self is most applicable to reality TV when programmes are designed to speak to viewers about issues that matter to them. Watching reality TV can be a reflexive process in the sense that the personalised stories and tips on living that feature in some reality formats are internalised by viewers, and stored for potential use at appropriate moments in their own lives. Reality programming has been criticised for its preoccupation with the individual rather than the social. Compared with traditional documentary, and its aspirations as a public form, reality TV can be seen as highly trivial, preoccupied with personal stories about personal lives (Dovey 2000). In terms of the content of much reality programming this is certainly true. Stories about health in *Children's Hospital* are stories about people's individual experiences of ill health and recovery, not the healthcare system; stories about holidays in *Holidays from Hell* are stories about individual experiences of good and bad holidays, not the holiday industry; stories about pop music in *Pop Idol* are stories about individual experiences of being a pop singer, not the music business. There are few reality programmes that attempt to look at the big picture, and other researchers such as Dovey (2000), Kilborn (2003) or Palmer (2003) have paid attention to why this is the case, and the impact of the privatised nature of much reality programming on factual television as a whole. But when we consider audience responses to certain types of reality TV, the focus on individual stories is something viewers are attracted to precisely because these particular programmes offer narratives they can relate to.

Health-based reality programmes typically contain an informative address to the viewer alongside personal stories. *999*, for example, mixes personal stories of accidents and emergency services rescue operations with general advice about first aid. In previous research, I examined *999* in relation to its communicative form and programme design, and its reception (Hill 2000a, 2000b). *999* uses stories of everyday accidents, such as a barbeque fire, to speak to viewers who may wish to learn how to prevent such accidents from occurring to themselves and their loved ones. *999* also selects stories with happy endings, and viewers value its life-affirming stories because they offer an idealised version of a caring society (Hill 2000c). When the programme offers advice about first aid these segments can be perceived by viewers as learning opportunities, where viewers may store information or ideas for later use. As this viewer explains: 'I watch *999* to, sort of, see what can I do in case of a fire, or, I break a leg, what first aid I could use, or stuff like that' (40-year-old female part-time secretary). Or, as this viewer describes: 'I think the best thing is, it's informative. You never know when you're going to find yourself in a situation that, maybe you've seen something the previous day where you thought that might come into practice at a later point' (37-year-old female secretary). In another example, a mother explained how she was able to use information from a health-based reality format to help her son: 'My son's tooth was knocked out ... it was the whole root and everything, and 'cos I'd seen it on the *Children's Hospital* that you were supposed to put it in milk, I did that and he's still now, six years on, got that same tooth. They put it back in!' (37-year-old housewife).

Consumer-based reality formats also typically contain an informative address to the viewer alongside personal stories. *House of Horrors*, for example, mixes personal stories of customers' experiences of unprofessional builders or plumbers, with general advice about consumer awareness and complaints procedures. Typically, a presenter undertakes to investigate customer complaints about particular trades people by going undercover, and hiring particular trades people to 'fix' various building problems, whilst secretly filming their often illegal activities. Once the hidden cameras have proven their guilt, these people are then confronted by the presenter and held to account. The 'horror' stories of unprofessional builders or plumbers are presented in an entertaining manner, but there is a clear address to the viewer to take caution, and learn from other people's bad experiences of rogue builders. This discussion by two male viewers illustrates the way audiences respond to consumer-based reality formats:

Bob: I think the programme is designed to try and educate the general public to be more careful in any trade.

Shaun: But, at the end of the day, to me, what it's saying is 'I won't get these deals from the paper anymore, I'll get somebody who my mate knows who they can trust'.

Bob: Some people will pick up on that and say 'From now on, I'll try and get people recommended'.

House of Horrors is 'designed' to encourage the public 'to be more careful' when employing builders, and viewers pick up on the didactic elements of the programme and perceive the stories as cautionary tales.

I'd like to look in more detail at lifestyle programmes in order to explore how such programmes specifically speak to viewers about their own lives, and how viewers respond to information or advice given in the programmes. Traditional lifestyle programmes are about popular leisure pursuits, such as DIY or cookery, and typically contain instructions on how to look after your garden, or how to make a meal. Charlotte Brunsdon, in her analysis of old and new lifestyle series, points out that the 'hobby genre' traditionally focused on 'skill acquisition' (Brunsdon *et al.* 2001: 54). For example, in the long-running British BBC series *Gardeners' World* 'we are shown appropriate spring pruning, how to divide herbaceous perennials, and the planting out of hardened seedlings in 20 minutes of continuous address … By the end of the programme the listener would know how to do something' (ibid.). Brunsdon argues that contemporary lifestyle programmes retain the didactic elements of earlier hobby or enthusiast programmes, but the didactic element 'is narratively subordinated to an instantaneous display of transformation', where the focus is less on the information provided by the presenter, and more on the before and after of ordinary people's homes, gardens and persons (2001: 55).

The makeover has become a staple of contemporary lifestyle series in the UK, the USA and Australia. Medhurst (1999: 26) goes so far as to argue that the 1990s was characterised by lifestyle TV that told viewers 'don't just watch us, copy us'. Although the makeover often featured in advertising and cookery programmes, its place in primetime television was unique to the 1990s, where advice, transformation and consumer awareness became part of the language of lifestyle television for popular audiences (Bonner 2003: 130–1). In the 2000s, the makeover has transformed itself and, no longer limited to homes and gardens, has expanded to incorporate ordinary people and their way of life. We can watch (and copy) ordinary people transforming their business practices, or personal relationships, as well as their living arrangements, or personal appearances. Indeed, personal makeover stories, or what the BBC calls 'narrative lifestyle', are fundamental to contemporary lifestyle formats that attempt to consider the transformation of the self, as well as the transformation of the home environment.[8] According to Bonner (2003: 136) 'makeover programmes are the most overt signs of the way television perceives itself to be engaged in a project of advising its ordinary viewers about their transformation into happier, more satisfied, more up-to-date versions of their selves'. Thus, contemporary lifestyle programmes offer 'narratives of the self' that are less about leisure pursuits, and more about life in general. The UK broadcaster, Channel 4, even categorises its lifestyle programmes as 'Life' to reflect the transformation of lifestyle programming from leisure to living.[9]

Perhaps, the best-known makeover series around the world is *Changing Rooms*, a BBC DIY series that mixes personal stories of home improvement, with general tips on interior design. Typically, *Changing Rooms* contains the story of two sets of neighbours who transform each other's living space according to a design brief, budget and timeframe provided by the programme. A presenter judges the progress of the two teams, and provides humorous commentary on the style changes taking place. There are also interior designers who assist the teams, and who compete against each other to make bold design statements to the ordinary people in the programme and to viewers at home. Rachael Moseley (2000: 314) has argued that makeover series such as *Changing Rooms* have a 'doubled audience structure' whereby the reactions of ordinary people in the programmes are as, if not more, important than the reactions of viewers at home. The programme presents an insider's view of the reactions of ordinary people to the changes made to their homes, and viewers monitor these reactions, judging those reactions thought to be 'authentic' or 'false'. This type of judgement of the behaviour of ordinary people in reality programming is something I discussed in the previous chapter in relation to the issue of performance and authenticity. For Moseley (2000), the 'doubled audience structure' is troubling because it collapses public and private spaces, giving viewers the opportunity to see private responses they would not normally be able to see in traditional lifestyle programming. *Changing Rooms* has capitalised on its ability to let audiences see into the private lives of ordinary people, as it is arguable the programme is about anything but the 'moment of truth' when the transformation is revealed to the home owners. *Changing Rooms* may contain a mix of personal stories and general advice, but the informative elements are subsumed under the narrative drive of people's emotional responses to dramatic changes to their home environment.

Television audiences have ambiguous responses to the idea of learning in contemporary lifestyle programmes. *Changing Rooms* is a common type of reality programme audiences associate with practical learning. And yet, when viewers talk about the programme, they are hard-pressed to come up with concrete examples of learning from watching *Changing*

Rooms, and instead refer to the 'idea of learning' in the programme. This would suggest contemporary lifestyle programmes offer more informal 'ideas', rather than formal advice about living.

Arguably, the shift from advice to ideas in makeover shows is a result of the history of lifestyle programming. Traditional leisure programmes contain direct advice to viewers, whereas contemporary lifestyle programmes contain the responses of ordinary people to ideas from experts in the programme (Brunsdon *et al.* 2001). And the ideas from experts are not necessarily ideas viewers would wish to apply in practice. An example of audience discussion of lifestyle formats will illustrate the difference between advice in traditional leisure programming, and the ideas in makeover series. The Beech family lived in the south-east of England, and owned a terraced house with a garden, as well as two televisions, and one VCR and a PC. Robert and Vivienne (a stonemason and part-time nanny respectively) have three children, all of whom attended primary school, and many after-school activities, such as drama and swimming. The family read a local newspaper, and regularly watched reality programmes about places, survival, pets and homes/gardens. The Beech family had definite views on the difference between old and new lifestyle programmes.

Sally:	Dad hates *Changing Rooms*! And *Ground Force* [laughs]. But Mum loves watching *Changing Rooms*!
Vivienne:	You make me sound so bright, don't you! [laughs] Uurgh! 'Gormless mother!' [laughs] One of those mothers, what can you do?
Interviewer:	What do you think about it?
Sally:	It's … just really boring, it's just about what colour they can put on wallpaper …
Vivienne:	Well, for someone who doesn't even tidy their bedroom, it wouldn't really be of interest to you, would it?
Robert:	I think it's 'cos it's done on a budget and done so cheaply, that's what I don't like about it.
Vivienne:	See, he sees the practical side, he sees the work side.
Interviewer:	Do you think you get any information from it?
Vivienne:	I think so, yeah, they do, if you're that way inclined you could probably get some good ideas off them, on how to do things on the cheap.
Robert:	Nothing expensive.
Sally:	But Dad, they've got … for *Ground Force*, and for *Changing Rooms* I think, they've got those books like you've got upstairs that tell you all about how to do it.
Rachael:	But could you be bothered?

Vivienne: I think you'd pick up a lot more with *Ground Force* than you would with *Changing Rooms* because they are actually making proper gardens, rather than ... these aren't proper rooms they're making, are they?

Robert: No.

Interviewer: Have you ever acted on any ideas that you've got?

Vivienne: No. I'm not very creative, really, I think everyone would agree!

Robert: The trouble with things like *Ground Force*, you don't get so many normal gardening programmes, *Gardeners' World*, and those sort of programmes. But, erm, that's the trouble..

Vivienne: What was *Gardeners' World*? Wasn't that the same sort of thing?

Robert: No. It would just show you different plants and different gardens.

Vivienne: Oh, yeah. That was more in the detail, these are more like garden makeovers, aren't they?

Robert: It's a rush job, isn't it, to make it look nice before the owner comes back.

Vivienne: Yeah, not so practical then.

Interviewer: What about when things go wrong in *Changing Rooms*?

Vivienne: Well, that's what I wait for really. There's that girl, what she does to people's houses, your average person would probably quite like, I think, it's not very wacky. But that Llewellyn fella, that's just done for television. I mean, who on earth is going to like it. Like a gothic living room in the middle of, you know, Clapham! [laughs]

This lengthy extract from the Beech family discussion of lifestyle programming offers rich insight into the way television audiences make distinctions between different kinds of learning opportunities in different types of lifestyle programmes. Robert and Vivienne have different tastes in lifestyle programming. Robert likes more traditional lifestyle programmes because they offer advice, and they show viewers how to make quality improvements to their homes and gardens. Vivienne likes contemporary lifestyle programmes not because of the attention to 'detail' but because of the makeover. There are gender, class and age issues that shape the family discussion. Vivienne is embarrassed that she might be perceived as a 'gormless mother' for watching *Changing Rooms*, and for enjoying the personal stories and the 'bad taste' of the interior designers who regularly feature in the series. There may be ideas about interior design in the programme, but these ideas are not really valued by Robert or Vivienne, as the ideas are mainly about 'how to do things on the cheap', and neither would wish to suggest they would makeover their own house in a similar fashion. *Changing Rooms* isn't about 'proper rooms', but about rooms made over for 'television'. For Robert, lifestyle programming is 'good' if it is primarily about 'the work side' of home improvement, whereas for Vivienne, lifestyle programming is good if it is a diversion from work. With regard to the children, they point out that there are informative elements to makeover series, including books that accompany the series, but learning how to do something is not the main appeal of watching makeover television ('could you be bothered?'). For the Beech children, lifestyle programmes are 'really boring', but this doesn't mean to say they don't watch the programmes with their parents. The appeal, or lack of appeal, of reality programming for family viewers is something I discuss in the next chapter. Suffice to say that the Beech children are more likely to watch *Changing Rooms* with their mum, than *Gardeners' World* with their dad, because one is perceived as more entertaining than the other.

Another example from a discussion about *Changing Rooms* will illustrate the subtle difference between learning and the 'idea of learning' in lifestyle programmes. The Palmer family lived in the south-east of England, and owned a large detached family home with a garden, and with five televisions, one VCR, one PC and a satellite subscription. Steven was an engineer, and Victoria was a part-time carer. They had four children living at home; the two eldest children (Richard and Sarah) worked full time, whilst the two youngest were still in school. The parents read the broadsheet newspaper the *Daily Telegraph*, and the young adults read the tabloid newspaper the *Sun*, and the family regularly watched reality programmes about motorway/driving, police/crime, and homes/gardens. The front room was redecorated at the time of visiting the family, and Victoria said she had redecorated the room in order to make it hers, a room where she would be able to watch the TV 'in peace'.

Interviewer: You said you loved *Changing Rooms*.
Victoria: Yeah, I watch that when I go to work.
Richard: My mum doesn't work!
Victoria: I do work … There are all sorts of things in that vein, whether or not it's *Changing Rooms*. They're very much of a muchness but I still love them all, I can't resist seeing what they're doing!
Sarah: You've got ideas …
Richard: Stop! They get cladding – cladding is it? – and they paint it brown or something, with a wood effect! [tone of disgust]
Victoria: Yeah, but for every twenty bad ideas, there's usually one that's handy.
Richard: You do watch it to get ideas.
Victoria: To find out how to do it yourself, really.

Interviewer: And have you actually used any ideas?
Victoria: Erm …
Sarah: You *imagine* ideas you'd like.
Steven: Blue paint [that Victoria used on walls in the garden].
Victoria: I think I heralded the blue paint, excuse me!

Like the mother in the previous extract, Victoria defends her taste in makeover shows to the rest of the family. She mixes criticism of the programmes with praise for the way makeover shows enable her to 'see' what other people are 'doing' in their homes. For Victoria and her daughter, the personal stories of home improvement offer 'ideas' rather than direct advice. But when the Palmer family consider the practical application of these ideas, they become imagined rather than real ideas. Thus, the format does not contain advice, or even ideas, but *imagined* ideas for home improvement. And Victoria even rejects the *idea* of the idea of learning from *Changing Rooms*. She wants to be perceived as 'heralding' her own creative ideas for home improvement rather than relying on 'bad' ideas in contemporary lifestyle programmes.

These extracts from family discussion of contemporary lifestyle programming suggest that television audiences do not readily pick up information or ideas from watching these programmes. The difference between health-based reality programmes and lifestyle programmes is worth mentioning because the confident manner in which viewers talk about the practical learning opportunities from health-based programming is quite different from the rather more ambivalent discussion of the way viewers could 'imagine ideas' from contemporary lifestyle series. One of the reasons I focused on lifestyle programmes in audience discussion of practical learning is precisely the ambiguity of what exactly is learning in contemporary reality programming. As the makeover series has shifted attention from didactic address to transformation and display, the opportunities for learning are restricted to 'ideas' rather than practical knowledge. Indeed, contemporary lifestyle programming illustrates how information has been transformed into the idea of learning, rather than learning itself. Although lifestyle programming contains 'narratives of the self' (Giddens 1991: 20) in the form of personal stories, audience responses are less about how to learn from these stories, and more about the idea of learning, if at all, from watching reality television.

SOCIAL LEARNING

The phrase 'people watching' is commonly associated with reality TV. For some critics, 'people watching' is another term for nosiness, and there is certainly a 'nosey sociability' (Corner 2000) to watching reality programming. In the previous section, viewers talked about their pleasure in watching what other people do to their homes in makeover programmes. There is a difference between voyeurism and people watching, as voyeurism implies a deviant character trait, whereas nosiness, or people watching, is a somewhat more socially acceptable form of behaviour. Reality TV invites viewers to look in on the world around them, and encourages viewers to enjoy watching ordinary people and their everyday activities. In this sense, the scopic function of television becomes part of the attraction for audiences of reality programmes. This viewer explained her attraction to docu-soaps like *Airport* as, 'I like just sitting on benches and just watching everybody walk past' (31-year-old female part-time carer). Many viewers in my research used similar analogies as a way of describing their 'natural' interest in watching other people on television: 'You do like to people watch in real life and that is just something you can do from the comfort of your own home. And I think that's why it's interesting because you just ... it's a natural instinct to want to see what other people do' (35-year-old female technical agent).

The activity of people watching is applicable to the concept of learning in reality programming because observation of social behaviour can be informative. John Hartley (1999), in his book *The Uses of Television*, refers to an assertion made by cultural historian Richard Hoggart in the 1960s that television can be an educator, or moderator of manners: 'television is a major source of "people watching" for comparison and possible emulation' (1999: 155). Hartley argues that television can teach us awareness of how different or similar we are to other people, and how different or similar our own culture is to other cultures. For Hartley, 'difference is understood as neighbourliness' and many television genres, such as 'the world's most gruesome police-chase videos' or 'neighbours from hell documentaries', have incorporated neighbourliness into the presentation of the stories, assuming that viewers at home will have an understanding of social behaviour and draw on their pre-existing knowledge when responding to the programmes (1999: 159–60). In reality programmes such as *Police Camera Action!*, 'moralistic discourses about getaway cars ... can only work for the audience on a prior presumption of neighbourliness and civility in personal, social and domestic comportment' (ibid.). Although Hartley links Hoggart's idea of the uses of television to political participation, or what he calls 'cultural citizenship', I am more interested in Hoggart's notion of people watching as a possible source of learning in relation to reality programming. The reality genre is rich with stories about socially appropriate and inappropriate behaviour. Whether audiences can learn from this is another matter, and I would be hesitant to make claims about potential uses of reality TV when the concept of learning is so openly criticised by viewers themselves.

As we saw in the previous section on entertainment, for the majority of viewers the idea of learning from something so entertaining as reality TV is laughable. Even viewers who are prepared to entertain the idea of learning from watching reality programming make a clear distinction between practical learning from lifestyle programmes, and more observational programmes: 'Some programmes you benefit from, say a cooking programme, you might, you might think "Oh, I'd try that tonight", or a decorating programme or whatever, you'd try something out. But things like *Ibiza Uncovered* or *Big Brother*, you just watch just for the laugh' (23-year-old female barrister's clerk). If, as Hoggart suggests, television can teach us about our own behaviour by watching how other people behave, then reality TV is a prime site for this type of learning. In the previous sections, we saw how the idea of learning from television programmes that openly set out to entertain us is problematic for viewers. For adult viewers, in particular, it is problematic to acknowledge that they can learn from watching people on TV because it implies a lack of knowledge about social behaviour. When this viewer spoke about *Big Brother* she rejected the idea of learning from watching people in the programme because 'You know I, sort of, I sort of know that, I know how people are anyway, nasty and vindictive, nice or whatever. It might open some people's eyes that don't go out, maybe' (27-year-old mother). Her suggestion that the only people who might learn from watching *Big Brother* are people who don't get out much sums up a general feeling amongst audiences of reality programming that if you need to watch reality TV to learn about life then this implies you don't have a life outside of watching TV.

When audiences discuss the idea of learning from watching people in reality programming they are hesitant to give concrete examples of what they have learnt themselves, and talk in more general terms about how other people may learn from watching other people's experiences:

'You can see the pressure of ... the thing is with *Airport* and all that, you can see the people, the pressure that people are put under and how they're coping with that sort of pressure and what they have to deal with. If, programmes like that, where the public is concerned, they can look at that, maybe see their job – whatever it might be in their part of a industry – will look at that and will, like, "Maybe I can learn how to handle pressure better if I handle it like that. Maybe I can take things from that and handle stress better."'

(34-year-old male bus driver)

This viewer's discussion of social learning in *Airport* is interspersed with qualifications regarding the possibility of learning at all from watching this programme. The viewer never directly claims that he has learnt something from watching *Airport*, but relies on second- and third-person pronouns ('you', 'they') to talk about how other people can learn from observing how airport employees cope with the pressures of the job. Even when this viewer does use the first-person pronoun it is a technique to talk as if he were the kind of person who 'can learn how to handle pressure better if I handle it like that'. Similar to the discussion of the 'idea of learning' in contemporary lifestyle programmes in the previous section, discussion of the idea of social learning is framed in relation to other people rather than actual examples of social learning.

Critics of reality TV would argue that audiences are hesitant to give examples of things they have learnt from watching reality programming because there is nothing to learn from them. Even when audiences are talking about practical tips and advice from lifestyle programming they are hesitant to give examples of ideas they have taken from the programmes themselves. But it is too simple to say that audiences don't learn from watching reality programming because there is nothing there for them to learn. When audiences talk about traditional lifestyle programming, or health-based reality programming, they are confident in their discussion of learning from the programmes, whether it is advice about first aid, or tips on how to plant shrubs. When the programme adopts a didactic tone, and tells audiences how to do something, then audiences are more open in their acknowledgement of learning from reality programming. There is something about more observational, people-centred reality programming that causes viewers to either talk in a tentative manner about social learning, or close down discussion of the idea of learning altogether.

If we look at the format 'extreme history' where ordinary people live as if they were in the 1900s, or the First World War, we can see how audiences are open to the idea of learning from social observation if there are clear didactic elements to the programme. Reality formats such as the *1900s House* (UK, Channel 4), or *The Edwardian Country House* (UK, Channel 4) and its American counterpart *Prairie House* (PBS), combine observational style footage within an educational/historical frame. Typically, a group of ordinary people agree to take part in a social experiment, and the series documents their experience as they struggle to come to terms with life in the past, compared with life in the twenty-first century. Thus, *The Edwardian Country House* (my personal favourite) involved the Olliff-Cooper family, who learned how to live as Edwardian aristocrats, and a group of unrelated people, who learned how to live as Edwardian servants (such as Mr Edgar an architect, who became the butler). Needless to say the servants had a much harder time coming to

terms with Edwardian life than Lord and Lady Olliff-Cooper. By the end
of the experiment the Olliff-Coopers were sad to leave life 'upstairs' as the
last living aristocratic Edwardians, whereas the servants couldn't wait to
leave behind the dirt, hard work, and social constraints of life
'downstairs' in order to embrace modern living. Similarly, in the *1940s
House*, a family lived life as Londoners during the Second World War,
balancing their ration book, and taking cover in their air raid shelter at all
times of the day or night. The series filmed their experiences over a six-
week period, and interspersed observational footage of life on the home
front with video diaries kept by the family members, and educational
inserts by historians who commented on the authenticity of the re-created
1940s house. The series also tied in with an exhibition at the Imperial War
Museum. There was also the *1900s House*, where a family lived as
Victorians in the suburbs of London.

Audience responses to these historical social experiments highlight
how social observation can be perceived as informative if the social
observation is presented within an educational frame. For example, this
family of five lived in the south-east of England and owned their own
home. The father (Shaun) was a policeman, the mother (Alison) a teacher,
and all three boys were still at school, aged 15, 11 and 8 at the time of
interview (2001). The family discussed programmes like the *1900s House*
and the *1940s House* in relation to learning about social history through
the eyes of ordinary people:

Shaun: This is a very interesting programme. I watched the *1900s House*,
which was good, and this was the subsequent one.
Alison: I heard they found it very, very difficult.
Brian: Yeah, they couldn't live without shampoo. They got egg in their
hair, and they had to use normal Victorian soap.
Tom: I watched the Victorian one, and they had to go to the toilet in the
garden, and they had to kill their own chickens, they did. And get
them to lay eggs.
Brian: This is history told from the point of view of someone.
Alison: The schools programmes tend to be done with some of it acted
out, and there is some information, so it's not too personal. It is
living history, but you are not emotionally involved.
Tom: You learn how hard it is to live in them days.
Shaun: Programmes like this, they relate history. The fact is that when we
go to breakfast we put our cereal out, and go to the fridge and get
eggs. They get the egg and the slab of butter and that's the week's
ration, and it comes home to you. We can relate to the tasks they
do, but we've got everything to hand, and they haven't.

Brian: You have to be in the right mood to watch some of these programmes. You can either think 'Oh yes, this is really good', or 'Oh no, not another one of them'.

Alison: I mean, if they did the 1960s you would still have the same thing, people without fridges and you know, having the first washing machines, and having to go down to the local shop everyday. It's such a short time, if we look at the ways things have changed.

The family 'relate' to the television family as they try to live their lives in the 1900s, or the 1940s. It is the little things that they notice, living without shampoo, or breakfast cereal. As one of the boys points out, they 'learn how hard it is to live' without modern comforts. The historical framing of this reality format ensures that the family are in no doubt about what the programme is trying to teach them – 'history from the point of view of someone'. And the mother's connection between this reality format and schools programming indicates how the family categorise these types of reality formats as informative and educational. The mother's final comment also indicates how historical social experiments allow audiences to critically reflect on 'the way things have changed' in society.

Earlier on I indicated that young viewers were likely to value entertaining rather than informative reality programmes. Young viewers claimed they would switch off the television if a reality programme advertised itself as a 'learning programme'. Although the young viewers in the above extract had watched the *1900s House* with their parents, the comment from the eldest son that he had to be in the 'right mood' to watch it suggests his ambivalence towards these types of historical social experiment reality formats. Young viewers are especially attracted to reality programmes such as *Police Camera Action!* or *Big Brother*. In discussion of these programmes, young viewers talk about the idea of learning from social observation. Despite having a natural aversion to 'learning programmes', young viewers are open to the idea of learning about life as a by-product of watching an entertaining reality programme. Take this discussion about crime by a group of young male viewers (aged 12–14):

Interviewer: Is there something about *Police Camera Action!* that you can learn from?

Mike: Don't steal a car.

Michael: There isn't really anything you can learn from it, it's just good to watch really.

Grant: Learn how to go at 130 miles an hour and not go into anything.

Richard:	You learn that you can't, you can't really get away with it, the driver knew he was being followed 'cos as soon as he got out the car, he looked up.
Mark:	It kind of, kind of gives the message that, erm, you shouldn't do stuff like that 'cos the police have all this new technology, like, in the helicopter, that they'll be able to track you down. And even though I wouldn't steal a car, after seeing that, people would probably be less likely to. And also, I think, they don't show some things on that programme 'cos the people who do get away, they probably wouldn't show on that programme.
Mike:	Yeah, 'cos it shows up the police force as not being good.

First, there is the usual joke about learning from *Police Camera Action!*, a favourite reality format for this group of viewers, and the usual dismissal of learning 'anything' from a programme that is 'good to watch'. But what follows on from this discussion is an exploration of how the programme can teach people 'that you shouldn't do stuff like that'. What is more, these young viewers have also learnt that the programme only selects successful stories of law and order in order to teach viewers not to engage in criminal activities. Here, the 'message' of the programme gets through to these viewers, and at the same time they critically reflect on how these crime stories are selected for viewers.

In another example, a group of young female viewers (aged 15–18) talk about social learning in relation to *Big Brother*, the favourite type of reality format for this group of viewers:

Interviewer:	Is there anything that is informative about *Big Brother*?
Angela:	Well, you learn about people.
Hilary:	No, it's only, like, you always get caught lying.
Laura:	No, it is informative when they go in that room and they start giving their opinions on people.
Angela:	I think you can learn a lot about people from that.
Laura:	Yes.
Angela:	You can see the way people behave, the way they behave around TVs, on their own, the way they deal with things 'cos they're locked up … I mean … When people think of it they think first of all 'Oh, no, you can't learn' but you can. Do you know what I mean? It's really interesting to watch people, you know, in an environment where everyone is seen all the time.
Sally:	I think *Big Brother* was a lot more interesting and more informative than *Animal Hospital*.

Emma: Yeah, it's, like, people skills, you learn to see how people react to certain situations and it's, like, they're shut in a house all the time, with each other, they can't get away from each other and it's, like, how they either put their difference aside and try and get on or they have stand-up rows, or … it's just how they get on and the way you relate to it really.

Nicola: Well, erm, what I got from people at school was that it wasn't for the informative part or anything it was just basically bitching about other people, they were just, like, 'I don't like him, I don't like her, I think he should win' … that was all basically it was, it was just entertainment.

Sarah: Definitely. It was a lot more light-hearted.

Angela: Yeah, it's like entertainment but you still can … you know what I mean, you can still, like, see things, you can learn things. No, you don't necessarily learn things from it but it shows you things like, you know, people's attitudes or whatever.

Again, there is the familiar dismissal of the idea of learning from watching *Big Brother*, this time framed in relation to gossip and entertainment. But there is also debate about how viewers can 'learn about people' by watching the activities of the contestants in the *Big Brother* house. Thus, the discussion moves backwards and forwards, assessing various responses to the series as 'light-hearted' or more serious, depending on the way viewers perceive the activity of 'people watching'. There is hesitation about what to call this type of learning ('you don't necessarily learn things from it but it shows you things'). But there is also an open debate about the idea of learning from watching a reality format such as *Big Brother*. For these young viewers at this stage in their lives, watching the way people behave in social situations is potentially informative because they are still forming their own understanding of socially acceptable and unacceptable behaviour. Although older adults mainly reject the idea of learning from people watching, younger adults have a vested interest in gathering as much knowledge as they can about 'the way people behave' because they are still learning how to conduct themselves in various social situations, in particular situations involving peers. Reality gameshows such as *Big Brother* provide a useful opportunity for young adults to learn about something that matters to them. As one viewer suggests, watching a contemporary reality format such as *Big Brother* can be more informative than a traditional reality format such as *Animal Hospital* because young adults can relate to the content of one more than the other.

Audience discussion of learning in contemporary reality programming highlights how the genre has 'primarily developed as a medium of entertainment and diversion, with its knowledge-providing role as a secondary function' (Corner 1999: 117). The majority of viewers dismiss the idea of learning from popular factual television precisely because they perceive it as 'mindless entertainment'. Their perception of reality TV relates to the stigmatisation of the genre as trash TV. Some viewers are likely to categorise traditional reality formats as informative when the entertaining elements are framed in an educational manner, and the didactic elements offer practical tips and advice viewers can use in their everyday lives, as in health-based reality programmes. Most contemporary reality formats are thought to be entertaining rather than informative, unless the formats frame the entertainment in an educational manner, as in historical social experiments. Only a minority of viewers consider contemporary reality programmes, in particular observational style programmes, as potentially informative in relation to social behaviour. Audience responses to information are complex because the didactic elements of more traditional popular factual television have transformed into more amorphous learning elements in contemporary reality programming. Even when young viewers discuss learning in contemporary reality formats, they make a distinction between formal and informal learning elements in the programmes, where learning becomes an optional rather than an integral part of the viewing experience. This is why the majority of viewers of reality programming talk about the 'idea of learning' rather than learning itself.

When Hartley (1999) talks about the uses of television in relation to its ability to teach the public, we should bear in mind the resistance on the part of audiences to being taught by popular factual television. The way that audiences dismiss or qualify the idea of learning from reality programming highlights a shift in understanding the role of information in traditional and contemporary reality programming. The difference between traditional health-based and leisure reality programming, and contemporary reality programming highlights how the more reality formats develop as entertainment and diversion, the more the role of knowledge becomes sidelined in the content and reception of the programmes. There are exceptions. Historical social experiments such as *The Edwardian Country House* combine a number of different elements – historical facts, social observation, personal experiences, time travel – to create an innovative popular factual programme that offers formal and informal learning opportunities for audiences about life in the Edwardian era, and life in the twenty-first century. Reality gameshows such as *Big Brother* combine a number of different elements – psychological facts, social observation, personal experiences, games – to create an innovative popular factual programme that offers informal learning opportunities for young audiences about being a young person in the twenty-first century. Such examples indicate the potential for contemporary reality formats to provide 'modes of casual, inferred knowledge' (Corner 1999: 117) for popular audiences. However, if audiences mainly perceive contemporary reality programming as entertainment and diversion then this suggests there is an imbalance between the different elements of entertainment and information in the programmes. The power of reality programming is that it can provide both entertainment and information at the same time, and if all contemporary reality programming can offer is the idea of learning then it has come a long way from its origins as infotainment.

Audience discussion of the idea of learning suggests there is a healthy debate about the balance between information and entertainment in popular factual television. Whether this is debate amongst adult viewers about practical learning in makeover shows, or debate amongst young viewers about social learning in reality gameshows, audiences are engaged in critical viewing practices. The fact that so many viewers are critical of the idea of learning would suggest that there is something they have learned from watching reality programming. The idea of learning therefore relates not only to how viewers might learn from popular factual television, but also to how viewers might learn to not value learning in popular factual television. On one level, viewers talk about how there is little they can learn from contemporary popular factual television. Here, audiences interpret learning as learning about something, whether this is formal or informal learning, and whether this learning is explicitly or implicitly addressed by a reality format. On another level, when viewers talk about the idea of learning about something from popular factual television their talk about the difference between traditional and more contemporary reality programmes is evidence of learning.

When audiences reflect on the idea of learning in reality programming they are reflecting on the development of the genre itself. The ability of audiences to see *through* reality television, and by that I mean witness events, as well as critique the process of selecting events, is fundamental to the development of the reality genre.

CONCLUSION

This chapter has examined the changing role of information in popular factual television. I assessed how audiences judge the informative elements in popular factual television, and whether information is valued in hybrid formats which draw on fictional or leisure formats for entertainment. My research indicates that audiences have contradictory responses to information in popular factual television. On the one hand, audiences value informative elements within the genre, and associate 'information' with the public character of factual television in the UK. However, audiences consider much reality programming to be entertaining rather than informative. Their discussion is framed by media coverage of reality TV as a stigmatised form of popular culture. When viewers discuss informative elements in traditional reality programmes, discussion centres on the deployment of knowledge, such as practical tips for viewers. For example, programmes about consumer issues, or health are thought to be informative because viewers can relate to them, and store information, or ideas, for later use. These reality formats provide practical and social learning opportunities within an entertainment frame. When viewers discuss informative elements in contemporary reality programmes, discussion centres on the idea of learning rather than learning itself. These reality formats do not provide clear practical or social learning opportunities, and instead foreground entertainment. Overall, television audiences are critical of the idea of learning from watching reality programming. However, such criticism is evidence of learning, as audiences debate the role of information within popular factual television, and display critical viewing practices, practices that are healthy for the development of the reality genre.

Chapter 6

Ethics of care

The ethics of reality TV is significant to our understanding of the production, content and reception of the genre as a whole. The relationship between ethics and reality programming is problematic, as reality TV is often criticised for its lack of ethics. Such criticism will often focus on the unethical treatment of ordinary people who participate in reality programmes, or unethical programme makers who use people's private stories for the purposes of public entertainment (Dovey 2000). This type of concern for the production of fair and responsible reality programming is part of a wider debate about the ethics of television production, and includes issues such as fairness, privacy, and taste and decency, issues at the forefront of content regulation (Winston 2000). Debate about the ethics of reality programming is important because non-professional actors have a right to be treated in a fair and responsible manner in reality programming, and programme makers have a responsibility to present stories of ordinary people and their experiences in an ethical manner. All too often ordinary people have little recourse to complain about the way they have been treated or represented in reality programmes (Kilborn and Hibbard 2000; Messenger Davies and Mosdell 2001). Rather than considering ethical practices within television production, I want to focus on ethics in relation to television reception.

Much content of reality programming is concerned with ethics. Reality TV, in the words of Gay Hawkins, has 'taken an ethical turn' (2001: 412). In this chapter, and the following chapter, I want to explore how certain types of reality programming, such as health-based reality formats or lifestyle formats, have taken ethical issues concerned with how we live our lives, and about how other people live their lives, and made such issues a central component of the programmes. In particular, I want to focus on an aspect of ethics related to care. An ethics of care is a form of moral reasoning that we use to understand how we ought to care for our home and family. How television audiences respond to the 'ethical turn' in reality programming is significant in that it illuminates ethical values as represented in the programmes, and as discussed by viewers. The type of reality programmes that attract family viewers, such as health-based reality programming, are also the type of programmes that contain implicit and explicit references to an ethics of care. This chapter, therefore, explores the concept of an ethics of care as applied to reality programming popular with family viewers. In the following chapter (7), I apply the concept of an ethics of care to a case study of the content and reception of animal-based reality programming in order to illustrate the significance of moral values to our understanding of the reality genre.

ETHICS

Ethics are part of our everyday lives. Ethics are concerned with moral values, with the right and wrong ways to live our lives. There are ethical theories of moral principles, and there is the application of these principles in our everyday lives. As Peter Singer notes: 'we cannot avoid involvement in ethics, for what we do – and what we don't do – is always a possible subject of ethical evaluation. Anyone who thinks about what he or she ought to do is, consciously or unconsciously, involved in ethics' (1993: v). Ethics means the study of morality, and is sometimes referred to as moral philosophy. Ethics also means morality itself. Thus, there are normative ethics which are associated with abstract ideas about how we ought to live our lives, such as virtue theory which is concerned with the type of virtues that we aspire to in order to be a 'good' person. There are also applied ethics which are associated with the application of ethical reasoning to practical moral issues, such as the application of virtue theory to personal relationships.

Ethics has its origins in ancient civilisation, and ethical writings from ancient Greek, Egyptian and Hebrew civilizations point to the development of ethical reasoning in small- and large-scale societies. There are a number of great ethical traditions, from Indian, Buddhist and classical Chinese ethics, to Jewish, Christian and Islamic ethics. In terms of Western society, the history of moral philosophy began with ancient Greek scholars such as Socrates, Plato and Aristotle, who searched 'for a rational understanding of the principles of human conduct'; and this search has continued through Roman times, and medieval and Renaissance times, to the present day (Rowe 1993: 121).

Modern moral philosophy has its origins in classical ethical writing, but is also somewhat different from traditional ethical reasoning. According to Annas, traditional ethical writing is about how we can achieve our own 'final good', how we can achieve personal happiness (1992: 130). This type of ethical inquiry is 'not the fundamental ethical question in modern theories'; such theories 'characterise morality in terms of concern for others, whereas ancient ethics begins with concern for oneself' (ibid.). Modern moral philosophy is concerned less with the 'problem of explaining and validating the morally autonomous individual', as exemplified by traditional ethics, and more concerned with moral values within groups or communities, and moral issues within socio/political contexts. For example, 'questions concerning abortion, environmental ethics, just war, medical treatment, business practices, the rights of animals, and the position of women and children occupy a considerable part of the literature and teaching considered to be [modern] moral philosophy or ethics' (Schneewind 1993: 156). Modern moral philosophy is therefore primarily about public good, and the development of moral values within particular social, political and cultural groups, and also within particular secular societies.

There are normative ethical theories that are useful in our understanding of contemporary everyday life. For example, modern virtue theory argues that 'modern societies have inherited no single ethical tradition from the past, but fragments of conflicting traditions' (Pence 1993: 251). Theorists claims that traditional ethical writing on virtue by the ancient Greeks, such as Aristotle or Plato, can help us to anchor modern moral philosophy in an understanding of human good, or personal integrity. Ethical questions can be asked about how a person may handle personal relationships, on the basis of whether they are a 'good' or 'bad' person. Ethical questions can also be asked about how particular cultures encourage or discourage particular virtues or vices:

> modern philosophers are pursuing many questions about virtue, such as the degree to which one is responsible for one's own character, connections between character and manners, connections between character and friendship, and analysis of specific traits such as forgiveness, loyalty, shame, guilt, and remorse.
>
> (Pence 1993: 257)

We might apply modern virtue theory to an understanding of good and bad professional practices, or good and bad character traits. We might also consider how our judgement of whether someone is 'good' or 'bad' is influenced by social and cultural contexts, or personal prejudices.

Another example of ethical theory is that of Kantian ethics, a form of ethical reasoning that claims rational human beings should follow universal laws of reason. Kant was an eighteenth-century European philosopher who argued that our thinking should be established on the natural, rather than the metaphysical, world. Kantian ethics are built on the idea of a general moral law, or categorical imperative. According to Kant, moral principles should be applicable to everyone – they should be universal. Modern ethical theorists influenced by Kant argue for universal moral principles that can be applied to issues concerning law, or human rights. Critics of Kant argue that universal moral principles are too abstract, and separate from socio-historic contexts. Kant was influential in the development of deontological theories of ethics, which argue that we ought to live our lives according to moral rules that should not be broken, even if the consequences are such that our lives would be improved if we ignored these moral rules. Deontological theories of ethics are the opposite of consequentialism, which argues that we should make decisions about how we ought to live our lives based on whatever has the best consequences for us.

Another type of ethical reasoning is that of the social contract tradition. A social contract approach to ethics is one based on social agreement. Social contractarianism requires that we 'join others in acting in ways that each, together with others, can reasonably and freely subscribe to as a common moral standard' (Diggs 1981: 104, cited in Kymlicka 1993: 186). According to Kymlicka there are two forms of contemporary social contract theory, both of which draw on Enlightenment philosophies. The first social contract theory is influenced by the ideas of the eighteenth-century philosopher Hobbes, who argued that a community agrees on common moral standards according to the principle of mutual advantage. For example, it is mutually advantageous for a community to agree that stealing is wrong because this ensures that the individuals within a community do not (in theory) have to spend valuable time and money defending their property. This form of social contract theory privileges those in power. Our understanding of moral values is shaped by the principle of mutual advantage rather than natural duty, and we therefore do not have a universal respect for the rights of others, but rather a respect for rights that are beneficial to ourselves, and the community. The second social contract theory is influenced by the ideas of Kant, who argued for 'a natural equality of moral status, which makes each person's interests a matter of common or impartial concern' (Kymlicka 1993: 188). This type of social contract theory is underpinned by the assumption that 'each person is entitled to equal consideration. This notion of equal consideration gives rise at the social level to a "natural duty of justice"' (1993: 191). Thus, a social contract theory influenced by Kantian ethics is one that does not privilege those in power, and reinforces the assumption that we have a natural duty to respect the rights of others. Modern ethical theorists have mainly been influenced by a Kantian approach to social contractarianism, for example in relation to the issue of social justice. Critics of social contractarianism point out that the ideals of moral equality and natural duty have no foundation, and are therefore abstract concepts that are difficult to apply to contemporary ethical issues.

Public service broadcasting is a useful example of the contemporary application of Kantian ethics and social contractarianism. Public service broadcasting is about three core ideas: diversity, universality, and impartiality (Collins 2003). In the UK, the BBC is the main public service broadcaster, and its mission to inform, educate and entertain the public is a mission that is founded on the principles of diversity, universality and impartiality. For example, BBC news should be available to all members of the public, it should address the interests of diverse members of the public (including ethnic minorities), and it should be impartial in its reporting of national and international events. The relationship between the BBC and its public is a social contract. The BBC exists for the public, and the public pay the license fee in return for a public broadcasting channel based on the general principles of diversity, universality and impartiality. Collins (2003: 45) suggests that a Kantian enlightenment philosophy underpins the historical premise of the BBC as a public service devoted to instructing public opinion and contributing to human well-being. Public service broadcasting also has its roots in the history of British politics, as the political assertion of the importance of the collective against the individual is an assertion founded on socialism, and indeed can be related to an ethics of care, as discussed in the next section.

Critics of the BBC would argue that the social contract between the BBC and its public is under threat. In a highly competitive commercial environment, the BBC could be perceived as operating in its own interests. The Lord Hutton inquiry into the BBC's reporting of the Iraq war in 2003 addressed exactly these ethical issues, and came to the conclusion that the BBC had not been impartial in its war reporting, and had been overly critical of the government's role in the Iraq war. Hutton suggested that the BBC had criticised the government in order to maximise ratings. The resignation of two leading figures (the Chair of Governors and the Director General) in the BBC as a result of the Hutton inquiry might suggest that the BBC was in breach of its social contract with its public. However, public opinion after the Hutton inquiry, and the resignation of Gavin Davies and Greg Dyke, suggested that public trust and support for the BBC had increased as a result of the inquiry. The level of public support for the BBC was partly due to the high value the British public place on public service broadcasting; the level of public trust in the BBC was partly due to public perception of the BBC as professional and impartial in its news reporting, and also their distrust of the government and its involvement in the Iraq war.

The social contract with the BBC and its public is a contract that is profoundly ethical. When we consider the BBC, we can apply ethical reasoning to the key concepts that underpin the remit of the BBC. Why should the BBC be impartial? What common moral standards can we apply to BBC broadcasting practices? How ought the BBC to address diversity in Britain? In order to answer these questions we can use applied ethics to help us come to an understanding of the role of ethics in our everyday lives and in contemporary society.

ETHICS OF CARE

An ethics of care is an established form of ethical reasoning that has its roots in traditional Buddhist social ethics, feminist ethics, and an ethics of rights. An ethics of care draws on traditional and modern ethical reasoning in order to promote a way of life grounded in the moral values of care and rights. How can we care for and how can we be responsible for ourselves and other people? How do we express our compassion, and our responsibility towards others? How much should we care? These are all moral questions that are at the heart of an ethics of care.

An ethics of care is associated with both normative and applied ethics. It is primarily related to two ethical positions, that of an ethic of care, and an ethic of rights. In traditional Buddhist ethics these two positions are fundamental to social ethics: 'the principles of humanistic altruism and the notion of righteous social, moral and political order...provide the ethical foundations of society' (De Silva 1993: 65). The family is central to Buddhist social ethics; and within the family females are traditionally associated with duties of care and compassion, whilst males are traditionally concerned with the value of righteousness. Contemporary Buddhist ethics, in particular Western Buddhist ethics, are strongly associated with virtue ethics (Whitehill 1994).

The focus on gendered social ethics in traditional Buddhist moral philosophy is tangentially related to certain aspects of feminist moral philosophy. There have been a number of feminist scholars who have argued that there are specifically female forms of virtue that can be characterised in relation to care. Some feminists have argued that

> the practices in which women engage, in particular the practices of childcare and the physical and emotional maintenance of other human beings, might be seen as generating social priorities and conceptions of virtue which are different from those that inform other aspects of social life.
>
> (Grimshaw 1993: 496)

In particular, the 'practices of caring for others' can offer 'an ethical model...which is very different from the competitive and individualistic norms of much social life' (ibid.). Noddings, in her book *Caring: A Feminine Approach to Ethics and Education* (1978), argues that there are distinctive attributes to female ethical thinking, and women take moral decisions based on detailed knowledge of the people and the situation involved (Grimshaw 1993: 492–3).

The idea of an ethics of care, as addressed in traditional Buddhist social ethics and feminist ethics, is problematic as it suggests that the practice of caring for others is distinctively female. A woman is often the primary carer in a household, and often represented as the primary carer in culture and society, but this does not mean to say that only women are capable of caring for others. That women are commonly engaged in the practice of care is related to factors such as class, income and ethnicity, as well as personal choice. Grimshaw points out that 'essentialist views of male and female nature are of course a problem if one believes that the "nature" of men and women is not something that is monolithic or unchanging, but is, rather, socially and historically constructed' (1993: 493). Grimshaw is referring to debate concerning gender role development. This debate is characterised by two positions: (1) that we are born with particular chromosomes and hormones that make us behave in masculine or feminine ways, or (2) that we are socialised to behave in masculine or feminine ways as we develop from children into adults. Although there is some evidence to suggest gender is determined by biological factors, this evidence is by no means trouble free (Gauntlett 2002: 34). Alternative research in gender role development suggests we learn about gender roles from our family or friends, we learn to imitate the behaviour of other males and females around us (Malim and Birch 1998: 518, cited in Gauntlett 2002: 34). Research also suggests that society reinforces particular gender roles and behaviour as more socially acceptable than others. What is more, social attitudes towards sexuality and gender change over time, and therefore what is considered to be socially acceptable gender roles and behaviour gradually changes over time (see Hill and Thomson 2001 for further discussion of changing social attitudes towards sex in the media).

Kittay argues that the role of the carer needs to be re-evaluated in contemporary society. She proposes a 'public ethic of care' (2001: 526). A public ethic of care draws on the concept of reciprocity: 'we are obliged to provide care because we have all, at some point in our lives, been the recipient of care' (2001: 535). Kittay calls for a collective, social responsibility for care that supports care workers and family members in the practice of care:

> an individual in need of care is like a stone cast in the water. Those feel the impact most immediately who are in closest proximity, but the effects come in wider and wider ripples. Even though the well-being of an individual may be the immediate duty of those who are closest, it is the obligation of the larger society to assure that care can be and is provided.
>
> (2001: 535)

Thus, a public ethic of care is one that draws on support from individuals, society and the state. Kittay argues that 'society benefits from those who work to care for dependents, whether or not the dependent individual is one for whose well-being we are most directly responsible' (ibid.). Kittay also contends that although carers are primarily female, society and the state should encourage males to participate in care work in order to ensure more equal distribution of care duties.

The idea of an ethics of care as being fundamentally female is based on the assumption that female behaviour is determined by biological factors. This idea of an ethics of care is not one that reflects contemporary understanding of the social construction of gender roles. The idea of an ethics of care as fundamentally social is more useful for analysis of contemporary social relationships and ways of living. If we frame the concept of an ethics of care in relation to contemporary gender role development and modern moral philosophy then an ethics of care can be understood in relation to moral values of compassion and responsibility within groups or communities, and moral issues of compassion and responsibility within particular social/political contexts.

An ethic of rights is based upon the concept that an individual has a natural and moral, and in some cases legal, right to live their lives in the same way as other people. According to the British eighteenth-century philosopher John Locke, everyone has a right to life, liberty and property, or the pursuit of happiness (Almond 1993: 260). Rights are most commonly associated with universal human rights. There are groups that campaign against human rights abuse, for example the non-governmental organisation Amnesty International campaigns for the release of illegally detained social and political commentators around the world. An ethic of rights also includes legal rights. For example, universal human rights were given legal force by the establishment of the United Nations Declaration of Human Rights (1948), after the Second World War. In addition, an ethic of rights also includes moral rights. For example, universal human rights are also moral rights, as a human being has the capacity to suffer and it is morally wrong to inflict suffering on others, unless there is prior legal and moral justification.

An ethic of rights is related to an ethics of care in the sense that rights are based upon social responsibility. The concept of universal human rights is applicable not just to ourselves but to other people as well – this is what makes it universal. Contemporary ethical thinking on rights has argued for greater application of rights to social issues, such as environmentalism, or animal rights (Almond 1993). If we take the case of animal rights, we can see how an ethics of care is bound up with an ethic of rights in moral reasoning on the treatment of animals in Western society. It is commonly agreed that animals have rights, and that 'there are no defensible grounds for treating animals in any way other than as beings worthy of moral consideration' (Gruen 1993: 352). The moral rights of animals have legal force in the EU Convention of the Protection of Animals. In order to ensure ethical treatment, animals should be cared for in such a way that they do not experience unnecessary suffering. There are arguments about how to enforce ethical treatment of animals, and organisations such as the Royal Society for the Prevention of Cruelty to Animals exist in order to care for animals that have been mistreated by humans. Nevertheless, animals have a moral and legal right to be treated in a responsible, compassionate and caring manner. I discuss further the dual ethics of care and rights in relation to animals in the following chapter on animal-based reality programming.

There are other types of ethics that espouse moral values of care, compassion, responsibility and rights. For example, virtue theory is about the integrity of an individual and how they attempt to live their lives in a 'virtuous' manner. The moral values of compassion or responsibility are commonly thought of as character building, and as positive attributes in modern society. Modern moral philosophy primarily locates an ethics of care in relation to social ethics, feminist ethics, and an ethic of rights. In the next section, I consider how ethics can help us to understand reality programming, before specifically addressing an ethics of care in health-based and lifestyle reality formats.

ETHICS AND REALITY TV

How can ethics help us to understand reality programming? Ethics are about morality in everyday life. There are many aspects of reality programming that raise complex moral issues concerning how we live our lives. For example, the premise of *Big Brother* – to lock people in a house, filming their every move 'twenty-four/seven' – is one that takes away an individual's right to freedom in return for the social and economic rewards of fame and fortune. Housemates and voters judge social interaction in the *Big Brother* house according to their perception of 'good' or 'bad' behaviour. Television audiences debate how true to themselves the housemates have been whilst in the *Big Brother* house. Audiences question how truthful programme makers have been in their representation of activities in the house. Television regulators question whether the ordinary people taking part in the programme have been treated in a fair and responsible manner. The popular press tests boundaries of fairness and privacy in their quest for the latest scoop from inside and outside the *Big Brother* house. These issues concerning the production, content and reception of *Big Brother* are all in one way or another moral issues, and our understanding of this reality gameshow is connected in one way or another with our understanding of moral values.

Participation in reality programmes

Contemporary reality formats, in particular reality gameshows, provide rich data for analysis of the ethics of participation in television programmes. Two studies conducted by the UK television regulatory body the Broadcasting Standards Commission, *Consenting Adults?* (Kilborn and Hibbard 2000) and *Consenting Children?* (Messenger Davies and Mosdell 2001), examine the ethical treatment of non-professional actors in television programmes. For example, UK regulation regarding the treatment of children in programming stipulates that children cannot participate in programmes unless the programme makers have acquired the consent of parents or guardians. The report recommends that in addition to the existing provisions and safeguards for the protection of children in television programmes, programme makers should provide 'a person on hand…to monitor and ensure the application of these guidelines for the welfare of the children during the course of production' (Messenger Davies and Mosdell 2001: 12). The report also suggests that 'parents may be more enthusiastic about seeing their children on television than the children themselves are, which reinforces the importance of children's consent to appear on television being sought independently of their parents' (2001: 13). Ultimately, the report recommends that in order to ensure the ethical and legal rights of children in television 'guidelines for programme makers should be based on current good practice in child and family law about the treatment of children and procedures for obtaining consent or not' (2001: 14).

In relation to contemporary reality programming, there are many examples of programmes which feature children that deserve close scrutiny in terms of ethics. For example, the reality social experiment series *Wife Swap*, made by independent production company RDF Media for the UK and USA, involves the participation of ordinary families in a challenging social experiment, where families with different lifestyles and values attempt to live together for two weeks. In one episode of the first series in the UK (Channel 4, 2003), a working-class white family swapped lives with a working-class black family. The 'white wife', who confessed her fears that the other family might be non-white, openly argued with her adoptive husband, and her eldest daughter openly argued with her adoptive mother, at one point calling her a 'black bitch'. Whilst the parents will have given consent for themselves and their children to participate in the programme, did the children know the type of experience they were letting themselves in for, and did they have recourse to complain about how they were represented in the programme once the programme had been aired? With such an emotionally charged social experiment as *Wife Swap* it is important that programme makers are regularly monitored on their ethical treatment of children in a reality programme for adult viewers, broadcast after the family viewing watershed of nine o'clock.

Similarly, although adults are given a choice as to whether to participate in reality gameshows or not, and sign consent forms allowing programme makers to film them twenty-four/seven whilst taking part in the show, they are not necessarily aware beforehand of how emotionally difficult their experience might be, or how they may feel after filming has been completed and the programme has been aired. Although programme makers claim that they receive thousands of applications from ordinary people to participate in reality gameshows, and that these people give informed consent, the very nature of reality gameshows is to 'play the game', even if the game asks people to make morally difficult decisions, and to engage in morally dubious activities.

For example, in the reality gameshow *The Bachelor* the name of the game is group dating, and a series of single women date one eligible bachelor who, through a process of elimination, chooses his soul mate. In the UK version of *The Bachelor*, aired on BBC3 in 2003, the single women were taken on what appeared to be romantic dates with the bachelor. In the finale of the series, it became apparent that the bachelor had become sexually intimate with several women during these dates. One woman in particular had found his advances unwelcome – he had entered her hotel room uninvited, and she repeatedly had to ask him to leave. She explained: 'He was trying to get me into his room and I said no. And then at four in the morning, drunk, in his pants, with a hard on, he tried to help himself to me.' The studio exchange between this woman, the presenter and the studio audience highlights the manner in which the programme makers represented this participant's claims to have been sexually harassed by the star of the show. Vanessa's experience was recounted in the studio to a male presenter and the studio audience, which included her mother, the other single women who participated in the programme, and friends of the bachelor. After describing what happened in the hotel room, the interview continued:

Presenter:	I take it that was an off-camera moment?
Vanessa:	Yes, unfortunately it was all off camera.
Presenter:	Impressed?
Vanessa:	Not really.
Presenter:	[laughing] I had to ask. Some people may say that you were a woman scorned.
Vanessa:	He still thinks no means yes … At not one point did I giggle and laugh and give him the impression that I was enjoying him trying to get in bed with me. I was furious. [off camera a member of the studio audience shouts something at Vanessa, and she asks 'What was that?']

Presenter:	Let's find out what your mum thinks.
Vanessa's Mum:	I've seen the way he has behaved with a lot of girls, led them on to believe they are very special and then voted them off. If a girl behaved like that she would be classed as a tart … I believe my daughter … I think he has behaved in a totally dishonourable manner. [the single women cheer]
Presenter:	[to friends of the bachelor] How would you defend him?
Friend:	I think David has just acted like any young man. Women are just not like us, are they?
Presenter:	[laughs] I'm glad you said that. Vanessa, final word?
Vanessa:	I think he is a bit of a slapper really. [heckles from the audience] He's a nice guy really … but I just think no means no.

The Bachelor illustrates the concept of virtue ethics, as applied to group dating. The format is based on character virtues and vices, such as honesty and trust, or dishonesty and sexual conquest. Typically, the eligible bachelor is shown making difficult choices – which girl to take on a date, which girl to eliminate. The single women are shown competing for his attention, and responding to the changing group dynamic – how to stand out from the crowd, how to maintain interest. In the programme itself, these moral choices are represented as illustrations of 'good' and 'bad' moral conduct, and we are asked to judge the bachelor and his dates according to their character traits. Is the bachelor honourable? Are the women honest? Off camera, the participants are also asked to make moral choices, and in the studio finale we learn that several of the women experienced emotionally challenging situations, especially concerning the issue of sex, that are not featured in the programme itself.

   The Bachelor reflects traditional social attitudes towards men as sexual predators, as the star is encouraged to be sexually active, and is rewarded for his behaviour. His vice is transformed into a virtue. As Vanessa's mother points out 'If a girl behaved like that she would be classed as a tart.' The single women are represented differently. The very fact that they have chosen to take part in the programme is perceived as a negative character trait. As the presenter points out, 'some people might say you were actually desperate to come on a TV show like this to find a man'. Thus, the programme reflects traditional social attitudes towards women as 'gold diggers'. Although the sister reality format *The Bachelorette* attempts to counteract such gender stereotypes, the different ways in which the male and female stars of the shows are represented only serves to underscore the gendered application of virtue ethics in this type of reality format. *The Bachelor*, and other reality formats such as *Joe*

Millionaire, constructs negative representations of single women, as it is the job of the single man to find the one honest woman amongst many dishonest women.

When it comes to participating in reality formats such as *The Bachelor*, non-professional actors deserve to be treated in an ethically informed manner. The finale of *The Bachelor* is an example of how women can be unfairly treated in reality programming. The participant's experience discussed here raises significant ethical issues about the rights of women that are not addressed satisfactorily by the programme itself. The practice of informed consent needs to be addressed by programme makers and programme regulators in order to ensure non-professional actors are treated with the respect they deserve, before, during, and after the transmission of the programme. It is certainly the case that television audiences regularly discuss the potential exploitation of ordinary people in reality programmes. Their discussion focuses not only on the misrepresentation of non-professional actors, or informed consent, but also how ordinary people should treat each other whilst participating in a reality programme such as *The Bachelor*. In Chapter 7, I examine audience discussion of the participation of pet owners and their pets in animal-based popular factual television

The content of reality programming

In terms of the content of reality programming, there is also rich data for analysis of ethics. Bonner points out that 'a whole panoply' of television programmes can be 'accused of rewarding greed or showing off, leading people to expect "quick fixes" to problems, advocating "shallow" interpersonal and sexual relationships and destroying community sentiment' (2003: 154). Gay Hawkins, in an article titled 'The Ethics of Television' (2001), argues that ethics has become entertainment, and television has found a variety of ways to entertain us. Talk shows such as *The Jerry Springer Show*, or reality programmes such as *Neighbours from Hell*, make a spectacle of ethical crises. In another related article, Hawkins suggests that reality gameshows such as *Big Brother* or *Temptation Island* invite 'us to enter into the world of ethical uncertainty, the zone where clear positions or sides are not necessarily evident' (2002: 1). Hawkins is critical of programmes such as *Temptation Island* that encourage audiences to take 'pleasure in the plight of others' (2002: 6).

The type of reality programming common to Fox TV, cable channel Reality TV, and digital channel Sky One, is a type of commercial reality TV that lends itself to ethical analysis. *Temptation Island* tests the fidelity of couples by tempting them to cheat on their partners. As one male contestant put it, 'I haven't come here to play scrabble' (*Temptation Island* (Series Two), UK, Sky One, 2002). *Joe Millionaire* requires that the eligible bachelor must deceive single girls into believing he is a millionaire in order to win a million dollars (USA, Fox, 2002) – 'his name's not Joe and he's not a millionaire'.[1] *Sex on the Beach* shows young British holidaymakers drunk and behaving badly (UK, Sky One, 2002). *When Good Times Go Bad 3* shows on-scene footage of car accidents, and personal injuries (such as a man's arm coming away from its socket in a game of tug-of-war) as spectacles for entertainment (USA/UK, Reality TV, 2003). We could analyse any number of these types of reality programmes from a number of ethical positions, such as the virtues and vices of ordinary people, or the ethical issues of privacy, or taste and decency.

If we consider the type of reality programming concerned with outrageous behaviour, such as *Ibiza Uncovered* or *Big Brother*, we can see how such programmes test the moral limits of acceptable behaviour. These reality programmes provide an opportunity to discuss socially acceptable, or unacceptable behaviour. In Chapter 4, I discussed how television audiences debated the behaviour of 'Nasty Nick' and Mel in the first series of *Big Brother*. When one woman commented on Mel's personal grooming habits – she plucked her pubic hairs in the garden whilst chatting to other housemates – she did so in order to point out that she found this personal grooming socially unacceptable. Similarly, the discussion in Chapter 5 regarding *Ibiza Uncovered* is also concerned with whether the two 'Jack the lads' who took part in this programme behaved in a socially acceptable manner. Whilst the male viewers who discussed the programme thought their behaviour acceptable in a private setting, they did not think it was appropriate for television, where their wives and children might witness their drunken and flirtatious behaviour.

In this section, I focus on particular types of reality programmes that are about taking care of oneself and others. For example, lifestyle programming such as *Gardeners' World* invites us to examine 'ways to live' (Hawkins 2001: 412). Lifestyle programming can teach us about the application of ethics in our everyday lives. These reality formats can 'show us that ethics is practical, various, creative, experimental and relational; that while ethics can be implicated with wider moral codes (they often are), they can also be relatively autonomous, a product of our own particular sensibilities, principles and micro-moral communities' (2001: 418). The stuff of the everyday in lifestyle programming can be transformed into moral instruction for audiences: 'television is now deeply implicated in shaping our ethical sensibilities, in marking out fields and activities that warrant ethical attention, in advising us on how to cultivate particular practices and conducts in the interests of realising ethical goals' (2001: 413).

Hawkins suggests the experience of watching ethics on television can encourage audiences to participate in 'quests for the truth of the self' (2001: 412). She refers in her research to a body of work concerned with the politics of the self. Michel Foucault, in his later work *The History of Sexuality*, volumes two and three (*The Use of Pleasure* and *The Care of the Self*, 1992, 1990), explored the idea of the self in relation to ethics. Ethics, Foucault suggests, is 'the kind of relationship you ought to have with yourself' (2000: 263). Foucault argued in *The Care of the Self* (1990) that ancient Greek and Roman moral philosophy could help us to understand our relationship with ourselves. The idea of the 'cultivation of the self' in ancient Greek and Roman ethical writing is best characterised by the phrase 'take care of oneself' (Foucault 1990: 43). This ethical principle of the care of the self is dependent on three related concepts: 'individualistic attitude', 'the positive valuation of private life', and 'the intensity of the relations to self' (1990: 42). By this Foucault means that the care of the self is dependent on moral values associated with the central role of the individual in society, the central role of the family in society, and the importance of self-improvement in relation to an ethical way of life. Foucault notes that the cultivation of the self in ancient Greek and Roman civilisation was 'not a rest cure', and in order to ensure care of the self one would be encouraged to undertake a variety of physical and mental activities associated with self-improvement (1990: 51). Foucault's idea of 'the self's relationship to itself' involves the principle of the care of the self, and the practical application of this ethical principle to the way we think and act, something Foucault calls 'technologies of the self (Gauntlett 2002: 124–8).

Hawkins argues that Foucault's idea of the shaping and regulating of the self is 'the stuff of infotainment' (2001: 417). The practical and moral instruction of lifestyle and makeover programmes provide external advice on how to improve our home, or our appearance, and internal advice on how to improve our relationship with ourselves. The idea of an ethics of care, as discussed in the previous section, specifically relates to Foucault's concept of the care of the self. However, the ancient Greek and Roman ethical principle of care of the self is somewhat different to contemporary understanding of an ethics of care. As I suggest in the previous section, an ethics of care draws on traditional and modern ethical reasoning in order to promote a way of life grounded in the moral values of compassion and responsibility for ourselves and other people. The ethic of rights is central to the principle of caring for ourselves in the same way we would wish to care for other people. An ethic of rights is absent from ancient philosophical writing about care of the self primarily because the self is the focus of such writing. Modern philosophical reasoning foregrounds the application of an ethics of care not just to individual ethical dilemmas but also to social groups and issues.

Reality programming occupies a complex position regarding care of the self and an ethics of care. On the one hand, the content of much lifestyle programming is about individual ways to improve care of the self. On the other hand, the content of much health-based reality programming is about how other people care for individuals in compassionate and responsible ways. Frances Bonner, in her book *Ordinary Television* (2003), addresses the complex relationship between lifestyle and health-based reality programming. She comments that 'lifestyle television addresses an individualised viewer with advice about consumption practices ostensibly designed to improve the quality of life in the area addressed by the programme' (2003: 106). She refers to Anthony Giddens, and his work on self-identity, in order to explain the way lifestyle programming addresses viewers as consumers: 'lifestyle can be defined as a more or less integrated set of practices which an individual embraces, not only because such practices fulfil utilitarian needs, but because they give material form to a particular narrative of self-identity' (Giddens 1991: 81, cited in Bonner 2003: 105). There are echoes of Foucault's concept of care of the self in Giddens' notion of lifestyle and self-identity. According to Bonner (2003: 104), lifestyle programmes 'alert viewers to the existence of more products and services for their utility in the endless project of the self'. A similar focus on the individual's interest in care of the self is also apparent in health-based reality programming: 'the individual to whom the advice is directed is concerned as being a body eager to be improved by dietary changes, exercise regimes, cosmetic enhancements and surgical corrections' (Bonner 2003: 107). Foucault (1992: 56) also noted in ancient ethical philosophy 'increased medical involvement in the cultivation of the self ... expressed through a particular and intense form of attention to the body'. This relationship between care of the self and the body is reflected in the relationship between lifestyle and health in reality programming.

Although lifestyle and health-based reality programmes address an individualised viewer about care of the self, they also address the viewer about how to care for others. The moral instruction of *Changing Rooms* or *Children's Hospital* is related to both the individual and the social. For example, in *Changing Rooms* the stories about home improvement are primarily about how ordinary people can benefit, or not, from professional advice about interior design. We see the before, during and after of the home improvement, and witness the 'reveal', as home owners react to the DIY transformation. A secondary part of these stories is that neighbours volunteer to transform each other's houses for the sake of home improvement (and participating in a television programme). Upon completion of the transformation, the responses of the home owners are in part a response to design intervention, and also the treatment of their home by their neighbours. Hence, we regularly see neighbours asking fellow neighbours 'not to paint the marble fireplace', or to take care of items of sentimental value, and if their wishes have been ignored then it is the neighbours, as well as the designers, who are responsible for unwanted changes to the home. Although the programme itself is more concerned with the entertainment value of design *faux pas*, there is an underlying emphasis on care and responsibility in the programme as a whole. In *Children's Hospital*, the stories about health crises are primarily about how ordinary people benefit from professional medical treatment. We see the diagnosis, treatment and (in most cases) recovery of sick children, and the reactions of the children and parents to the various stages in their recovery. A secondary part of these stories is about the caring profession: the doctors, nurses, and emergency services personnel who devote their lives to caring for others, and the parents who care for their children in times of acute illness. Thus, a story of the successful recovery of a child from acute illness is in part about the strength and bravery of the patient, and also about the informed care of medical professionals and parents. This focus on the health and well-being of children is central to the programme's emphasis on individual and social care, and responsibility for children.

In my audience research, the concept of an ethics of care incorporates traditional ethical reasoning regarding care of the self within a wider understanding of social ethics and rights ethics. As we shall see in the next section, and in Chapter 7, when watching such programmes, audiences store information or ideas for the care of their family, friends and home environment. As Hawkins and Bonner have suggested, we can interpret these audience responses in relation to the concepts of self-identity and care of the self, as outlined by Giddens and Foucault. Audiences also discuss lifestyle and health-based reality programming in terms of a more socially orientated idea of caring for others as well as the self. I have suggested in the previous section and here that we can interpret these audience responses in relation to compassion and responsibility, as outlined in philosophical moral reasoning on ethics of care.

ETHICS AND AUDIENCES

British lifestyle and health-based reality programmes appeal to family viewers. Families are defined by *Social Trends*, the official publication of British demographic and social trends, as 'a married or co-habiting couple with or without their never married children (who have no children of their own), or a lone parent with such children. People living alone are not considered to form a family' (Social Trends 1999: 43, cited in Hughes and Fergusson 2000: 50). In 2000–2001 the average household contained 2.4 people (Social Trends 2002). The types of people living in households were mainly couples with children (39 per cent), or couples without children (24 per cent). Twelve per cent of the population were classified as people living alone, and 6 per cent as lone parents (Social Trends 2002). In terms of time spent on various activities in the home, women spent an average of 2.2 hours per weekday watching the television and VCR, 2.5 hours per weekday involved in household and family care, and 0.2 hours per weekday on childcare (Social Trends 2003). In comparison, men spent an average of 2.4 hours per weekday watching the television and VCR, 1.8 hours per weekday involved in household and family care, and 0.1 hours per weekday on childcare (Social Trends 2003). At 8pm on weekdays, most households were involved in leisure activities (57 per cent), or housework and childcare (15 per cent) (Social Trends 2003). This statistical snapshot is useful in indicating who might be at home, watching television and/or engaged in other household or leisure activities during the time period when reality programming about lifestyle and healthcare is scheduled. As television commissioners and schedulers pay attention to demographic and social trends, it is not unreasonable to assume that weekday evening reality programming has been designed to target the largest group of viewers watching television at that time – families.

According to research in the sociology of the family there is evidence to suggest that 'although the two-parent family remains numerically dominant today, this institutional form no longer defines so exclusively what it is to live in a family, or what a family is' (Hughes and Fergusson 2000: 57). David Morgan comments that 'notions of "family" are rarely static but are constantly subjected to processes of negotiation and re-definition' (1999: 18). For Morgan, the concept of the family is related to family practices that involve caring for other family members and being responsible for their needs (1996). Allen and Crow (2001: 2) argue that there should be greater precision about how the terms 'family' and 'household' are used. The household, in which family members may or may not live together, can be characterised as the 'division of responsibility and workload between household members', whereas the family can be characterised as 'the solidarity and conflict developing between people who are linked through kinship' (2001: 6). The household and the family overlap when people who are linked by kinship live together under the same roof (2001: 7). Most family households, therefore, will often involve family practices related to care of the family and the household. The idea of social ethics is significant to the family household, as family members are expected to care for each other and the home, and be responsible for each other and the home. An ethics of care, as discussed in the previous sections, is a form of ethical reasoning that can be applied to the care and maintenance of family households.

In a national survey in 2000, adults (aged 16–65+) living in households with children watched particular types of reality programmes (Hill/ITC 2000). For example, the types of reality formats watched regularly and occasionally by adults with children in the household included programmes such as *Changing Rooms* (78 per cent), *Police Camera Action!*

(75 per cent), *999* (63 per cent), *Animal Hospital* (62 per cent), and *Children's Hospital* (60 per cent). If we look at the programmes children (aged 4–15) watched most often during the same period we see a correlation between the viewing habits of parents and children. The types of reality formats watched regularly and occasionally by children were programmes such as *Changing Rooms* (84 per cent), *Animal Hospital* (83 per cent), *Police Camera Action!* (71 per cent), *Children's Hospital* (66 per cent), and *999* (58 per cent).

In terms of gendered preferences for reality formats, men were as likely as women to be occasional viewers of these types of programmes. For example, there was little difference between the percentages of men and women who occasionally watched programmes such as *Changing Rooms* (43 per cent and 39 per cent respectively), *Animal Hospital* (36 per cent, 37 per cent), *Police Camera Action!* (48 per cent, 47 per cent), *Children's Hospital* (33 per cent, 37 per cent), or *999* (42 per cent, 44 per cent). But women were far more likely to be regular viewers of lifestyle and health-based reality programmes than men. For example, there was a difference between the percentages of men and women who regularly watched programmes such as *Changing Rooms* (18 per cent and 35 per cent respectively), *Animal Hospital* (17 per cent, 30 per cent), and *Children's Hospital* (12 per cent, 25 per cent). For crime reality programmes, such as *Police Camera Action!*, the gender split for regular male and female viewers was equal (24 per cent and 25 per cent respectively). It's a similar story in terms of social class. A greater percentage of people in the social category C2DE (skilled and working class, and lowest level of subsistence) than ABC1 (upper to lower middle class) regularly watched lifestyle and health-based reality programmes, but there was not much differentiation by social class in terms of occasional viewing. For example, the breakdown for people who occasionally watched programmes like *Children's Hospital* was AB – 34 per cent, C1 – 35 per cent, C2 – 36 per cent, and DE – 35 per cent, whereas the breakdown for regular viewers was AB – 12 per cent, C1 – 17 per cent, C2 – 21 per cent, and DE – 23 per cent.

These figures suggest that parents and children watch lifestyle, emergency services and health-based reality programmes together. One reason why families tend to watch these types of reality programmes is because they happen to be on at a time when families are relaxing after work and school, and are looking to watch television together. As this 14-year-old schoolboy commented 'I watch *Changing Rooms* every week. I'm a bit sad really … I always watch that with anyone else who's in the room, usually my mum'. The figures also indicate mothers and fathers watch these types of programmes occasionally with their children, whilst mothers in the C2DE social category are more regular viewers of these programmes. One reason why mothers tend to watch these types of programmes is because they spend more time watching television with their children than men. As this 35-year-old housewife explained, 'I tend to watch *Children's Hospital* and *Animal Hospital* with my two little girls, and then *Changing Rooms* ... those ones like that, all of us would watch them, the family really'. The fact that these mothers tend to be in the C2DE social category is in part to do with their low income status as full-time mothers, as well as the income status of their spouse or partners.

The survey results also indicate that parents and children like similar programme elements, such as stories caught on camera (75 per cent of adults with children in the household, 67 per cent of children). One difference in the likes and dislikes of programme elements for parents and children is that parents most like information in reality formats (82 per cent of adults, 49 per cent of children), whilst children most like animals in reality formats (72 per cent of children, 63 per cent of adults). This difference in preferences for programme elements in reality formats is related to the fact that parents tend to like programmes they can learn from, and watch animal-based reality programming primarily so that they and their children can learn more about how to care for family pets, whereas children tend to like animal-based reality programming above all other types because they like stories about animals (see Chapter 7 for further discussion). Overall, the results suggest lifestyle and health-based reality programmes appeal to parents and children because they contain potentially informative stories, especially about animals, that are caught on camera for television.

How audiences talk about ethics in lifestyle and health-based reality programming is associated with how they watch these programmes as a family. The content of these programmes is designed to appeal to family viewers, as the stories about ordinary people and home improvement or health crises are stories about the care and maintenance of members of the family and the household they live in. Gay Hawkins comments that lifestyle programming:

> Transforms wider questions about how we should we live, about ways of being, into technical advice. How should we be in our garden, how should we relate to food, to our lovers, to our pets? This technical advice is never purely technical – it is also at the same time ethical because it involves giving privilege to certain conducts over others, the classification of certain conducts as good.
>
> (2001: 418)

I would extend this observation about emphasis on good conduct in lifestyle programming to health-based reality programming, as advice about health is also about privileging certain lifestyles, eating habits, and ways of being, over others. The way that family viewers discuss ethical issues in lifestyle and health-based reality programming reflects the 'ethical turn' in television to situate advice and ideas about ways of being into ethical reasoning about good conduct within the family and the household.

For example, this family of five lived in the south-east of England, and owned their own home. The father was a stonemason, and the mother a part-time child-carer, and they had three girls, aged 10, 8 and 5 at the time of the interview (2001). The mother and children were regular viewers of lifestyle programmes, such as *Changing Rooms*, as well as programmes such as *Children's Hospital*, *Animal Hospital* and *999*. The father was an occasional viewer of these programmes. In a discussion about the appeal of lifestyle programming they reflected on good and bad practices in the home:

Sally:	'Cos sometimes they have kids and they do their bedrooms and I like it when they come and see if they like it, the different designs. When they go back to different houses and see if they've kept it that way, then that's quite good.
Vivienne:	Why do I think the children like it? I think it's the transformation, isn't it? It's all very quick, isn't it? It's not going on for hours.
Robert:	And they know there's going to be a surprise.
Interviewer:	Have you two ever helped your parents with the decorating?
Robert:	They've wanted to.
Rachael:	Well, I have painted on the wall, like doing in pink, by accident ...
Robert:	By accident!
Rachael:	But then Daddy painted green over it.

One of the reasons the eldest daughter watched programmes such as *Changing Rooms* was because she liked to see how other children reacted to their redesigned bedrooms. As her mother points out, it is the way homes can be transformed in a matter of minutes that appeals to children. But, just as there are good and bad designs for children's bedrooms in the programme, so too are there good and bad ways to transform the home. Thus, when the youngest daughter talked about her contribution to the changing colour scheme of her bedroom her father was quick to point out that this was not his idea of help with home improvements.

In another family discussion of lifestyle programming, the idea of good and bad conduct within the home was expanded to include the idea of an ethics of care for the home, and by extension the family. This family of five also lived in the south-east of England and owned their own home. The father (Shaun) was a policeman, the mother (Alison) a teacher, and all three boys were still at school, aged 15, 11 and 8 at the time of interview (2001). The mother regularly watched programmes such as *Changing*

Rooms, and was an occasional viewer of *Children's Hospital, Animal Hospital, Police Camera Action!* and *999*. Their eldest son, Brian, was an occasional viewer of *Police Camera Action!*, but rarely watched other reality programmes, although he used to be a regular viewer of *Changing Rooms* when he was younger. Tom and Steven, their younger sons, regularly watched programmes such as *Animal Hospital* and *Changing Rooms*, and occasionally watched *Children's Hospital, Police Camera Action!* and *999* with their mum and dad. The father regularly watched *Children's Hospital*, and occasionally watched other reality programmes with the family. The following extract is an example of the kind of rich discussion that arises from watching lifestyle programmes:

Tom: I like to see how they change the rooms so quickly and …
Alison: They particularly like *Ground Force*.
Tom: But the people from *Ground Force*, they actually have personalities. The people from *Changing Rooms* [in boring voice] 'Oh, we're going to change that TV over there, put that over there …'.
Alison: Yes, we get what you mean! You get to know the people who are running the programme, yeah?
Brian: It's a little bit more in-depth, less artificial.
Shaun: Steven, why do you like *Ground Force*?
Steven: Errr … I don't know! [giggles]
Brian: When it first started *Changing Rooms* was good but now …
Interviewer: What did you like about it when you used to watch it?
Brian: The way you could see how they changed it. It was, I don't know … it was entertainment! If it was on you would watch it. You maybe wouldn't … say make a special effort. If it was on 'cos, like, they were watching it, I'd be, like, 'Oh, it's on, I'll come and sit down.'
Alison: When it's on, they'll sit and watch it even if I'm not. They'll sometimes have re-runs and they'll sit and watch it … I don't know if they watch it because I tend to watch those things, whether they watch it with me because they know I do the decorating and the gardening … they know I have more aesthetic sense and I will change things.
Brian: This room's been decorated about six times!
Alison: No, it hasn't.
Interviewer: Have you guys ever done your bedrooms?
Brian: I did my bedroom, was it Easter?
Interviewer: Was any of it based on anything you might have seen on the telly?

Brian:	No. Actually, you maybe pick up ideas just subconsciously by watching it. You just remember little bits and you think 'Oh, yeah, I might use that'.
Alison:	I did his room last year, and discussed ideas with him.
Brian:	Which is pretty cool.
Shaun:	If there's stuff to be done, DIY round the house, or the garden ... for me personally, my father would be 'Help me do this in the garden' and I'd be holding the can of paint and that was as much as I did! But everything we do around the house, they say 'can we take part?' and as much as it can take you twice as long to do, we try to get them involved.
Alison:	Yeah, I always used to help my mum. I just like to feel they'll be involved in their home from helping us because otherwise they never take pride in anything. I think the more you're involved in something, the more you're likely to care about it.
Tom:	We're always trying to rub down the walls ... maybe not the painting, but we help.
Alison:	They help in colour choice.

There is a natural progression from discussion about their family viewing practices, and preferences for lifestyle programming to discussion about their own way of life as a family household. As with the previous extract, the younger members of the household like the way the stories in lifestyle programmes are about transformation. But they are also critical of more contemporary lifestyle makeover formats, such as *Changing Rooms*, for being too formulaic and lacking in character. Even though the eldest son previously enjoyed watching *Changing Rooms*, he is quick to point out that he wouldn't choose to watch it, it is just something that is easy to watch with the rest of his family. Their mother has a strong interest in lifestyle programmes. Her comment 'I will change things' indicates her personal interest in advice and ideas in lifestyle programming that she can put into practice in her own home. Both parents make a connection between taking responsibility for the maintenance of the household and the maintenance of the family. They draw on their own somewhat different experiences of helping their parents around the home in order to illustrate the importance of 'helping out'. When their children help out with home improvement they are 'involved' in the family. The mother's choice of words 'the more you're involved in something, the more you're likely to care about it' is illuminating as she suggests that the more her children are involved in caring for the home the more they will be involved in caring for the family. The above extract highlights how watching lifestyle programming can give the family not only ideas about home improvement, or ways of living, but also ideas about good and bad family practices.

In health-based reality programming, audience discussion about programmes such as *Children's Hospital* suggests an explicit link between reality programming and an ethics of care. In previous work on *Children's Hospital*, I argued that viewers value life-affirming stories of successful treatment and recovery in specialist children's hospital units (Hill 2000c). Viewers know programme makers have edited the stories in *Children's Hospital* in order to ensure happy endings, and they have come to expect, and indeed want, the programme to concentrate on positive stories at the expense of a more realistic portrayal of healthcare in Britain. Part of the reason why viewers like to watch stories of children's acute illness is because the stories are melodramatic, and offer an emotional roller coaster ride that usually has a positive outcome. As this 36-year-old mother comments: 'I like *Children's Hospital* and I always end up in tears watching it but I always still watch it … I can't turn off. I know it's going to upset me.' Or, as this 15-year-old schoolgirl explains: 'the children in *Children's Hospital*, they're ill but they're really sweet … It's like the up side of life. Even though they're ill, they're still happy.' The mixture of sad and happy stories in the series makes for powerful melodrama, and viewers feel compassion for the children and their fight for survival.

The stories have a dual role in *Children's Hospital*: to entertain viewers with melodramatic stories of acute illness, and to inform viewers about the medical treatment and care of children. As this 41-year-old father points out:

'Yeah, I mean you've got the kids pulling heart-strings and things and also every medical condition seems to be something new. So it's not the same, every kid they treat they seem to find a new illness or new treatment and you think "Oh, god, I didn't know they could do that", so you're learning as well. So, it's two roles if you like, in one.'

Viewers can feel compassion for the children featured in the programme, and they can also learn about how the medical profession cares for other people's children and how parents care for their own children in times of need. The stories of ordinary parents and children coping with acute illness also have another role, as they remind many viewers at home about other people less fortunate than themselves. This 37-year-old motor tradesperson and father of three explains why watching *Children's Hospital* gives him perspective on his own life and that of his family:

'Yeah. I feel it's a very good programme and it does upset me quite a lot to watch it but it is a programme I do like watching … because it makes you realize that maybe yourself or other people round you, you haven't really got a problem at all … until you look at someone like that. And then it makes you start thinking, why am I worried about my car when, er, the person you've just watched the night before, their 6-year-old son is dying of cancer … I think the majority of people on the outside world haven't really got a clue of what a problem is until they see something like that and, erm, I think it must be really hard to deal with something like that if it ever happens to you, which I hope it doesn't … So I think the programme is good 'cos you do actually see what other people, out there, are going through. And I think you do need reminding that it does go on.'

The sad stories of acute illness can be transformed into life-affirmative stories that viewers can learn from. The stories may be upsetting, but they are also life lessons. For this father, *Children's Hospital* is a 'good programme' because it reminds him how healthy and well cared for his own family is compared with 'other people, out there'.

Health-based reality programmes such as *Children's Hospital* encourage viewers to think about care and responsibility for the health and well-being of themselves and their family members. The programme's explicit emphasis on an ethics of care is reflected in the way viewers talk about their responses to the stories of acute illness. The fact that viewers feel compassion towards the people featured in the programmes suggests they care about other people, and the fact that viewers can learn from other people's experiences suggests they feel responsibility for care of themselves and their family. Similarly, lifestyle programmes such as *Changing Rooms* encourage viewers to think about care and responsibility for the household, and by extension family members of the household. The programme's implicit emphasis on an ethics of care is reflected in the way viewers talk about home improvement in relation to good and bad conduct, and good and bad family practices. Lifestyle and health-based reality programming can potentially give viewers the opportunity to learn about an ethics of care, and to apply an ethics of care in their everyday lives.

However, these kinds of reality programmes are problematic in that they contain stories about other people's private lives, and other people's suffering. The way in which lifestyle programmes, especially makeover programmes, offer us a window into the private lives of ordinary people raises issues for programme makers regarding the ethical treatment of these people in emotionally difficult situations. Although reality formats such as *Changing Rooms* are principally about the makeover of people's homes, the reveal is an emotionally charged moment because people are often emotionally invested in the way their homes look and feel to themselves and other people. In dating makeover formats such as *Would Like to Meet* the stories are about the makeover of people's lives, and therefore more likely to show people in emotionally difficult situations. Lifestyle programmes raise issues for viewers in terms of the ethics of watching people's private lives on television. The representation of suffering in health-based reality programming raises issues for programme makers in terms of the ethical treatment of ordinary people in times of acute distress. The representation of suffering also raises further issues for viewers in terms of the ethical dilemma of watching the suffering of others on television. In the next chapter, I consider audience responses to representations of suffering in pet reality programmes in order to explore further the complex relationship between an ethics of care and reality programming.

CONCLUSION

In this chapter, I have argued that just as 'we cannot avoid involvement in ethics' (Singer 1993: v), we cannot avoid involvement in the ethics of reality programming. Ethics informs our understanding of the treatment of ordinary people by programme makers, the content of many stories about people's private experiences and dilemmas, and the way audiences respond to the representation of these stories in reality programming. Although some people might argue that ethics are absent from reality programming, in fact ethics are at the heart of reality programming. Rights to privacy, rights to fair treatment, good and bad moral conduct, and taste and decency are just some of the ethical issues that arise when examining the reality genre. I have chosen to focus on an aspect of ethics, an ethics of care, in particular types of reality programming, lifestyle and health. The concept of an ethics of care incorporates traditional ethical reasoning, regarding care of the self in ancient Greek and Roman ethical writing, within a wider understanding of social ethics and rights ethics in modern moral philosophy. An ethics of care can also be understood in relation to the concepts of self-identity and care of the self, as outlined by the sociologists Anthony Giddens and Michel Foucault. Lifestyle and health-based reality programming has 'taken an ethical turn' (Hawkins 2001: 412), and stories about home improvement or acute ill health are constructed in such a way that they implicitly and explicitly address viewers about good and bad ways to live their lives, and good and bad ways to care for themselves and other people. Lifestyle and health-based reality programmes are popular with family viewers, and the way parents and children talk about an ethics of care is connected with the way they often watch these programmes together. Viewers relate the stories of ordinary people and their experiences to their own family practices, and their own understanding of care and responsibility for the family and the family household. Thus, these programmes can encourage viewers to apply an ethics of care in their everyday lives. However, the relationship between ethics and reality programming is complex, and although there are reasons for a positive reading of the 'ethical turn' in lifestyle and health-based reality programmes, there are also causes for concern. These programmes raise ethical issues regarding privacy, and the representation of suffering in reality TV. A more critical reading of the 'ethical turn' in health-based reality programming is considered in the following chapter on audience responses to the suffering of animals in pet programmes. This chapter, therefore, is the first part in a more detailed examination of an ethics of care in reality programming, and one that I hope leads to further discussion about ethics in the reality genre.

Chapter 7

Pet deaths

Some of the most popular types of reality programmes contain stories about humans and companion animals. There are observational formats such as *Vets in Practice* (BBC, 1994–), infotainment such as *Animal Hospital* (BBC, 1994–2004), and advice formats such as *The Pet Psychic* (Animal Planet, 2002–) or *The Dog Listener* (Channel 5, 2001–2002). There is even a cable TV channel targeted directly at pets; Miow TV includes visuals that appeal to cats, along with information for cat owners. Given the variety of reality formats for pets on television, the content is surprisingly similar: most formats are concerned with pets in crisis. In this chapter, I want to explore popular factual television concerned with the ill health, ill treatment, recovery, and, in extreme cases, death of companion animals. This chapter applies the concept of an ethics of care, as discussed in the previous chapter, to a case study of the content and reception of animal-based reality programmes. Programmes such as *Animal Hospital* are popular with family viewers, and regular viewers of these programmes tend to be mothers and children. When audiences talk about programmes such as *Animal Hospital* they frame their responses in relation to compassion and responsibility towards pets in the home, and socially acceptable treatment of pets. The stories of pets in crisis highlight the morally charged arena of human–animal relations, and mark the transformation of the cultural meaning of pets in the late twentieth century from 'lifestyle accessories' to valued 'members of the family'. In addition, such stories of pets in crisis raise ethical issues concerning the politics of suffering, and the politics of viewing suffering on television.

HUMAN–ANIMAL RELATIONS

The history of human–animal relations is a history of changing social attitudes and behaviour towards the co-existence of humans and animals within the natural world. Adrian Franklin, in his book *Animals and Modern Culture*, summarises the main theoretical approach to human–animal relations as follows:

Most sociologists and historians of human–animal relations have been influenced to a greater or lesser extent by an earlier body of anthropological work which found that human conceptualisation, classification and theorisation of animals signify or encode social thought. First, social structures and morality are routinely extended into the animal world to provide a logical ordering to this parallel metaphorical society. Second, the socially constituted animal world is then used to think through or resolve social tensions, conflicts and contradictions ... Animals are uniquely positioned relative to humans in that they are both like us but not like us ... humans are intimately involved with animal worlds everywhere; so much so in fact, that human and animal societies are often believed to exist on the same plane and to be socially and morally, as well as physically, interactive. Animals are therefore good to think about what it is to be properly human.

(1999: 9)

Human–animal relations therefore tell us something about who we are as human beings, and who we are in our social, cultural and natural environment.

A brief overview of the historical development of human–animal relations suggests that contemporary attitudes towards animals have arisen from changing social attitudes towards man and nature. For example, in Tudor England 'the Christian theological orthodoxy maintained the view that God had given humans absolute rights to use animals as they saw fit. This included domesticating them, eating them, and sporting with them – fairly or otherwise' (Franklin 1999: 11). However, Keith Thomas (1983) has argued that this anthropocentric view of animals changed during the seventeenth and eighteenth centuries. One of the reasons why attitudes towards human–animal relations changed was that developments within natural history and the biological sciences opened up understanding of the natural world as a world that does not 'exist for man alone' (1983: 166). Another reason for changing attitudes towards humans/animals was rural to urban migration during the nineteenth century. As more people became less dependent on animal power as a result of industrial-technical development, attitudes towards animals became more sentimental, and 'the old way of treating animals ("badly") became increasingly unacceptable to urban sensibilities' (Franklin 1999: 12). It was during this period that campaigns developed to stop cruelty to animals, and various anti-cruelty legislations were passed. By the twentieth century, a discourse of animal rights had emerged, along with greater understanding of animals in their natural environment.

This brief and selective history of human–animal relations illustrates how social attitudes towards animals gradually changed from an anthropocentric to anthropomorphic understanding of animals. However, this transition is not as consistent as the above historical overview suggests. For example, at a time when nineteenth-century society condemned cruelty to animals, rural animal sports, such as hunting and angling, flourished (Franklin 1999: 16). Nineteenth-century reform of human–animal relations therefore was a reform about working-class animal sports, such as cockfighting, and not upper-class sports such as foxhunting. This contradiction between legislation regarding animal cruelty and upper-class sporting practices is one that is still present today. Debate about foxhunting reflects a 'web of relationships involving wild animals, domesticated animals, and humans' (Marvin 2002: 154). Foxhunting is not 'a natural encounter between predator and prey', but a 'sporting cultural event', and as such is 'an event that is both alternately and simultaneously natural and artificial' (2002: 152–3). The natural elements of foxhunting include man's right to hunt animals just as animals hunt each other in the wild. These natural elements are contradicted by the artificial elements of a staged cultural event, where humans rely on horses to take part in the event, and the hounds are trained to hunt for humans rather than for themselves in the wild (Marvin 2002).

Sociologist Norbert Elias, in his book *The Civilising Process* (1994), argues that the social formation of manners and taste is connected with social restraint of the body, in particular restraint regarding violence towards human beings and animals. The civilising process is a gradual historical process that involves self-restraint, and awareness of socially acceptable codes of behaviour. Elias (1986) used the case of foxhunting to indicate the gradual civilisation of the sport from a violent contest between humans and animals to a violent contest between animals. Franklin takes up Elias' argument about sport and violence as one explanation of social attitudes towards cruelty to animals. For Franklin, foxhunting indicates changing thresholds of tolerance for violence towards animals. In the eighteenth century, thresholds of tolerance for violence towards animals changed, and this in turn led to a change in the way humans hunted foxes for sport, removing human involvement in the ritualised killing of the fox. In the twenty-first century, thresholds of tolerance for violence towards animals have changed to the extent that there is a political campaign to ban foxhunting altogether. On the one hand, the debate about foxhunting can be seen as an example of changing social attitudes towards the humane treatment of animals. In this sense, the campaign to ban foxhunting is a campaign that illustrates 'animal protection, animal rights, and the civilising of manners' (Franklin 1999: 25). On the other hand, the fact that foxhunters vigorously defend their right to hunt in rural areas illustrates the contradictory nature of human–animal relations, as humans continue to assert their dominance over animals in the natural environment.

In terms of the history of human–companion-animal relations, there has been a transformation of cultural and social attitudes towards pets and their owners. According to Thomas (1983), it wasn't until the Enlightenment that people began to keep pets in earnest. Although the upper classes kept pets, it took the advent of the industrial revolution for pet keeping to filter down to the masses. During the nineteenth century 'pets were significant in society as much for their qualities as positional goods and entertainment value as showy, fashion accessories or intelligent competitors, as for their companionability' (Franklin 1999: 88). During the twentieth century, there has been a gradual increase in the value of animals in human leisure, particularly in Western societies. For example, in postwar culture, close companionship with pets was often subject to disapproval, a stand-in for 'normal' human relationships, but today people, especially children, are often encouraged to develop close relationships with their pets (Serpell 1986).

The social construction of pets as companions illustrates how the boundary between humans and animals is gradually blurring; the more we perceive pets as sharing the same physical, emotional and psychological needs as humans, the more likely we are to accept pets as members of 'our family' (Franklin 1999). Research by Salmon and Salmon (1983) in Australia indicates that people who have experienced the loss of a relative, or live alone, are more likely to own a pet, to value their companionship above all other qualities, and to anthropomorphise their pets' activities. A similar study in the USA by Albert and Bulcroft (1988) predicted that pet keeping will increase in urban households as a result of social changes to the make-up of family units. Research by Bodmer (1998: 237)) on the impact of pet ownership on the well-being of adolescents with few familial resources indicates that 'pet owners report a higher level of well being and more familial resources than non-owners'. Franklin argues that 'the nature and extent of human surrogacy and anthropomorphism from the 1980s is a major landmark in the social history of the family and the home' (1999: 97). Pets can provide social benefits not readily available in modern society: 'familial friendship, neighbourhood and community ties … are relationships which provide the day-to-day norms and cultural exchanges for most people' and yet these relationships are 'most at risk from … new flexibilities and freedoms in the creation and dissolution of domestic relations' (1999: 4). For Franklin, pets provide security at a time of social risk, confusion and unpredictability.

The earlier example of foxhunting relates to discussion of the transformation of social attitudes towards companion animals. Just as foxhunting is an example of contradictory attitudes towards wild animals, so too pet keeping is an example of contradictory attitudes towards domestic animals. On the one hand, the history of the relationship between humans and companion animals indicates the transformation of social attitudes towards domestic animals as companions rather than accessories. However, although pet populations have risen exponentially over the past few decades, cruelty towards pets has also risen to the extent that there are thousands of animal shelters for mistreated and unwanted pets. I refer to the relationship between pet ownership and pet cruelty in more detail in the next section in order to set the scene for contemporary representations of pets in popular factual television.

The following case study of the content and reception of pets in popular factual television in Britain is a case study that draws on the history of human–animal relations. The way pets are represented on television is indicative of the anthropomorphism of animals in Western society. It is also indicative of an increasing sentimentalisation of companion animals, and the legal and moral framework to human–animal relations in the twenty-first century. For example, many pet programmes report on the work of anti-cruelty campaign groups such as the Royal Society for the Prevention of Cruelty to Animals (RSPCA). These reports blur boundaries between humans and animals, and present stories of animal suffering in a sentimental and moralistic manner. Thus, our understanding of companion animals, as represented in the media, is framed according to the wider moral and legal context of human–animal relations in contemporary society. The fact that many of these pet programmes are about animal suffering indicates a connection with Franklin's argument about social attitudes towards thresholds of tolerance for violence towards animals. In these programmes, animal suffering caused by humans is socially, morally and legally unacceptable. By watching such programmes, viewers are encouraged to empathise with the animals, and to condemn inhumane pet-keeping practices. As such pet programmes can be seen as an example of changing social attitudes towards the humane treatment of companion animals, and also an example of changing thresholds of tolerance for violence towards companion animals.

In this case study, I examine domestic pets in Britain. The nationally specific nature of these representations of companion animals is significant in that Britain is a nation with a large urban population, and a large domestic cat and dog population. British people are famous for being 'pet lovers' (Franklin 1999). Pet programmes draw on these cultural and social factors in their representation of pets and their owners. A case study of British pet programmes, by its very nature, focuses on particular aspects of human–companion-animal relations. This case study excludes other significant aspects of British pets, such as pet keeping in rural areas, working dogs and their owners, and exotic pets. It also excludes wild animals, and farmyard animals. By focusing on Britain, the case study also excludes the representation of companion animals in other countries. All of these areas deserve serious academic attention. Given the constraints of this case study, I hope the following analysis will be useful in opening up debate about the content and reception of pets in popular factual television, and will illuminate understanding of cultural responses to human–companion-animal relations in contemporary Western society.

PETS AND PEOPLE

Before looking at popular factual programmes about pets, we should first assess the development of the pet industry, and pet organisations. The pet industry and pet organisations have developed in postwar Western society as a result of an increase in pet populations and a related increase in the value of animals in human leisure. In the USA, more than half of all households own a pet dog or cat. In 1981, there were 44 million pet cats, and over 50 million pet dogs; by 2001 dog ownership had increased to over 60 million, and ownership of cats to 75 million.[1] In Australia, 60 per cent of households own a pet (Franklin 1999). Approximately 55 million Europeans own at least one pet – 41 million dogs, 47 million cats.[2] The growth rate for ownership of dogs and cats has increased dramatically in Britain. Between 1963 and 1991 the number of dogs rose by 66 per cent, and the number of cats, by over 70 per cent (Franklin 1999: 89). In 2002, just under half of the population owned a pet, with ownership of cats and dogs totalling 14.5 million. Cat ownership is at its highest in the 35–44 age group (27 per cent) and dog ownership in the 45–54 age group (30 per cent).[3] With so many dogs and cats in the world, pet food manufacturers have experienced rapid economic growth. According to Franklin (1999: 89), 'the British spent more on pet food in 1993 (£1.3 billion) than they did on fresh fruit and vegetables for themselves (£1.2 billion)'. In 2000, dog owners in the UK spent over £800 million on prepared pet food, and cat owners spent £700 million – even bird owners spent over £3 million on seed.[4] In Europe, there are 450 pet food companies, selling 5 million tonnes of pet food, valued at Euro 8.5 billion.[5] Pet food manufacturers have capitalised on current attitudes to pets as companions and sell products by promoting awareness of the health and therapeutic benefits of pet ownership. Companies outline the various ways pets play significant social and psychological roles in today's society, drawing on current studies of pets and healthcare that suggest pets can help to prevent illness and aid recovery from ill health (Franklin 1999). Claims are made that pets ease loneliness, improve family relationships, provide playmates for children, provide security for singles, reduce blood pressure and anxiety levels, and combat depression and inactivity amongst the elderly. According to Garrity and Stallones (1998), a review of research suggests that the benefits of pet ownership relate to physical, psychological, social and behavioural issues.

Emphasis is placed on valuing pets by buying prepared pet food. For example, the Pet Food Institute (PFI) in America is dedicated to 'promoting the overall care and well-being of pets'. The PFI believes 'a healthy pet is a happy pet', and by spending 'tens of millions of dollars ... to develop and enhance pet foods to provide the best possible nutrition' pets can live long and healthy lives.[6] Media advertising echoes such rhetoric. An advert for 'Whiskas® with Lifecare' cat food depicts a single white female and her tabby cat, reading the paper together, with the caption 'Long live those who help us to take life a little slower'.[7] This product has a 'unique, new immune-strengthening formula', and promises essential nutrients 'proven to keep [cats] healthier for longer'. Rival products include the 'Friskies' "see the difference in three weeks, or your money back" Vital Balance range, and the Iams "reverse the effects of aging" range'.[8]

This type of public relations exercise for the pet food industry crosses over into general pet services, which draw on the 'pet as companion' rhetoric to create a range of services, from the poodle parlour to pet cremation, which are primarily extensions of human amenities. Pet services combine two approaches to pets: pets are companion animals on the one hand, and on the other, positional goods. Thus, there are pet selection agencies that operate on the same principles as human dating agencies, pet nannies to look after animals whilst their humans are at work, and pet psychiatrists for pets and their owners. Other services include pet pampering, pet holidays, pet hotels (room service optional) and pet fashion, such as the 'Cosipet' jogging suit for dogs. The 'Burberry' line of designer gifts for dogs (the 'Burberry' bean bag, a 'classy gift', retailing at £92)[9] illustrates how human fashion is extended to include pet fashion.

Alongside changes in social attitudes to pets from playthings to companions, there has also been an increase in animal rescue organisations in Western society. This central paradox in the human–companion-animal bond mirrors the paradox of animals in modern cultures – alongside an increase in understanding of animals as a cultural species, there has been mass destruction of animals in their natural environment and in agricultural industry (Franklin 1999).[10] In the USA, there are over 1,000 official animal rescue centres, fifty in New York alone.[11] It is estimated that a third of the dog population in the USA are sent to animal shelters (Garner 1993: 82). Although some of these destructions occur due to medical reasons, many are the result of owners' treatment of pets as 'throwaway objects to be discarded when they become inconvenient or cease to give pleasure' (ibid.).

The Royal Society for the Prevention of Cruelty to Animals (RSPCA) is the oldest animal welfare organisation, founded in 1824. Although it has been subject to criticism, the RSPCA is the most high-profile organisation in the UK, and is linked to the most popular pet series on television, *Animal Hospital*.[12] According to the RSPCA Annual Review for 1999, they received 1,572,344 phone calls, investigated 132,021 complaints, rescued 9,929 animals, and prosecuted 701 humans at a cost of £1,812,465 million (RSPCA 1999: 7). In the same year, the RSPCA re-homed nearly 100,000 unwanted animals, and humanely destroyed nearly 90,000 (1999: 9). Other animal welfare organisations in the UK include the National Canine Defence League (NCDL), which rescued/re-homed 11,000 dogs, and the Cats Protection League, which rescued/re-homed 70,000 cats in 2000. These organisations all rely on donations and legacies from the public: the RSPCA received incoming resources of over £57 million in 1999, £45 million of which came from legacies and donations; NCDL received a total income of £16.9 million in 2000, £13 million in legacies and donations (RSPCA 1999; NCDL 2001).

PET CARE

The previous overview of the pet industry and pet organisations highlights the value of companion animals in human leisure. The value of companion animals involves both economic and moral value. The many pet services now available to feed, groom, train and maintain pets all testify to the increasing economic costs of pet keeping. Pet services primarily draw on the moral value of pets to persuade owners to spend money on items once thought non-essential, and now perceived as essential to the health and well-being of companion animals. In many ways this is a social contract, and the symbolic appeal of these pet services is that owners who buy into the maintenance of the human–animal companion bond are responsible, loving pet owners. The contradiction in the rise in pet populations, pet services *and* pet cruelty highlights this social contract, as those humans who care for animal welfare donate money towards rescuing animals from irresponsible, uncaring humans.

Viviana Zelizer (1985), in *Pricing the Priceless Child*, studied the changing social value of children through insurance policies and legislation. Her research draws on the work of Phillippe Aries and his sociological and historical study of childhood (1962). Zelizer argues that social attitudes towards child mortality changed during the Enlightenment, and especially during the nineteenth century in Europe. Prior to the eighteenth century, the death of a child was 'met with a mixture of indifference and resignation', and the child's burial probably took place 'in the backyard, as a cat or dog is buried today' (1985: 24). However, during the nineteenth century, a 'dramatic revolution in mourning children had taken place'. Bereavement literature, burial monuments, insurance policies and legislation all indicated a transformation in the cultural response to death (1985: 27). Zelizer explains:

> Insuring children became big business at the turn of the century. But it was a unique commercial enterprise, profoundly shaped by the sentimental value of its young customers' lives. As children were excluded from the workplace, insurance benefits from the death of a child could hardly be justified in economic terms, that is, as a replacement of a child's lost wages. Insuring the sacred, economically 'useless' child turned into a semi-ritualistic business. At the turn of the century, it provided funds for a child's proper burial; later on, it served as a symbolic expression of parental love and concern.
>
> (1985: 137)

Zelizer's work is particularly useful in considering institutional discourses and how these discourses indicate changing social and cultural values. Her analysis of the economic and moral value of children can be applied to the economic and moral value of companion animals in human leisure. In the same way that nineteenth-century legal documents asked the question 'how much is a child's life worth to its parents?', so too twenty-first century legal documents ask 'how much is a pet's life worth to its owner?'.

The pet insurance industry is the third largest insurance industry in the UK. There are over sixty different insurance companies offering pet insurance, from PetPlan, the largest pet insurer with over 40 per cent of the UK's pet insurance market, to animal charity RSPCA, or retail company Marks and Spencers. The pet insurance market is worth more than £160 million. There were 1.8 million pet insurance policies in 2003 in the UK. According to the RSPCA:

> 40 per cent of the costs incurred from owning a pet come from unexpected vet bills, averaging around £250 per year per pet. With veterinary inflation running at 11 per cent a year – thanks largely to advances in the medicines and technology used to treat animals – conditions previously left untreated such as cancer, are routinely dealt with by expensive procedures such as chemotherapy.[13]

The RSPCA also advise pet owners that 'treatments are becoming more expensive which is why it's so important for people to take out pet insurance to ensure they can meet the cost of all eventualities'.[14] The most common ailments claimed for include arthritis, lameness, dermatitis, heart disorders and tumours. It is more expensive to buy insurance for a pedigree pet. For example, PetPlan charge £155–326 for pedigree dog insurance, in comparison with £119–246 for cross-breed dogs. There are more insurance claims for pets than there are for housing or car insurance.[15] In 2002, 'claims for dog bites cost insurance companies $310 million' in the USA and many companies have altered their coverage to exclude breeds with bite statistics.[16]

Pet insurance is based on the premise that pet healthcare is similar to human healthcare. Pets can get urinary infections, heart disease, arthritis, and responsible pet owners should prepare for such eventualities by spreading the costs of veterinary healthcare. Pet insurance foregrounds the moral choices faced by pet owners. Insurance companies offer a variety of packages which include holiday cancellation due to pet illness, recovery of lost animals, death benefit from illness or accident (up to £750 in the UK), and third-party cover if a pet should cause accident or injury (up to £1 million in the UK). The Kennel Club Healthcare Plan offers 'peace of mind' for all dog owners because 'owning a dog is a great source of pride and pleasure, but it can also cause great anxiety and expense if illness or injury should arise'.[17] The adjective 'great' is the key here. For the small price of 40 pence a day, a dog owner can insure against the potentially large veterinary fees, and claim up to £5,000 for accident or illness. The Kennel Club helpfully outlines the 'rising' costs involved, with case studies of past veterinary treatment, such as the English Springer Spaniel who needed 'X-Rays and emergency surgery to repair multiple fractures, following a traffic accident' (cost £1,442), which is the most common form of accident for dogs.[18] As pet insurance companies remind us, there is no NHS for pets. Thus, companies promise to help pet owners through the 'difficult times', and 'take the worry out of pet ownership by making sure that owners never need face agonising choices about whether or not they can afford the best treatment for their pet'.[19]

In relation to the loss or death of companion animals, pet insurance policies offer a range of services that cover advertisements for missing pets, burial costs and bereavement counselling. The insurance company Royal & Sun Alliance ensure pet owners have access to 'a 26-strong team of bereavement counsellors to help them through the emotional torment following the death of a much-loved family dog or cat'.[20] This business initiative followed on from a successful £20 million advertising campaign for the Royal & Sun Alliance arm More Th>n, which advertised its pet insurance via a widespread poster appeal for information about a lost dog called Lucky. The campaign was so successful members of the public called the telephone number to help locate Lucky, only to find they were the victim of an advertising hoax. These pet insurance services indicate the price pet owners are prepared to pay for the care of their companion animals. Pet insurance policies not only provide the necessary funds for veterinary treatment, but they also provide symbolic expression of pet owners' love and concern for their companion animals.

The success of the pet insurance industry is connected with the increase in pet populations, and the increase in the sentimentalisation of companion animals in postwar Western society. Another industry to benefit from the increasing value of pets in human leisure is the pet mortuary industry. Whilst some pet owners still rely on discreet burial in the back garden, there are increasing numbers who wish to draw on professional services, related to burial and/or bereavement counselling. According to Franklin (1999) pet cemeteries have increased since the 1970s in Western societies. In the UK and USA humans can be buried alongside animals – it is illegal in Australia (Franklin 1999: 93). In such cases, animals are 'laid to rest', although a more popular alternative for owners is pet cremation. Farewell Pet Cremation Services (UK) sell caskets, hand carved in the shape of a cat or kennel; in the USA, Angel Paws™ sells pet memorials, with phrases such as 'a very good dog' inscribed in stone. These monuments to companion animals symbolise immortality. They also signify an increase in awareness of the impact of pet death on humans, which in turn signifies an increase in the core values of the human–companion-animal bond (Seale 1998).

Despite an increase in the pet mortuary business, there remains a social stigma to pet bereavement, and owners can often feel isolated after the death of a pet. The Society for Companion Animal Studies (SCAS) launched a pet bereavement telephone support line in 1994, and claim to have helped over 4,000 pet owners cope with the loss of a companion animal in the UK. SCAS supports bereaved pet owners because there is little social support available:

> Grieving for the loss of a pet, whether through death or enforced separation, can be a very sad and difficult experience. Life, once filled with the love and friendship of a pet, may suddenly seem very empty. Feelings of despair, loneliness and even depression can be overwhelming. There may also be a strong sense of guilt and self-doubt, particularly when a decision has been taken to euthanase a pet. These feelings are normal and a testimony to the special bond between people and their pets. Unfortunately, not everyone understands this grief, and it can be a very lonely experience.[21]
>
> (SCAS 2002)

Pet bereavement services have gradually increased in recent years, with some insurance companies offering bereavement counselling, as well as animal societies, and selected veterinary practices. There is a growing body of literature on pet bereavement for owners, such as *Goodbye, Dear Friend* by Virginia Ironside, or *Companion Animal Death* by Mary Stewart, a practical guide for veterinary teams, who, despite performing euthanasia on a regular basis, receive little formal training in effective strategies for managing pet owner bereavement.

Animal welfare organisations originated at the same time as child welfare organisations. During the twentieth century attitudes have gradually changed towards animal cruelty, and preventable pet mortality is now perceived as a social crime in Western society (Zelizer 1985: 24). Legislation on companion animals states that to cause an animal unnecessary suffering, to ill treat or terrify an animal, is an offence of cruelty and owners can be prosecuted under the Protection of Animals Act (UK), and the EU Convention of the Protection of Animals. Such legislation does not stop animal cruelty, but it does frame the legal and moral context of animal welfare. Animal welfare organisations utilise the rhetoric of the priceless pet in their promotional material. In an advert for NCDL, a dog asks 'How much do you love me?' This type of emotive advertising illustrates social attitudes towards thresholds of tolerance of violence towards companion animals. The message of the advert is that humans are morally culpable for their treatment of companion animals, and that care of companion animals should not be measured in economic terms.

For Zelizer, the legal evaluation of children as having sentimental worth worked alongside the moral evaluation of children's rights (1985: 227). There are parallels to be drawn regarding the sentimental worth of companion animals and their rights as a 'social group'. However, animal rights activists would argue for the separation rather than coming together of humans and animals, because they believe all animals are distinct from humans and should be allowed to live in their natural, i.e. non-human, environment. According to Garner (1993: 79), 'the keeping of animals as pets *per se* would not seem to be a problem from the perspective of the moral orthodoxy regarding animals'. However, problems occur in the mistreatment of pets and the destruction of healthy animals. As we saw in the previous section, many animal rescue organisations operate a destruction policy. It is legal to humanely kill an animal under the Protection of Animals Act (so long as the animal is killed without unnecessary suffering, and the owner's consent is obtained). But from an animal rights perspective this destruction is morally wrong. According to the moral orthodoxy, animals are sentient beings, and therefore humans have moral obligations to ensure that animals are not unnecessarily harmed. A more radical position, adopted by new animal rights groups, is one which argues we should treat animals as if they are humans (Garner 1993). The most common position adopted in Western society is that of moral orthodoxy. Most products related to companion animals, whether this be pet insurance or pet cremation, emphasise the close emotional ties humans have with their pets, but at the same time emphasise the responsibility humans have to care for pets, to behave in an ethical manner towards pets, always with the understanding that humans are autonomous beings and animals are dependent on humans for their welfare.

The moral orthodox position in animal rights connects with moral reasoning regarding an ethics of care. As discussed in the previous chapter, an ethics of care is an established form of ethical reasoning that has its roots in ancient Greek and Roman ethical writing on care of the self, Buddhist social ethics, feminist ethics, and an ethics of rights. An ethics of care draws on traditional and modern ethical reasoning in order to promote a way of life grounded in the moral values of care and rights. How can we care for and how can we be responsible for ourselves and other people? How do we express our compassion, and our responsibility towards others? How much should we care? These are all moral questions that are at the heart of an ethics of care. Feminists within the animal protection and liberation movement have argued that caring theory is significant to understanding human–animal relations. Donovan and Adams explain: 'caring theory developed out of unequal relationships, where the carer has more power than the cared for ... values the emotions and considers sympathy, empathy, love – feelings that often characterise humans' responses to animals' (1996: 15–16). The concept of an ethics of care, therefore, is useful in understanding the relationship between humans and companion animals, a relationship characterised by the legal, moral and sentimental evaluation of the value of companion animals in Western society.

When we consider pet insurance and anti-cruelty legislation, the legal and moral framework for companion animals is based on an ethics of care. Pet owners are encouraged to pay for non-essential items in return for 'peace of mind' regarding the care of their animals. Bereavement literature, burial monuments, and insurance policies and legislation all indicate a transformation in the cultural response to the death of companion animals (Zelizer 1985: 27). Whereas in the past, pet bereavement was largely ignored, or went unnoticed, in the twenty-first century there is a public acknowledgement of a need for greater understanding of pet bereavement. This is closely associated with an ethics of care. The cultural response to pet death is one characterised by sympathy and empathy for companion animals.

When we consider popular factual programmes about pets, the premise and narrative drive of the stories in the programmes is based on an ethics of care. Individual cases of animal ill health, cruelty and suffering are presented to viewers within the moral context that humans should treat their companion animals in a sympathetic and empathetic manner. In the following sections, I examine how pet suffering and mortality is represented in reality programmes, and how viewers respond to representations of animal suffering. My argument is that pet programmes construct sentimental stories of pets in crisis in order to elicit sympathy and empathy from viewers, and in order to foreground socially responsible care of companion animals. The way viewers respond to these stories of animal suffering is framed in relation to their compassion for companion animals, and their understanding of animal rights.

PETS, VETS AND TV SETS[22]

In an article published in *Broadcast* in 1999, Nikki Cheetham (managing director of Bazal and creator of *Pet Rescue*) prophesied that the trend for UK animal-based reality programming was about to end. She was right. The 1990s proved to be a decade in which animals dominated television screens and scored high ratings in prime time slots, regularly appearing in the top 30 programmes in the UK. Post-2000, only a few remain, and these are stalwart programmes such as *Animal Hospital*, which began the trend in animal-based reality programmes. This is not to say that pet programmes will disappear from television screens, the growth in pet ownership and pet services testify to the economic strength of pet products, but the particular type of pet programmes of the 1990s may be due for a makeover. The BBC's *Death by Pets* (2003) is one possible indication of the direction pet programmes could take in the 2000s. However, given the BBC's own admission that '*Death by Pets* was meant to be a joke – but as it was it wasn't a very good joke' it is unlikely there will be many more humorous reality formats about animal mortality.[23]

Television has always shown an interest in animal-based factual programmes, from natural history series, or documentaries, to children's programmes which feature pets and exotic animals. However, the rapid rise in pet keeping during the 1980s and 1990s ensured a rapid rise in pet programmes that proved to be ratings winners. *Pet Rescue* was one of the first series to tap into audience interest in pets, with an average viewing share of 16 per cent, more than the average share (10 per cent) for Channel 4 throughout the day (Carter 1999: 16). *Animal Hospital* was also a ratings winner for the BBC, attracting over 7 million viewers during its first and subsequent series, and a viewing share of up to 40 per cent. Similarly, *Vets in Practice*, also for the BBC, attracted 8 million viewers, with an audience share of over 30 per cent. Table 7.1 outlines the ratings success of pets in selected popular factual series.

Table 7.1 Ratings for selected pet programming (UK)

Series	Average audience (million)	Average share (%)	Network	Time
Animal Hospital	10.17	43	BBC1	20:00
Animals in Uniform	9.31	37	BBC1	20:00
Vets in Practice	8.09	39	BBC1	20:00
People's Vets	6.59	33	ITV	20:00
Animal Rescuers	6.45	29	ITV	20:30
Battersea Dog's Home	6.25	24	BBC1	20:30
Barking Mad	6.13	30	BBC	20:00
Dog Squad	5.73	24	ITV	19:00
Animal Detectives	5.34	25	ITV	20.30
Animal People	4.90	24	BBC1	19:00
Animal Hospital Roadshow	4.69	30	BBC1	18:30
Animal Police	4.28	24	BBC1	21:35

Source: BARB 1995–1999[24]

A brief overview of audiences of pet programmes in the UK in 2000 illustrates the general all-round success of these programmes (Hill/ITC 2000). Out of all types of popular factual television, formats such as *Animal Hospital* rated highly with adult viewers – 61 per cent of the general public watched such programmes on a regular or occasional basis. Pet programmes were popular with female viewers (67 per cent compared to 53 per cent of male viewers), appealed to audiences across age ranges (16–65+), across social categories ABC1 (upper to lower middle class) and C2DE (skilled and working class, and lowest level of subsistence) (58 per cent of ABC1, compared to 62 per cent of C2DE), and across educational levels (school, college and university). Families were particularly likely to watch pet programmes. Sixty-two per cent of households with children watched such programmes on a regular or occasional basis, and over 80 per cent of children (aged 4–15) watched animal-based reality programmes, although interest tapered off in the young adult age range. The profile of regular viewers indicates gender, social category and age are also significant factors. Regular viewers are more likely to be female (30 per cent females, compared to 17 per cent males), in the DE social category (29 per cent DE, compared to 16 per cent AB), and under the age of 16. However, the profile for occasional viewers suggests that pet programmes have broad appeal, especially with children and parents.

Scheduling is a key factor in the success of pet programmes. Although some series, such as *Pet Rescue*, are often shown in a traditional scheduling slot for children, it is the peaktime scheduling of series such as *Animal Hospital* which garnered family viewers, fresh from watching popular soap operas such as *EastEnders*, and looking for something to watch in the 8–9pm slot (Brunsdon *et al.* 2001, Ellis 2000). Of course, scheduling is not the only reason for the popularity of animal-based reality programmes. When a programme focuses on companion animals there is a strong chance viewers will tune in. Carter sums up the success of pet programmes from the point of view of television producers:

> The interaction between pet owner and pet has a strong emotional appeal,' says Channel 4 daytime strategy director Julia Le Stage. 'It's to do with caring – there's a need to feel needed nowadays and these shows tap into that,' says Richard Edwards, executive producer at Element Productions, which makes HTV's *People and Pets*. 'It shows the nation how caring we are,' adds Elaine Hackett, executive producer at Bazal, which produces *Pet Rescue* and *Animal SOS*.
>
> (Carter 1999: 16)

With an ethics of care in mind, pets are packaged into programmes which focus on dramatic narrative structure, each personal story framing a moment of crisis, when pets need to be cared for by owners, rescue organisations and veterinarians.

In many ways, pet programmes make use of existing formats in health-based reality programmes, which in turn make use of medical drama. In an overview of medical drama in the USA, Turow (1996) outlines the main dramatic formula in health-based television series, which consist of three basic ingredients: the definition, prevention and treatment of illness. This narrative formula began in 1960s popular medical drama such as *Dr Kildare*, where the central plot revolved around acute physical illness that dramatically escalates, and requires immediate surgery at the end of each episode. Minor changes were made to the formula, such as the 'urgently relevant' drama of 1970s series such as *Bold Ones, Emergency!*, with a focus on cutting-edge emergency medical procedures, but the basic plot remained the same. Turow comments 'by acting out tales of life and death … TV fiction about healthcare can present compelling scenarios about what caregivers might do'. But he is also critical of US medical drama's failure to discuss and critique 'the real-life political and economic battles' in the policy and provision of healthcare (Turow 1996: 1240–2).

Popular factual programmes about healthcare are similar to medical drama in that they focus on the definition, prevention and treatment of illness, and often overlook political and economic issues. Brunsdon *et al.* (2001: 42) note that reality programming 'uses the codes of entertainment, rather than documentary, in representing the real'. Health-based reality programmes, such as *Children's Hospital*, use the codes of medical drama to create a character-based, sympathetic representation of human healthcare, which at the same time tells real stories of human suffering, bravery and recovery. In previous research I conducted in audience responses to *Children's Hospital*, the very fact that the series almost always showed successful treatment of children's illness was a primary reason for watching the series in the first place. In this case, 'viewer enjoyment is linked to an unreal depiction of successful rescue and medical operations which creates a more pro-social, positive portrayal of society than viewers know to exist in real life' (Hill 2000c: 207). Pet programmes also seek to replicate this life-affirming viewing experience. Brunsdon *et al.* discuss how *Children's Hospital* and *Animal Hospital* 'are essentially concerned with transformations' and 'the trauma of tragedies that occur to ordinary people (and animals) can be vicariously enjoyed in a condensed narrative that guarantees a favourable outcome' (2001: 43).

It is because of the transformative qualities of these programmes that Brunsdon *et al.* argue that 'the narrative structure … is much closer to the format typical of the make-over or cookery show than the traditional documentary or current affairs programme' (2001: 43). The alchemic transformation of the negative event of critical illness into positive life-enhancing experience is similar to the physical transformation of a person or environment, whereby the emphasis is usually on the negative to positive experience. However, the stories in health based popular factual programming have a moral agenda often missing from lifestyle series. In some ways the transformation from negative to positive experience mirrors the dominant cultural scripts Clive Seale associates with discussion of death in Anglophone countries (1998: 127). For Seale, discussion of death as heroic journey provides opportunities for people to 'imagine that their experiences belong in a wider, indeed, universal, community of care' (1998: 144). The dramatic formula of health-based reality programmes – definition, prevention and treatment of illness – would suggest that the transformative characteristics of such programmes primarily relate to an ethics of care. In pet programmes, the transformation is provided within the narrative arc, so that critical illness leads to recovery and recovery reaffirms a community of care, in this particular instance a community of animals, vets and their owners, but in the wider sense a community of carers and dependants.

In order to illustrate the caring component of pet programmes I want to analyse two series in detail. The first is *Animal Hospital*, made for a public service broadcasting channel (BBC1), and the second is *Animal ER*, made for a commercial channel (Channel 5, now known as Five). I am particularly interested in acute illness, when the melodramatic moment of the pet and pet owner's story is at its most intense and the high level of care required for the recovery of the pet most warranted. If the narrative drive of pet programmes is to focus on the transformation from negative to positive experience, providing a life-affirming story for viewers, what happens when this narrative breaks down? As we shall see, the factual representation of the death of a pet is not generic, and public service broadcasting and commercial imperatives are noticeable in the different treatment of pet deaths in *Animal Hospital* and *Animal ER*. *Animal Hospital* uses an informative address to the viewer to frame its representations of pet mortality, whereas *Animal ER* uses a more sensational address to the viewer.

Animal Hospital

From the outset, *Animal Hospital* was popular with viewers. John Ellis commented:

> Initially, *Animal Hospital Week* had been a weekly 'stripped' special event which followed the work of a vet's practice, fronted by Rolf Harris, by then an over-the-hill children's presenter … It was the quintessence of popular public service broadcasting as the BBC conceives it, providing information about animal care in an entertaining format. After its unexpected success, it was re-commissioned as a weekly half hour for Thursdays at 8.00pm … in this new weekly form, it had more pronounced soap aspects. It developed regular characters, plenty of chat and speculation and week to week cliff-hanger suspense about 'how the animals will do'.
>
> (2000: 141)

The series was re-commissioned over ten times during the 1990s, and led to various spin-off products. These include the BBC video '*Animal Hospital* with Rolf Harris' which contains 'heart-warming stories' of 'some of the hospital's memorable patients', the number one bestseller *True Animal Tales*, a collection of stories about heroic and remarkable animals around the world (Harris *et al.* 1997), and *A Year in the Life of The Animal Hospital*, the story of David Grant ('television's best-loved vet') and his day-to-day dealings with pets and their owners at the RSPCA's Harmsworth Memorial Hospital (Grant 1998).[25]

The locations for *Animal Hospital* are various RSPCA veterinary clinics that operate rather like an NHS for pets, offering free veterinary healthcare for urban pet-owners. The charitable work of the RSPCA acts as a backdrop to the programme's focus on the sentimentalisation of pets as companion animals. According to Lorraine Heggessy, the executive producer of the first series, when 'people saw the German Shepherd being put down and Rolf crying live on national television … the next day it was the talking point of the nation. The next night our rating shot up to nearly ten million'.[26] Rolf Harris accompanies the pets to the treatment rooms and operating tables as an animal lover, rather than an animal expert. His questions are primarily directed at the vets, and serve as a prompt for information and advice on pet healthcare. Each episode begins with the theme tune, an upbeat, high-pitched horn providing the key sound, which can be slowed down when necessary to achieve a more melancholy effect. The first person we see is Rolf Harris, who often begins by saying 'G'day, and welcome back to *Animal Hospital*' before launching into new stories and updates on previous stories. Each story is relatively short, with six to eight stories featuring in any one episode, usually depicting a variety of pets, exotic animals and wild animals, both in the RSPCA hospital and on location. The staple visual style is that of the close-up, usually a close-up of a sick animal, but also of the owner, the vets or nurses. The close-up is used as an emotional device that works alongside the story structure, which usually comprises the arrival of the sick animal, treatment, and recovery, where the pet is reunited with their owner, often in the 'privacy' of their own homes. For example, in the case of Snowy the poodle, we begin with the diagnosis of the stray dog at the hospital (it has been badly mistreated, and has mange), cue close-up, cut to the treatment of the dog (it is shaved), and then finish with a shot of the dog playing in a garden with its new owners – chosen from 'hundreds of people [who] offered Snowy a home'.[27]

The narration is vital as the subjects of the stories are silent, and the animals, whilst clearly able to show their suffering, cannot talk to the camera about their anxieties regarding their illness and hopes for recovery. The programme makers use narration to frame the stories in relation to animal care. Thus, Rolf Harris translates animal behaviour for humans who *care* about animals. For example, when Spike, a Great Dane with an internal testicle, wakes up from his operation, the camera closes in on his miserable expression, then cuts to Rolf who reassures us that the dog is fine – 'he'd just come round from the op there so he's looking a bit groggy'.[28] The narration also serves to heighten tension and to emphasise an ethics of care. In one episode, Rolf talks to camera in the waiting room of the surgery: 'it is always worrying if our pets fall ill, but if they have straightforward symptoms we can usually take them to the vet, get something to make them better. But it is very frightening when your pet has dramatic symptoms' – cue a dog with convulsions.[29] Or, in another episode, he tells us that the outcome is 'touch and go' for Sammy the puppy who swallowed rat poison.[30] These stories serve to emphasise the commonalities of existence between humans and companion animals. Animals have similar illnesses and accidents to humans, and we watch stories about animal suffering because we care about their welfare, because we are humane.

The ethics of care in *Animal Hospital* is most compelling when the animal illness is most acute. Although pets often die from serious injury or illness, such dramatic incidents are rarely shown on *Animal Hospital*, where the recovery rate is far higher than in most veterinary hospitals.

When a story of pet mortality does feature in the series, the programme makers attempt to balance the melodrama of the story with factual details of the reasons for the death of the pet. The example of Susie the kitten will illustrate the treatment of pet death in *Animal Hospital*. Often the viewer is prepared for an acute case with a general warning, in this instance 'the pressure is never off for vets', which acts as a reminder that accidents and illness can occur any time. We move directly to the story of Susie, who has an intersesection, which is when part of the stomach turns in on itself and becomes infected.[31] First, we begin with the diagnosis, and the close-up of Susie looking distressed and in need of urgent medical attention. The owners are not present and Rolf Harris stands in as concerned pet owner. Next, we cut to the treatment of Susie, who is lying on the operating table, her future bleak. The vet informs us of the procedure, showing us how she is removing the infected part of the gut, and sewing the healthy parts together. There are close-ups of the surgical procedure, highlighting the seriousness of Susie's case and functioning as a reminder of the professional skills of the vet. We move to Susie's recovery, with Rolf Harris informing us that Susie is still alive, and evidential shots of the kitten meowing, and eating morsels of food. This is the high before the low – cut to a close-up of Susie lying listlessly in her cage. This is the last time we see Susie, and the scene is an emotional one, underscored by the melancholy music that accompanies the final close-up of the kitten, and the confirmation that 'Sadly, Susie died.' We finish with an informative address to the viewer by Rolf Harris who asks the vet to demonstrate the intersesection with the visual aid of a rubber glove. This demonstration serves a double purpose; it emphasises the public service component of the story, and also re-enforces an ethics of care, as Rolf comforts a visibly upset vet who acknowledges she has 'sleepless nights' when coping with animal mortality.

In relation to the representation of suffering, *Animal Hospital* provides, in the words of Luc Boltanski, 'a window on the place of the heart' (1999: 85). This window is clearly constructed. According to Boltanski, when a representation of suffering is obviously designed to be 'moving', the representation fails 'because emotion is anticipated by the "visible strings" fixing it to the images, sounds and words in the way a property is attached to a product' (1999: 83). One way to overcome possible failure is to blend two kinds of report within a representation:

> One which describes the unfortunate's suffering and which turned towards the outside world can be termed an *external* report, and another which can be termed an *internal* report in the sense that, devoted to inner life, it seeks to depict what takes place in the heart of the reporter, the states through which the heart passes.
>
> (1999: 85–6)

In the example of the story of Susie the kitten, Rolf Harris and the vet provide an external report, charting the kitten's progress, explaining medical procedure. The internal report is provided by the non-verbal cues, the non-diegetic music, the close-up shots of the kitten, and by the visual and verbal responses of the narrator and vet, who along with their technical observations, offer an apparently more spontaneous response to suffering. It is this balance between the internal and the external report which allows *Animal Hospital* to tread a fine ethical line between the use and misuse of suffering in popular factual television.

Animal ER

Channel 5 tapped into the success of established animal-based factual programmes by replicating the format for *Animal Hospital*. The series *Animal ER* was first broadcast in the winter of 1998, scheduled from 8.30 to 9pm, with an average audience of over 1 million, and a net share of up to 7 per cent. The first series was successful enough for Channel 5 to commission two more series, and repeat the first in the autumn of 1999, scheduled at the earlier time of 7.30pm. At a glance, there is little to differentiate *Animal Hospital* from *Animal ER*: both are based at veterinary hospitals, both invite empathy with animal victims of accident and illness, both stress an ethics of care. However, *Animal ER* is based at a private veterinary practice, rather than a charity practice. In addition, the commercial context of Channel 5 ensures that each programme contains more stories of acute illness in order to maximise ratings. In *Animal ER*, death is an everyday occurrence. These factors make watching *Animal ER* a different viewing experience from *Animal Hospital*.

According to Tom Brisley, the series producer, 'the programmes delve into the gritty world of real-life veterinary work ... and it's not always a happy ending' (Knowsley 1999: 3). Reverend Graham Stevens, then president of the National Viewers' and Listeners' Association commented: 'the traditional vet programmes are fun, helpful and good family viewing, but this is grotesque'. A national broadsheet newspaper, the *Daily Telegraph*, accused Channel 5 of producing a shocking documentary that 'has prompted renewed accusations that the network is overstepping the boundaries of taste and decency' (ibid.). Another national newspaper, the *Express*, summed up critical response to the series as follows:

> If you like seeing rehabilitated animals on TV, in *Vets in Practice*, say, chances are it's because they offer cute, heartwarming triumphs of the spirit. On the other hand, if you watch *ER*, it's likely to be for the fast moving drama and not for the gore. But here we are in a vets' practice ... with X-certificate shots of horses' guts, a calf with its eye hanging

out and a cat with a rank and rotting womb. Delightful. Who is this aimed at exactly?[32]

The opening credits set the tone, as an urgent piano sound accompanies a montage of animals in crisis. Narrated by the actor Tom Conti, the programme cuts between approximately three stories of acute accident and illness, editing between stories to heighten tension. The camera utilises the close-up on pets, owners and vets, but whereas in *Animal Hospital* the camera is fairly static, in *Animal ER* it is energetic, switching back and forth from the point of view of the pet/owner/vet. Similar to *Animal Hospital*, death can occur as a result of accident or illness, but in *Animal ER*, death can also occur as a result of neglect and financial constraint. Thus, there is a confrontational aspect to *Animal ER*, and a high rate of mortality – usually one death per episode. In many ways, the series borrows successfully from drama such as *Casualty* or *ER*, and viewers are encouraged to use strategies learned from medical drama when watching animal-based reality programmes. For example, regular viewers of the series can second-guess the outcome of the stories because of the expectation that at least one animal will die in each episode. The difficulty with this interchange between medical drama and factual programmes is that the deaths in *Animal ER* are real, and raise moral issues that are difficult to resolve within the programme.

In *Animal Hospital*, stories concerning cruelty to animals are a regular feature in the series. As we saw in the previous section, when the RSPCA rescue an animal, often the story is one of hope; although the animal has been abused, it recovers from its physical and emotional injuries with the help of the RSPCA and responsible pet owners. In *Animal ER*, stories concerning pet cruelty regularly feature in the series, but these stories are often moral lessons in irresponsible pet ownership. For example, the story of an abandoned dog runs alongside that of the birth of a calf, thus juxtaposing life and death in the same episode.[33] The dog has been neglected for many years. It has extensive wounds, and large balls of matted fur encase its body. The vet comments: 'it is the worst case of cruelty I have ever seen in my life ... I just cannot believe that people can stoop to this depth.' The camera zooms in on the dog as it is examined by the vet, who talks about the extent of the injuries inflicted, the suffering the dog has endured, before stating 'I feel obliged to have it euthanased.' Piano music accompanies images of the dog; and as the vet gives the dog a lethal injection the camera monitors its breath as it slows down and eventually stops. The dog is then placed in a body bag, ready for disposal.

Similarly, the story of Jodi the dog highlights moral issues related to private veterinary healthcare. Jodi has an injured spine, and after X-rays determine the serious nature of the injury, the dog undergoes an operation.[34] Music accompanies the diagnosis of the dog, creating a soft, melancholy mood. After inter-cutting with two other stories (a horse with bowel problems, a calf with an injured eye), we return to Jodi, as the vet surgically explores the spinal injury, and tells us that the dog will need a complicated operation to release pressure on the spinal cord, an operation that will cost thousands of pounds. The vet takes time out from surgery to call Jodi's owners who opt for euthanasia. Cue close-up of Jodi, still under anaesthetic, the nurse stroking the dog's head. Once again, two other stories interrupt the narrative, and when we return to Jodi, it is to witness her final breath. This representation of pet death highlights the economic factors in pet healthcare, and raises important ethical issues concerning the rights of companion animals, issues not addressed by the vet or commentator in the programme itself.

Another example of the representation of pet death in *Animal ER* highlights ethical issues concerning the right to privacy for pet owners and their pets. In a scene involving the death of a kitten, we see the owners struggle to come to terms with the decision to euthanase their pet. In this instance, the position of the camera is illuminating, as at first the camera records the kitten and its owners inside the treatment room, providing close-ups of the owners as the vet informs them that the kitten has a serious bowel condition, and there is no hope of recovery. Cue tearful reaction shots of the owners to the bad news. As the vet leaves the room, he forces the camera crew to leave with him, physically closing the door to ensure a degree of privacy for the pet owners. However, a round window in the door provides an opportunity for further filming, and the last image we see is of the owners hugging each other, and the kitten, accompanied by melancholy piano music. Thus, an essentially private moment is made public, and the programme makers test boundaries of privacy and taste and decency by choosing to film 'through the keyhole'. In this instance, the privacy issues relate to the pet owners, but in other scenes in *Animal ER*, there is a case to be made that the animals themselves have a right to privacy in the final moments of their lives.

In *Animal ER*, the stories of pet death highlight ethical dilemmas regarding pet ownership and animal rights. The series attempts to show the reality of pet healthcare in a commercial veterinary practice. The representation of pet death in *Animal ER* is different to that in *Animal Hospital*. In accord with Boltanski (1999), the vet and the commentator provide external reports of the pets, the reasons for their acute illness and suffering, and procedures involved in euthanasia. There is no direct informative address to the viewer, but the commentary attempts to tell us what is going on and why certain action is taken. The internal report of suffering is provided by non-verbal cues, the non-diegetic music, and the close-up shots of animals in distress. The use of sentimental music accompanying images of dying animals serves to emphasise the emotionally charged nature of pet death, in particular where death is often a result of human actions. The absence of a presenter is significant, as without an internal report from someone such as Rolf Harris, an animal lover, these representations of suffering appear distant, observed from afar, rather than experienced by someone who visibly cares about animals, and who shares their experience with viewers. Thus, there is an imbalance between the internal and the external report of suffering in *Animal ER*. Although stories of pets in crisis in *Animal Hospital* and *Animal ER* appear similar, there are subtle and not so subtle differences in the treatment of suffering that raise issues about the viewing experience of pet death in reality programming. These representations of animal mortality invite viewers to consider ethical issues related to the care of companion animals.[35] In the final section of this chapter, I examine how television audiences respond to representations of suffering in *Animal Hospital* and *Animal ER*.

WATCHING PET DEATH

The stories of companion animals in reality programming underscore the value of caring for others. In the case of animal mortality, such stories may be distressing, but can allow children (and parents) to 'face up to the reality of death' (Seale 1998: 71) through watching second order experiences of pet death on television. The negative event of a pet death can be transformed by relating such experience to 'a wider, indeed universal, community of care' (1998: 144). If we look at audience responses to animal mortality, the experience of watching pet death is framed in relation to audience criticism of representations of suffering, or what Boltanski (1999) calls the politics of suffering. Children and parents are critical of programme makers for exploiting animals for the purposes of making entertaining popular factual programmes, and critical of themselves for watching such suffering. Thus, although there are potentially positive aspects to watching pet death in reality programming, such as learning about caring for animals, television audiences are mainly critical of the idea of showing animal mortality on television.

Audience responses to representations of suffering are often framed in relation to the concept of compassion. Compassion can be experienced at an explicit or latent level, depending on the representation of suffering. 'Compassion fatigue' is a term used to describe the idea that television audiences fail to feel compassion towards the suffering of others because the representations present human suffering as more or less equal, and therefore fail to take into account different types of suffering and the causes of suffering in the world (Tester 2001: 51). The idea of compassion fatigue assumes that audiences remain impassive to stories of suffering, such as news stories of the plight of refugees, and 'any possibility of a moral bond between audiences and the suffering and miserable others will be avoided' (2001: 56). The problem with this assumption is that representations of suffering vary across different genres, and programmes. As we saw in the previous section, programmes that contain similar stories of animal suffering vary in the way they present this suffering to audiences. In light of audience research presented in this chapter, it is more helpful to consider compassion in relation to an ethics of care, rather than drawing on the idea of compassion fatigue. Contemporary research suggests that we experience compassion when representations of suffering are 'harnessed to the moral voice of justice or to the moral voice of care'. This research also suggests that our experience of compassion is gendered: 'while men tend to uphold an ethic of justice and fairness, women tend to uphold an ethic of care and responsibility' (2001: 69, 66). In relation to animal-based reality programmes, discussion of representations of suffering is framed in relation to an ethics of fairness and to an ethics of care and responsibility. In my research, gender and age are significant factors in understanding audience discussion of scenes of animal suffering and mortality in *Animal Hospital* and *Animal ER*.[36] Children tend to frame their responses to pet death in relation to an ethics of fairness and the issue of animal rights, whilst mothers tend to frame their responses in relation to both an ethics of fairness and an ethics of care and responsibility. These responses to animal suffering are similar in the sense that both types of viewers feel compassion for the pets and their owners in the programmes. However, children's responses are different to parental responses because children are far more critical of representing animal mortality on television than their parents.

Viewers draw on their knowledge of the subgenre of animal-based popular factual programming when discussing particular stories of pets in crisis. Viewers make distinctions between stories in *Animal Hospital* and *Animal ER*. These distinctions are based on the difference in channel (public service versus commercial channel), narrative arc (happy or sad endings to stories), and the presence of a presenter. The general narrative drive of stories about pets in crisis is familiar to viewers, as this 14-year-old schoolgirl indicates: 'All they do really is show ... an animal being cut open and then they close the thing and it lives or it's dead.' In addition, viewers are aware that *Animal Hospital* predominantly has stories with happy endings, unlike *Animal ER*:

'*Animal Hospital* ... you knew what was going to happen. It was like, animal comes in, it's half dying, cure it, go home.'

(15-year-old schoolboy)

'I don't find *Animal ER* very appealing 'cos it's, like, you just see people, like cats coming in and dogs coming in and having their stomachs untied and stuff [laughs]. And then they put them back together and then they just die.'

(12-year-old schoolgirl)

Viewers, especially parents, perceive *Animal Hospital* as containing stories of animal illness and recovery that are more appropriate for younger audiences because they contain optimistic messages. Parents consider Rolf Harris an important factor in the compassionate presentation of stories about animal suffering:

'Rolf Harris does a good job ... you know, he shows a bit of compassion and what have you.'

(41-year-old male carpenter)

'Rolf is so good on *Animal Hospital*. He's ever so emotional ... but you can believe him.'

(32-year-old female underwriter)

'With Rolf Harris, whenever you get like a thing that dies, the next segment is a thing and it goes good, so he always ... always leaves it on a, on a good note.'

(39-year-old male importer)

One viewer claimed that his father was upset after meeting the actor Rolf Harris at an RSPCA hospital, because his father was expecting Harris to be sympathetic towards his father's pet dog who was critically ill, and found Harris to act differently from his on-screen personality: 'he's, like, all caring [gestures this is an act] and when my dad actually met him, he was, like, [acts disinterest], he didn't care' (26-year-old male plasterer). A similar comment was made about the vets in the programme. One viewer commented on how important it was that the vet in the story about Susie the kitten showed she cared: 'she obviously cares for the animals and she's doing a job that she really likes, she likes the animals and ... she really wants it to live. You could see that she was sad, that the animal hadn't lived' (41-year-old female childminder). Another viewer claimed to have met a vet in *Animal Hospital* and had expected him to be like his on-screen personality, but instead found him to be 'miserable'. Audiences, therefore, place a great deal of importance on the presence of an empathetic presenter and vet, and viewers are likely to be more critical of a pet programme that lacks empathetic presenters and vets because these programmes would be perceived as lacking compassion.

The way viewers expect *Animal Hospital* to be different from *Animal ER* is partly to do with the type of stories common to the series, and also to do with the identity of the BBC and Channel 5. For example, this mother and daughter (aged 9), were critical of the way Channel 5 showed 'sad things' compared to the BBC:

Vanessa: Channel 5 just try to push everything a little bit further, don't they? I don't think they would have done that on *Animal Hospital*.
Sarah: That's just horrid, showing that.
Vanessa: I think it is.
Sarah: It was only a kitten.
Vanessa: It was just unnecessary, wasn't it? I know they are just trying to show things real, because obviously that does happen, doesn't it? You do get lots of kids watching these programmes. I mean my lot are not overly sensitive that way, but I know lots of children are ... The music just adds to it, makes it more sad ... They show sad things on *Animal Hospital* but I think it's done more tastefully.

Here, the BBC and *Animal Hospital* serve as a yardstick for 'tasteful' treatment of pet illness and mortality. The mother criticised Channel 5 for pushing boundaries of taste and decency, and she was especially critical because she knew such programmes were popular with young children. When I showed the story from *Animal ER* about the owners' decision to euthanase their kitten, as discussed in the previous section, the daughter was visibly upset by the programme, and her comment – 'that's just horrid' – illustrated her instantaneous response to the story.

In another example of family discussion of *Animal ER*, a mother and son (aged 9) express similar concerns about the treatment of animal mortality in a commercial television programme.

Tom: Channel 5 always do rubbish stuff – like Channel 5 news [in tone of newsreader] 'Someone's just bought a new pair of socks!' [laughs]
Amy: I don't know if that is an appropriate thing to show on television.
Tom: It's upsetting.
Amy: I know it's tugging at your heartstrings. In some respects I think maybe it's appropriate in that it explains to children that sometimes it is a necessity.
Tom: I don't like it. It's upsetting.
Interviewer: Is there anything informative about it?
Tom: No.
Amy: I think what they are trying to get across is that medical science can only go so far, and we do expect miracles, we expect them to solve everything, don't we?
Tom: Apart from kittens look cute.

Amy: No, no, we do expect to go to a doctor or vet and say this is the problem and this is how we solve it. So, maybe that is informative for youngsters so they can see, yes, there sometimes are occasions ... But the thing is, there are times when you don't want to be intruded upon – you know if you are really emotional, whether it is about a person or an animal.

Tom: You don't want it broadcast on TV.

This discussion of *Animal ER* highlights how parents, especially mothers, and their children respond to the representation of pet death. Here, the son is critical of the channel, the programme, and the story itself. He makes fun of the channel for its low production values, and its focus on trivial stories. His strong reaction to the story of the kitten in *Animal ER* (as discussed in the previous section) leaves no room for doubt as to his aversion for stories such as this – he doesn't like it, it upsets him, there is nothing beneficial (i.e. informative) about it, in fact the story shouldn't be broadcast at all. His mother is more ambivalent in her response, and although she is critical of the intrusive nature of the story, she is also willing to think about potentially beneficial aspects to the story, as children may learn about caring for animals through watching disturbing scenes such as those presented in the programme.

If we look at discussion of the story of Susie the kitten in *Animal Hospital* (see previous section) we can see similar responses from young and older adults about the ethical treatment of animal mortality in reality programming. Although in general viewers find *Animal Hospital* more sensitive in its treatment of animal suffering, and more appropriate for children in its emphasis on successful treatment and positive outcomes, when a story of animal mortality does occur in the series audiences are mainly critical of such representations. In particular, children and young adults are critical of representations of acute suffering, and frame their responses in relation to an ethics of fairness and responsibility, and the rights of animals to privacy in times of acute illness. For example, this 16-year-old schoolgirl makes her position quite clear – 'Watching animals die doesn't appeal to me!' Or, as this 14-year-old schoolgirl describes: 'It's, like, [the kitten is] really young and it's, like, vulnerable and for some reason you almost feel responsible for it. Like, when it dies you feel, like, really bad.'

Stories of pet death in *Animal Hospital* raise ethical issues regarding the use of pets in reality programmes. Many young viewers are unconvinced that acute animal suffering is acceptable television viewing, especially when the suffering results in mortality. The following comments illustrate how young viewers pick up on the moral context to representations of suffering:

'Things like that, I don't think really should be put on TV because, like, whether it's *Children's* or *Animal Hospital*, it's, like, it's kinda different from, like, watching *Big Brother* 'cos it's their lives but it seems, like, private, kind of. I can't really explain but it's their private lives, seeing operations and stuff and that's more private and shouldn't be on TV for everyone to see ... It's too personal.'

(16-year-old female student)

'It's much too personal, I think it's wrong.'

(17-year-old female student)

'I think that sort of thing they should keep private.'

(16-year-old female student)

These young viewers articulate their views regarding the rights of animals in reality programmes. The repetition of the words 'private' and 'personal' highlights, in Boltanski's terms, 'the politics of suffering', as their compassion for the suffering of the kitten turns into indignation at its treatment by the programme makers. Rather than drawing on an ethics of care, as vocalised in the programme itself, these viewers draw on an ethics of justice, and they raise issues about the fair treatment of animals in reality programmes.

In contrast, parents, especially mothers, discuss the representation of suffering in *Animal Hospital* in relation to an ethics of care and responsibility. Most mothers claimed they didn't watch pet programmes out of choice, but instead watched because of their children:

'I only watch it because my children like it, I wouldn't choose to watch it.'

(36-year-old housewife)

'Yeah, you wouldn't turn it on yourself really, would you? They want you to watch it with them. My son always calls me and I'll come and watch it, 'cos he wants to watch it but I think he likes me to be there [laughs].'

(40-year-old female pre-school advisor)

'In case something happens to the dog, or something [laughs].'

(40-year-old female part-time secretary)

The joke about the dog touches on several issues. For children, concerns about animal mortality can highlight their own feelings of vulnerability, and parental presence is one means of reassurance. For parents, stories of animal mortality can, in theory, be a second order experience of pet death that can help children to learn about the reality of caring for animals (and by extension, humans).[37] As this 41-year-old female childminder explained: 'I think it's ... quite a good experience, really, 'cos it's life, isn't it? And if you have got your own animals, I think, sometimes, it can prepare them for when your own animals go and, sort of, die ... it does happen, they do die! [laughs].'

Whilst children themselves find little positive to discuss when watching representations of pet death, parents are more likely to discuss children's experiences of watching pet death in a more constructive manner. The above quote echoes the narration in *Animal Hospital*, which places emphasis on learning how to care for companion animals. Parents do express concern about the treatment of animal suffering on television, but they also consider how such negative stories can be transformed into positive morality tales for younger viewers. This group of mothers discussed their concerns about children watching scenes of animal suffering and mortality:

Sally: Children would take that badly, wouldn't they?
Margaret: Yeah, my son would be mortified.
Ellen: You could almost get attached to it if you follow a story through, like the vet did.
Sally: I think, you know, it should always have a happy ending.
Margaret: But that isn't life.
Marion: That isn't life but then putting it on at that time of night, I think it's a bit too sad for children!

For these mothers, their concerns focus on the reactions of children to such stories as 'too sad for children'. Although in the real world, stories of animal suffering don't always contain happy endings, the mothers worry that children should not be exposed to the reality of pet care.

This mother explained her response to stories of animal illness and mortality:

'I suppose if you've got an animal, then it's informative, isn't it? I think ... I don't know really! [laughs] Not to say that your animal was ever going to have that but I just think, it's, everyone likes to know, um, if their animal has got a problem, or ... and you think "Oh, it might be this or it could be that", just as in the same way, I suppose, if you do love animals, like you would with your children – "I wonder if it's got a cold, or I wonder if it's this?" Um ... I don't know, really, I think it's nice just to see that they're doing their best for the animals ... my son watches it and he doesn't find it gory, but ... If something ... if an animal comes on that's been mistreated and it's ... it's got signs of being mistreated, that upsets me but, actually seeing the guts out on the table, I think maybe they're trying to help the animal so they've got to do that to help it. But, otherwise, it would distress me if it's, you know, infested or something like that, that does upset me.'

(37-year-old housewife)

She relates the stories of animal suffering to the role of companion animals as family members, and frames her compassion for the suffering of animals in relation to an ethics of care and responsibility. She also underscores the public service address within *Animal Hospital*, in particular how viewers can potentially pick up information and advice that is useful for the care of their own pets (and by extension, families). But she is also ambivalent about her response to representations of suffering ('I don't know', 'I think maybe', 'I suppose'), and emphasises her compassion for animals with references to stories that do 'distress' or 'upset' her.

In another example, a mother discusses how children's experiences of watching stories of animal suffering can teach them to feel compassion, and in particular engage with their emotions:

'With my children, when we have watched it, and an animal has died, they're very ... [pulls face] ... I don't know how other people's children react, whether they're the same? You know, they're blinking hard and I think "Ah", so they know it really happens and I think it's hard to see it happen but I think it's also good for them to see it happening, 'cos we've got pets and there's going to come a time where the animals will die. I just wonder, 'cos, you know, they do ... you know, they're blinking hard and it is really sad, isn't it? You know, I've got tears in my eyes too, so that they know it's alright, you can get upset when things die.'

(35-year-old female technical agent)

Here, this mother draws on a 'vocabulary of sentiment' (Boltanksi 1999: 91) in order to explain how her children respond to something that is 'really sad'. For this mother, stories of pet death can teach children how to respond in an appropriate way to suffering. Another example illustrates how mothers perceive these pet programmes as opportunities for their children to learn compassion for animals:

Martha: My daughter absolutely adores animals and she never misses a programme, so I watch it ... I can't watch the gory bits like the operation but I would have been really sad had I been sitting at home watching that with her 'cos I know she would have been really sad.

Natalie: Our son gets really emotional as well, I've seen him in tears
before now when an animal's died! Very much, I think, he doesn't
hide his feelings … his heart's on his sleeve.

Just as Rolf Harris is seen to cry at sad stories of animal suffering and
mortality, so too can viewers openly express their compassion for the
suffering of others. For these mothers, watching sad stories together with
their children is one way moral values can be passed on from parents to
their children.

In summary, adult viewers, in particular mothers, believe that the BBC
is sensitive in its treatment of animal suffering because it deals primarily
with uplifting stories of animal recovery from acute illness. When animal
suffering is shown in *Animal Hospital*, viewers value an empathetic
presenter such as Rolf Harris, who is able to provide both an internal as
well as an external report of the suffering to viewers. His apparent
compassion and care for the animals ensures that even when the
programme shows rare cases of animal mortality, these stories can be
transformed from a negative to a positive experience for viewers. Mothers
discuss their responses to representations of suffering in relation to an
ethics of care, and stress how children can potentially learn how to care
for their pets, and by extension other family members, through watching
such stories in *Animal Hospital*. These viewing strategies for
representations of suffering are guided by the way programme makers
construct stories of animal illness and death. *Animal Hospital* presents
stories of animal illness and recovery, and in extreme cases death, as
moral tales whereby we can learn how to care for our own animals
through watching the suffering of other animals. Such moral messages are
problematic because by their very nature they rely on the suffering of
animals to make dramatic and sentimental stories for popular factual
television. But, nevertheless, they are necessary in order to teach children
about the emotional reality of caring for family pets.

When animal suffering is shown in *Animal ER*, adult viewers find the
stories too negative, and too sad for younger viewers. Stories in *Animal ER*
highlight moral and economic issues concerned with pet ownership and
animal rights, and such stories are not well received by parents (and pet
owners). In *Animal Hospital*, the message is that pets are priceless, and
because the programme is set in a charitable veterinary practice there are
no references to the economic reality of caring for pets. In *Animal ER*, the
message is that pets come at a price, and because the programme is set in
a private veterinary practice there are frequent references to the economic
value of pets. Parents prefer their children to watch *Animal Hospital*
because it places emphasis on the moral and sentimental value of pets.

This somewhat idealised representation of companion animals mirrors
the representation of pets in the pet food and insurance industry. A

healthy pet is a happy pet, and the pet industry attempts to persuade owners of the moral and sentimental value of their pets in order to ensure owners perceive non-essential items, such as gourmet food, or insurance, as essential fare for the caring pet owner. In the same way that *Animal Hospital* emphasises an ethics of care for companion animals, so too does the pet industry emphasise the cost of caring for the family pet. As Franklin (1999) has argued, companion animals are perceived as members of the family by their pet owners, and, with contemporary domestic relations in a state of flux, pets can be seen as loyal and constant companions within the home. On the one hand, pet programmes do little to reassure family members of this constancy, as the repetitive theme of pets in crisis only serves to highlight the vulnerability of companion animals. But, on the other hand, series such as *Animal Hospital* situate the stories of pets in crisis within a wider community of care. Caring for animals, caring for animals as if they were humans, and caring about the way humans treat animals all work to emphasise a positive, life-enhancing aspect to what is essentially a negative experience for the animal, the carer and the viewer.

In contrast, young viewers have somewhat different responses to the experience of watching animal suffering and mortality in reality programming. Young viewers are critical of the use of animal suffering for the purposes of making a television programme. These viewers (and pet owners) feel compassion towards the suffering of animals, and vocalise their compassion in relation to an ethics of fairness and animal rights. In their view, it makes little difference if the story of pet death is shown on BBC or Channel 5, the story should not be shown at all. Young viewers reject outright the idea that there can be anything positive or educational about watching pet death on television, no matter if the story is represented in a sensitive and compassionate manner. In their view, when a companion animal experiences acute suffering, the animal (and its owner) has a right to privacy.

It is worth returning to the work of Zelizer (1985), and her observation that the legal evaluation of children as having sentimental worth worked alongside the moral evaluation of children's rights in the twentieth century. A generation of children are growing up watching pet death on television. Will their children be watching similar pet programmes in the future? Pet programmes mark an early stage in the transformation of cultural responses to animal mortality in contemporary Western society. Pet programmes also mark an early stage in the transformation of social attitudes towards the humane treatment of companion animals. The difference in the way children respond to the representation of companion animal suffering compared to an older generation suggests that attitudes towards human–companion-animal relations are gradually changing, as one group of viewers frame their responses in relation to a rhetoric of animal care, whilst another frame their responses in relation to a rhetoric of animal rights. These cultural responses to the moralisation of companion animals and the evaluation of animal rights call into question the treatment of animals in popular factual television.

CONCLUSION

The rise in pet populations in Western society has led to a rise in the pet industry and pet organisations and services. With approximately half of the population of the UK, USA and Australia owning a dog or cat, the pet food industry, pet insurance industry, and pet mortuary industry have benefited from large numbers of humans keeping domestic animals, especially in urban settings. These pet industries utilise the rhetoric of the pet as a companion animal, a valued member of the family, and as such a member of the family who needs to be cared for in a similar manner to the care of human members of the family. In particular, the legal and moral framework for pets and their owners in Western society indicates that humans should be responsible for the health and well-being of their pets, and should not cause unnecessary harm to their companion animals. This attitude towards companion animals is connected to a more general understanding of human–animal relations, where animals have gradually become anthropomorphised in Western culture during the nineteenth and twentieth centuries. It is within this environment that popular factual television about companion animals has flourished. These pet programmes were popular on British television during the 1990s. The programmes were especially popular with children and parents. One common feature of animal-based reality programmes is the narrative of the diagnosis, treatment and recovery of pets in crisis. In the majority of cases these stories of acute animal suffering have a happy ending; however, in extreme cases the stories are about animal mortality. What all the stories share is an emphasis on the care of companion animals, but how humans care for animals is presented somewhat differently in pet programmes on public service and commercial channels. Audience responses to representations of pet death are framed in relation to the concept of an ethics of care. Audiences feel compassion and empathy towards the animals, and talk about human responsibility to care for animals in a socially appropriate manner. In this sense, pet programmes can teach pet owners that they have a responsibility to care for their pets. However, there is a difference in the way children and mothers respond to representations of animal suffering in reality programming. Mothers are concerned about how their children might be upset by these 'sad stories', and at the same time perceive that such stories can teach children about compassion and caring for others. Children on the other hand do not perceive any social benefit from watching animal suffering, and are critical of the programme makers for exploiting animal rights for the purposes of television entertainment. Thus, audience responses to the representation of pet death on television suggest changing cultural responses to human–companion-animal relations. Audience responses to pet programmes also suggest the significance of an ethics of care to our understanding of popular factual television.

Chapter 8

Story of change

In order to understand audience responses to reality programming we need to consider how audiences categorise the reality genre, and how they judge the performance of ordinary people and the representation of authenticity within different types of reality programmes. We also need to consider how audiences understand the idea of learning from watching reality programmes, and how they think about ethics in relation to reality programmes. I would like to critically reflect on each issue in turn in this concluding chapter, before opening up debate about audiences of popular factual television to wider discussion of television audiences and television genres.

One point I would like to raise at the start of this chapter is the issue of cultural specificity. Much of the discussion in this book has been about British popular factual television and its audience. This is because the research I conducted was in the reception of British popular factual television. I have tried, wherever possible, to open up debate about reality TV in relation to other countries, in particular the USA. Nevertheless, the findings in this book could be perceived as findings about the British viewing experience of reality TV. I hope the general points made in this concluding chapter are taken in the spirit with which they are intended, which is to further our critical understanding of the production, content and reception of popular factual television. Although the findings are undoubtedly influenced by my experience of reality TV in Britain, I trust that readers can interpret these findings in relation to the broader picture of reality TV around the world, and can find similarities and differences with the viewing experience as outlined here, and the viewing experience for these programmes in other countries. As more audience research is conducted around the world, we will be able to construct a rich and diverse database for the reception of popular factual television.

CATEGORISATION

First, let me begin with the categorisation of the reality genre by the television industry, scholars and audiences. Within the current television climate, popular factual programmes cut across several areas of production, including investigative journalism, documentary, lifestyle, light entertainment, and new media. The question of what precisely constitutes popular factual television is a difficult one. Much of the debate about popular factual television has rightly concentrated on its relationship with documentary. How similar or different are reality programmes to documentary television? And how do audiences make a distinction between different types of factual programming?

It is clear from the television industry's perspective that there is much to be gained from opening up definitions of documentary and popular factual television. The climate for factual programming is changing, and this is a result of innovative programme development, and the ratings success of popular factual in peaktime schedules. The 2004 Factual Forum advertised itself to the British television industry as 'maximising opportunities in television's fastest growing genre'. But what is a factual genre? On the one hand, each broadcaster categorises factual programming similarly as all factual programming is essentially non-fiction programming. On the other hand, each broadcaster categorises factual programming differently, based on internal production histories, and internal management practices. Categorisation can get in the way of the business of television, as each broadcaster is in the business of putting 'eyeballs in front of the screen'.[1]

Over the past decade, documentary practitioners have argued that popular factual formats have taken over peaktime schedules at the expense of general and specialist documentary programmes/series. Brian Winston argues that 'the [documentary] form is no longer a discrete and valued genre. Despite a growth in its popularity, paradoxically its very continued existence is under threat because it has been subsumed by a new amorphous category, "factual programming"'(2000: 1). Jane Roscoe points out that popular factual has much to offer documentary in terms of how the 'real' can be represented as 'engaging, entertaining and informative', how popular factual can engage younger audiences in factual television, and how popular factual can encourage public engagement with 'social and political issues…through the experience of being entertained'.[2] But she also goes on to say that it is important to acknowledge the differences between documentary and popular factual television: 'they offer different opportunities for documentary as a form, and for documentary practitioners. They involve different aesthetics choices that stem from the demands of subject matter, and the approach of the practitioner. They are constructed around different institutional practices, and construct their audiences in quite distinct ways.'[3] Thus, Roscoe and Winston claim the categorisation of popular factual and documentary television needs careful consideration in terms of the differences and similarities across both genres and programme cultures.

Corner has argued that the term 'documentary' may have reached the end of its usefulness as a broad generic category (2000). He has also argued that the term 'reality TV' 'has become stretched a little (!) beyond analytic usefulness' (Corner 2003: 291). Similarly, Kilborn maintains that the term reality TV has 'probably outlived [its] critical usefulness' (2003: 55). What both authors refer to is a point in the evolution of documentary and reality programmes whereby we can mark the 'widespread dispersal' of these programmes 'across a much larger area of audio-visual culture' (Corner 2000: 688; Kilborn 2003: 6). The difficulty that television audiences have with defining popular factual programmes suggests that broad generic categories such as documentary or reality are shorthand for much more complex and varied formats within factual television.

A case in point is the development of popular documentary in contemporary British television schedules. Examples of popular documentaries include *Life of Grime* (BBC1) and *Jamie's Kitchen* (Channel 4). *Life of Grime* is categorised by the BBC as a contemporary documentary series. In *Life of Grime* the series follows a group of people who work for an environmental health department in London. The series relies on observational filming, combined with participants' direct communications to camera. *Jamie's Kitchen* is categorised by Channel 4 as an observational documentary series. In *Jamie's Kitchen* the series follows the celebrity chef Jamie Oliver and a group of young people who are training to become chefs in Oliver's new restaurant in London. The series relies on observational filming, combined with participants' direct communications to camera. Scholars writing about either series may well categorise either or both as docu-soaps. Kilborn describes the characteristics of the docu-soap, such as 'larger than life characters' or 'occasional dramatic outbursts', as 'essential features of popular factual entertainment' (2003: 102, 89). Both *Life of Grime* and *Jamie's Kitchen* contain just such characteristics. Television audiences might describe either series as documentary or reality TV, but more likely they will describe both series in relation to the treatment of a topic – behind the scenes of an environmental health department, behind the scenes of Jamie's kitchen.

We could say that television audiences do not really care if a factual programme is categorised as documentary or reality. What audiences care about is whether the factual programme will interest them. But much of my analysis of the viewing experience of popular factual television has been about how much audiences care about factual programming, and how much they care about how to categorise factual programming, especially reality programming. When television audiences talk about popular factual programmes they do so with a sliding scale of fact and fiction in mind. This fact/fiction continuum (Roscoe and Hight 2001) is a way audiences make sense of the range of factual programming available to them. At the far end of the fact/fiction continuum are more traditional types of factual programming such as news and current affairs, whilst at the other end of the scale are new reality programmes such as *Big Brother*, or *Joe Millionaire*. A myriad of other types of factual programming, from popular documentary, to hidden camera formats, are somewhere in the middle of the fact/fiction continuum. Even at the further end of the continuum, reality formats are categorised according to a sliding scale. Traditional reality formats such as *999* or *Children's Hospital* are categorised as more factual than lifestyle formats such as *Changing Rooms* or *Would Like to Meet*. The fact that audiences apply a sliding scale of factuality to reality programmes suggests one of the ways they have learned to live with this genre over the past decade. Audiences watch popular factual television with a critical eye, judging the degree of factuality in each reality format based on their experience of other types of factual programming. In this sense, viewers are evaluators of the reality genre, and of factual programming as a whole.

If the categorisation of factual programming is important to viewers, then it should also be important to the television industry and scholars. If audiences watch popular factual television with a critical eye, and this is the most common form of factual programming they will watch on a regular basis, then it may be the case that audiences turn their critical eye to documentary and news. We have seen this already in the way audiences responded to the documentary fakery scandals in Britain. The consequences of the fakery scandals were such that audiences became distrustful of the truth of what they were seeing in observational documentaries. My current research in audience attitudes towards accuracy of information and actuality in British factual programming indicates that audiences value accuracy of information and truthfulness in news, current affairs and documentary more than in popular factual programmes.[4] However, audiences are critical of news and current affairs, and documentary for not being accurate or truthful enough in the provision of information and representation of real events.

Audience criticism of factual programming can be a good thing, and something I discuss later on in relation to critical viewing strategies. But it is essential that there are distinctions made between investigative journalism and documentary, and more popular factual programmes. Just as Roscoe argues that it is important to consider the differences and similarities in the production, content and reception of documentary and popular factual television, so too is it important to consider the differences and similarities in the truth claims of news and current affairs, documentary and popular factual programmes. For example, the introduction of a current affairs drama-doc producer in the current affairs department of the BBC's Factual and Learning division indicates a move within the BBC to attract a different kind of audience to current affairs, an audience that traditionally has been attracted to popular factual, light entertainment and drama programmes. Drama-doc uses the codes and conventions of drama to recreate real events, and audiences primarily watch drama-doc as fictional dramas rather than as factual programmes; current affairs uses the codes and conventions of investigative journalism to represent real events, and audiences primarily watch current affairs as informative factual programmes rather than as fictional dramas (Paget 1998). Although there is hybridisation across the genres, in the use of the codes and conventions of drama and documentary, or the use of news stories as the subject matter of drama-docs, or the use of dramatised reconstructions in current affairs and documentary, there are still differences in the way audiences judge the truth claims of these types of factual programming.

Charlotte Brunsdon (1997: 108) argues that the aesthetic judgements used to assess the quality of television programmes are often based on an assessment of the quality of the programme itself (is it a good or bad programme?), and also the quality of the genre (is it a good or bad genre?). In the case of reality TV, the genre is commonly perceived by audiences as low quality television, but there are good and bad programmes within the genre. Brunsdon refers to John Mepham's three criteria for the judgement of high quality television – diversity, usable stories, and 'the ethic of truth telling' (Mepham 1990: 59, cited in Brunsdon 1997: 108). Audiences of popular factual television apply an ethic of truth telling to their judgement of good and bad reality programmes. Time and again we have seen audiences make distinctions between different types of reality formats, and different types of programmes within those formats, according to the truth claims of the formats/programmes. For example, in Chapter 4 we saw viewers debate good and bad reality programmes based on an ethic of truth telling – *Children's Hospital* was perceived as more truthful than *Big Brother*, and was therefore perceived as a 'good' reality programme according to this particular criteria. Although audiences apply other criteria to judge the quality of reality programmes, for example characterisation and storytelling, an ethic of truth telling is by far the most common type of criteria used to judge the quality of popular factual programming as a whole.

The quality criterion of characterisation and storytelling is often absent from discussion presented here. This absence is primarily because when viewers evaluate and interpret reality TV they criticise it in relation to other kinds of factual television. This is why performance and authenticity is so important to viewing strategies for different types of reality programmes. If viewers value factual television for its truthfulness, then this shared value has a significant influence on their criteria for assessing reality programmes as factual programmes. I would argue that characterisation and storytelling are significant to the way viewers respond to reality programmes. However, for viewers to foreground these elements they would perhaps need to value reality programmes for their drama and entertainment. In my research in 2000–2001, when viewers talked about reality TV as entertaining they were being critical of the genre. However, it may well be the case that as the reality genre develops, viewers highlight the positive entertainment value of reality TV (see next section for further discussion).

Audiences value the truthfulness of factual programming. The more fictionalised factual programming becomes, the less viewers value it. The truth claims of different types of factual programming are strengthened or weakened by the use of the codes and conventions of drama or light entertainment. If the distinctions between news and current affairs, documentary and popular factual become so blurred that audiences are distrustful of everything they see on television, then the television industry's categorisation of factual programming will cease to be meaningful to viewers. Regular research into changing attitudes towards factual programming will assist the television industry and scholars in the triangulation of evidence, from audience research, industry commissioning practices, and scholarly articles, that is necessary for meaningful categorisation of factual television.

PERFORMANCE

One of the significant ways that audiences evaluate the reality genre is by questioning the truth claims of various different reality programmes. Ellis (2002) argues that there is a 'community of understanding' of factual genres. The idea of a community of understanding is useful in thinking about how viewers debate the truth of what they see on television, both internally and with other viewers. The very tension between truth and fiction in reality formats is part of the experience of watching popular factual television. 'One of the pleasures offered by the new reality formats is the knowledge that what is being offered for consumption is manifestly "staged reality"' (Kilborn 2003: 149). The degrees to which a reality format is staged and the degrees to which it is real are issues audiences talk about on a regular basis.

On the one hand, audiences value witnessing events caught on camera, and judging events based on degrees of actuality in popular factual programming. On the other hand, viewers judge the performance of real people in relation to the actuality of a programme. The more people perform in front of cameras, the less 'real' a programme is. They expect non-professional actors to 'act up' in many popular factual programmes. Audiences have therefore developed viewing strategies that assess the improvised performance of 'real' people by looking for 'moments of authenticity' when the performance breaks down and people are 'true' to themselves. Such moments usually occur during scenes of emotional conflict and are often to be expected in reality formats such as *Big Brother*.

Roger Silverstone comments: 'we live in a presentational culture in which appearance is reality' (1999: 69). He is referring to the work of Erving Goffman, and the concept of the presentation of the self in everyday life (as discussed in Chapter 4). Silverstone (1999: 70) points out: 'the success of performance, in everyday life as on the bounded space of stage and screen, depends on the judgements and acceptance of an audience'. We judge the quality of performance by referring to our own social behaviour, our own performances in everyday life, and also the performances we see in the media (1999: 71). In Chapter 4, audiences assessed the performance of non-professional actors in reality programmes according to how 'realistic' their performance appeared to them, based on their own personal experiences, and knowledge of reality programmes. If we refer to Mepham's criteria for quality television, we can see audiences assess good and bad performances in reality programming according to 'the ethic of truth telling' (1990: 59). The improvised performances of non-professional actors in *Big Brother* are judged as good or bad performances based on how authentic they seem to viewers, how truthful to their experiences in everyday life. The fact that audiences know that much reality programming is 'made up' does not stop them from assessing the success of the performance of ordinary people in the programmes according to how authentic it appears to them. However, another way in which audiences judge performance in reality programming is to consider characterisation and storytelling, or what Mepham calls 'useable stories' (ibid.). Thus, a performance may be considered bad because it is not truthful, and it may also be considered good because it is dramatic.

If television audiences debate the truth claims of reality programmes then we might well ask why do they watch them in the first place? As Kilborn points out, reality programmes are multivalent: 'viewers may, at one level, treat the unfolding drama as having a degree of credibility ... at another level, however, they are sufficiently media literate as to be aware that everything played out before them has been contrived to meet their perceived entertainment needs' (2003: 82). Viewers enjoy the staged reality of many popular factual programmes. *Wife Swap* is a successful format because it stages the reality of two participating families, ensuring both families are different enough to create drama and conflict during the experiment. When audiences watch *Wife Swap* they do so on one level as a social experiment, and on another level as an unscripted social drama. Audiences are able to switch from appreciation of these ordinary people and their experiences, to awareness of the staged nature of their experiences created for television.

At another level audiences do not want to see too much reality or too much drama in popular factual television. There is a fine balance between a popular factual programme being too realistic, and too unrealistic. For example, audiences of *Animal Hospital* know that the BBC pre-select stories of animal illness in order to ensure that the majority of the stories have a successful outcome. Audiences have come to expect stories with happy endings in this programme. The stories may be realistic in every other sense – they are accurate accounts of these particular animals and their medical conditions. But they are unrealistic in that the stories mainly report successful medical treatment of animals with acute illness. When a successful outcome is not forthcoming, audiences are critical of the programme for showing animal mortality (see Chapter 7). Similarly, in life experiment formats such as *Faking It*, audiences know that the programme makers pre-select the people to take part in the experiment, and they pre-select the type of employment these people are expected to 'fake'. It is a more satisfying experience for the viewer if the experiment is a success. The narrative drive is one of transformation, and as such the transformation from, say, a classical cello player to nightclub DJ is only really complete when the end result is success as a nightclub DJ. When the transformation is not a success, the programme ends on a flat note. As viewers, we know the chances of a classical cello player successfully becoming a nightclub DJ are slim, especially in a short timeframe, but nevertheless we want to see the story as life affirming. If this means the programme makers have to work hard to ensure a likely positive outcome by pre-selecting someone who has a high chance of succeeding, then many viewers would accept this constructed element of the programme in return for a successful outcome. If the programme makers were to make adjustments to other areas of the programme, such as someone pretending to be a classical cello player when really they were an actor, audiences would complain. Reality can be staged, but the staging has to be clearly marked by programme makers for audiences.

The way audiences negotiate the staged reality of popular factual television is a testament to their understanding of the way reality is put together (Schlesinger 1978). Audiences assess the authenticity of real people's stories and situations within the performative environment of popular factual television. This viewing strategy involves criticism of the truth claims of reality programming, but also some degree of trust in the old adage 'truth will out'. This viewing strategy also involves expectation that reality programming will dramatise real people's stories and their situations, and that this will enhance the viewing experience. Both of these types of viewing strategies rely on programme makers sending clear signals to viewers about their claims to the real (Winston 1995). As long as these signals are clear, then there is an unwritten contract between audiences and programme makers that a certain degree of staging is expected in popular factual television. For example, when a drama-doc claims to be based on real events, and uses a caption informing viewers about the proximity of the drama-doc to its subject matter, this is a clear signal to viewers as to the truth claims of the programme. Similarly, when a lifestyle format such as *Queer Eye for the Straight Guy* undertakes a makeover in a specific timeframe, in this instance the programme makers claim it is one day, then viewers understand that the makeover, no matter how dramatised, actually occurs in the challenging timeframe of one day in the life of its participants.

The social contract between popular factual television and its audience does not necessarily apply to other types of factual programming. For example, when audiences watch the news or an investigative documentary they expect these genres to be accurate and truthful (see Chapter 4). In terms of documentary, the story is somewhat more complicated, as some scholars have argued that documentary's contract with its audience is based on the false premise that documentary can tell the truth in the first place (see Winston 1995). But public response to the documentary fakery scandals in the 1990s indicates that audiences do expect documentary to tell the truth (on the whole), and are critical of documentary when this contract is perceived to be broken. It is therefore important to remember that although audiences apply a fact/fiction continuum to factual programming, they have developed different viewing strategies for different types of genres within factual television.

LEARNING

Popular factual programmes can provide both entertainment and information at the same time. However, audiences mainly perceive reality programming as entertainment. This puts into question the knowledge-providing role of popular factual programmes. Can people learn from watching reality programmes? And, if they can, do they want to learn from watching reality programmes?

Audiences are dismissive of the knowledge-providing role of popular factual television because they perceive it as 'mindless entertainment'. This common phrase used by viewers when describing reality programmes echoes common phrases used by critics of reality TV in the media. When audiences watch reality programmes they do so with prior knowledge of social attitudes towards reality TV as trash TV. It is not surprising, therefore, to find audiences rejecting the knowledge-providing role of popular factual in favour of its entertainment-providing role. The communicative form and design of reality programming tends to re-enforce this perception of the genre as 'mindless entertainment'. The use of visual styles and narrative techniques associated with light entertainment, soap opera, or drama help to paint a picture of popular factual as entertainment. However, the content of much reality programming contains informative elements. These informative elements may not be the primary elements in the programme, but they are nevertheless part of the programme. For example, the lifestyle makeover format *Changing Rooms* functions as entertainment, and also as information. There is the drama of the style transformation, and the spectacle of the reveal, and there are the practical tips and advice on interior decoration. In more traditional reality formats such as *999*, the informative elements of the programme are made more explicit, as the stories of dramatic rescues are framed as stories viewers can learn from in order to protect their own family or loved ones in case of an emergency.

The balance between information and entertainment in popular factual television has shifted over the past decade. Whereas in traditional reality formats the relationship between information and entertainment was fairly explicit (in particular, crime, health and emergency services formats), in contemporary reality formats the relationship is more implicit (in particular, documentary gameshows). This distinction between traditional and contemporary reality programming in relation to information is reflected in the way audiences talk about learning from reality programming. When I analysed audiences' responses to more traditional reality programming such as *999* and *Children's Hospital* in the mid-1990s, audience discussion of the stories of rescue operations and acute health problems were framed in relation to what they could learn about life from the programmes (Hill 2000c). Viewers were quite clear that by watching these types of stories in *999* and *Children's Hospital*, they could learn how to apply first aid in case of family emergencies, or learn about how families cope with medical trauma. As the genre of reality TV has transformed to include other types of hybrid formats such as reality gameshows, audiences are less clear about what they can learn from watching these programmes. This is why in my research in 2000–2001 the majority of viewers talk about the 'idea of learning' rather than learning itself. Although some contemporary reality programmes do present stories of ordinary people in an educational frame (extreme history formats, for example) these are in the minority. Most contemporary reality programmes retain a connection with information; there is the idea of learning, but these programmes subsume the idea of learning within an entertainment frame.

The concept of the idea of learning raises issues about what we mean by learning. For television audiences, their idea of learning is related to formal learning. We can learn about world events from news. We can learn household tips and advice from lifestyle. These types of factual genres provide formal learning opportunities for audiences. For younger television audiences, their idea of learning is related to school learning. If a programme advertises itself as a 'Learning Programme' then these viewers will switch off. Younger viewers also associate the idea of learning as related to learning about life. A programme may advertise itself as an 'Entertaining Programme', but you might learn something along the way. These types of popular factual programmes provide informal learning opportunities for younger audiences. Research in young adults and education indicates that young adults learn in a variety of formal and informal ways (Kirwan *et al.* 2003). This is reflected in the difference between the more flexible manner in which young adults associate the idea of learning with popular factual programming, and the more inflexible manner in which older adults think about learning from popular factual television.

If we open up the idea of learning to include a range of formal and informal learning opportunities, there is potentially much to learn from watching popular factual television. We can talk about learning in relation to general learning. This might include general knowledge about the world and the way we live. For example, a clip show such as *World's Wildest Weather* can help us to learn about the natural environment. We can talk about social learning. This might include learning about world or national events, or social issues and public opinion. For example, a life experiment programme such as *Wife Swap* can help us to form opinions about subjects such as racism. We can talk about practical learning. This might include learning about health, or DIY, or personal improvement. For example, an animal-based reality programme such as *Animal Hospital* can help us to learn how to care for animals. We can talk about emotional learning. This might include learning about people's every lives and day-to-day experiences. For example, a documentary gameshow such as *Big Brother* can help us to learn about other people's lives.

Given the level of audience criticism of the idea of learning from popular factual television, I am cautious about making general claims that audiences do learn from watching these kinds of programmes. It is certainly the case that audiences choose to watch many popular factual programmes to be entertained rather than informed. There are other types of factual programming that audiences explicitly watch for information, such as news. However, although I am cautious of making general claims based on what audiences say about the idea of learning, I think audiences can learn about a variety of things from popular factual television if they choose to do so. I base this observation on the way audiences critically reflect on the idea of learning. Their critical reflection on popular factual television is evidence of learning (Livingstone and Thumim 2003).

The idea of learning therefore relates not only to how viewers might learn from popular factual television, but also to how viewers might learn not to trust the truth claims of popular factual television. On one level, viewers talk about how there is little they can learn from contemporary popular factual television. Here, audiences interpret learning as learning about something, whether this is formal or informal learning, and whether this learning is explicitly or implicitly addressed by a reality format. On another level, when viewers talk about the idea of learning from popular factual television their talk about the difference between traditional and more contemporary reality programmes is evidence of learning. Viewers have learned that they can learn more from *999* than from *Big Brother*. Viewers have learned to trust the truthfulness of what they see in *999* more than *Big Brother*. Thus, viewers show knowledge of how reality programmes are put together, in terms of editing techniques, characterisation, presentational styles; they show knowledge of the hybridisation of reality programming, such as the impact of soap opera or gameshows on reality formats; they show knowledge of the truth claims of different reality formats; and they show knowledge of the uneasy relationship between information and entertainment in popular factual television.

The way audiences critically reflect on the knowledge-providing role of popular factual programmes suggest the different ways audiences judge knowledge. The fact that audiences rarely use the term 'knowledge', and prefer to use the term 'learning' is also suggestive of the way audiences judge knowledge as something formal, something educational. The difference between the way young adults and older adults talk about learning highlights different ways of judging the knowledge-providing role of popular factual television. If young adults carry over more flexible attitudes to learning into adulthood, then we can expect to see more discussion of formal and informal learning in popular factual television in future years. This in turn would open up discussion about the idea of learning from television, a discussion that is much needed if we are to understand the importance of television as a knowledge provider for future generations of viewers.

David Buckingham, in his research on young adults and the news, argues that there is a need for 'fundamental rethinking' of the presentation of news for young adults, both in terms of the 'formal strategies of news, and what is seen to count as news in the first place' (2000: 210). Young adults like news that is innovative in its presentation, that makes them interested in news events that are of relevance to them, that is polemical rather than neutral – as one girl puts it: 'it gives you room to agree with them or disagree with them, and therefore you think about it more' (ibid.). This type of qualitative research is important to our understanding of information in factual programming. Buckingham argues that young adults will be more likely to respond to news if it 'invites scepticism and active engagement' (ibid.). Similarly, my argument is that we need to rethink what counts as learning in popular factual television. If audiences are sceptical of the reality of contemporary reality programmes, if audiences are actively engaged with the truth claims of reality programmes, then we should consider how to include such viewing strategies in our assessment of the idea of learning from popular factual television.

My current research on television audiences and factual programming considers how audiences learn from different types of factual programming, such as news and current affairs, documentaries, and popular factual programmes. I am using quantitative and qualitative research techniques – national survey, focus groups and in-depth interviews – in order to find out what younger adults and older adults understand as learning from different types of factual programming. One of the primary research questions is: what do audiences value about factual television? One of the ways to answer this question is to examine the knowledge-providing role of factual television. In the same way that I discussed how audiences use an ethic of truth telling as a criterion in their assessment of good and bad reality programmes (see previous section), so too audiences can use learning as a way to positively value factual television. If audiences are critical of the idea of learning from specific types of factual television, in particular popular factual, then these programmes will be less valued than others. One of the things I expect to find out in this research project is that audience understanding of learning from factual television will be different to broadcasters' understanding of learning, and different again from academic understanding of learning. This is because audiences will use different criteria from those used by broadcasters or academics as to what they perceive as learning, and what they perceive as factual television. Audience assessment of learning in factual television will be based on their understanding of the generic form of different types of factual programmes. Audience assessment of learning in factual television will also be in transition, as the programmes themselves continue to draw on a variety of fictional and factual genres, and utilise a variety of platforms – terrestrial channels, digital channels, radio, print media and the internet. And audience assessment of learning in factual television will also be contradictory, as the way they have learned to live with factual television will have been influenced by the inherent tensions and contradictions within the development of factual television.[5]

ETHICS

Carrying on from the previous section, the concept of the idea of learning can be applied to audience understanding of ethics in popular factual television. Although some people might argue that ethics is absent from reality programming, in fact ethics is at the heart of reality programming. Ethics informs understanding of the treatment of ordinary people by programme makers, and the content of stories about people's private experiences and dilemmas. Rights to privacy, rights to fair treatment, good and bad moral conduct, and taste and decency are just some of the ethical issues that arise when examining popular factual television. In Chapters 7 and 8, I applied the concept of an ethics of care to health and lifestyle reality formats. An ethics of care is about care and responsibility for ourselves and other people. I argued that much of the content of health and lifestyle reality formats is framed in relation to an ethics of care. I also argued that one of the ways viewers talk about these types of reality formats is in relation to their understanding of care and responsibility towards the family and the household.

One of the issues arising from audience discussion of health-based reality programmes about companion animals and their owners is the level of criticism directed towards programme makers in their treatment of animals. Younger adults in particular talked about animal rights, and were critical of programme makers for not allowing animals a right to privacy in times of acute distress. The idea of learning becomes relevant when we consider how audiences talk about the ethical treatment of companion animals in popular factual television. If ethics is about right and wrong ways to live our lives, then we can learn about moral values from watching and talking about popular factual programmes. In this sense, reality programmes can offer life lessons to audiences.[6]

There are two levels at which audiences can learn about moral values from particular popular factual programmes. At one level, viewers can learn about moral values as represented in the programmes. In the case of *Animal Hospital*, the programme represents companion animals as valued members of the family, and shows us how to be compassionate and understanding towards companion animals, and how to care for animals in a responsible manner. At another level, viewers can learn about moral values as articulated in discussion arising from the programmes. In the case of *Animal Hospital*, young viewers were in agreement with the programme's emphasis on an ethics of care, but took this one stage further in criticising the programme makers for not being caring enough towards the rights of animals. Adult viewers, in particular mothers, were also in agreement with the programme's emphasis on an ethics of care, but were critical of the programme makers for showing animal mortality at a time in the evening when children would be watching. By watching and talking about *Animal Hospital* viewers can express their understanding of ethics.

There are other ways in which we can learn about ethics from popular factual television. Take the example of *Temptation Island*. Here is a programme criticised for its lack of ethics. The premise of the programme is that couples compete to remain faithful to each other. The format is based on virtue ethics; the programme makers test the integrity of participants and how they attempt to live their lives in a 'virtuous' manner. Audiences can learn about virtue ethics by watching the couples as they struggle to remain faithful to their partners. We could say that some audiences learn how to cheat on their partners, or learn that if the opportunity arises it is acceptable to cheat. We could also say that some audiences learn there is a high price to pay for infidelity. When audiences talk about the programme, they are critical of the participants for taking part in a reality gameshow where their relationship is on the line. Audiences are also critical of the way the participants show their true colours, they are not honest about their relationships, they lack integrity. There are other reasons why people choose to watch *Temptation Island*. The promise of sexual transgression, the semi-naked men and women, the tropical location, are all reasons people watch this programme. But another reason for watching the programme is to be critical of the behaviour of the participants, and to judge the characters according to their virtues and vices. A reality programme such as *Temptation Island* tests the limits of acceptable social behaviour, and can provide an opportunity for audiences to discuss socially acceptable or unacceptable behaviour towards other participants in the programme.

Much popular factual television implicitly and explicitly addresses viewers about good and bad ways to live their lives. From a positive perspective, certain reality programmes can encourage viewers to apply an ethics of care in their everyday lives. This is a form of ethical reasoning that encourages people to take care of themselves, and their family, and is closely associated with traditional ethical writing about how we can achieve personal happiness, or self-improvement. An ethics of care as presented in lifestyle programmes is primarily about care and responsibility of individual households. In health-based reality programmes, we see a more public ethics of care, based on the concept of reciprocity where we, as individuals and as members of a society, are 'obliged to provide care because we have all, at some point in our lives, been the recipient of care' (Kittay 2001: 535). Sometimes lifestyle programmes attempt to address a public ethics of care, for example when the *Changing Rooms* team makeover a children's care home. Sometimes health-based reality programmes address a private ethics of care, for example when family members are shown caring for their loved ones. It would be good to see more reality programmes promote an ethics of care based on the concept of reciprocity, where we can learn a way of life grounded in the moral values of care and rights for ourselves and other people.

From a negative perspective, certain reality programmes can exploit ordinary people for the purposes of entertainment. Although there is some evidence that viewers are critical of programme makers for unethical treatment of their subjects, this is on a relatively small scale, and mainly restricted to the treatment of animals and children, two social groups perceived as 'vulnerable', and therefore cause for concern. Audiences tend to perceive adults who take part in reality programmes as consenting adults (Kilborn and Hibbard 2000). However, adults are not immune from unethical treatment. One particular case in point is the treatment of adults with mental health problems in popular factual programmes. There are examples of programmes where the adult participants are emotionally and mentally vulnerable, and this vulnerability is exploited to make an interesting story. Although programme makers would argue that these adults have signed consent forms, and they have been treated with sensitivity, it is sometimes all too evident that these people have mental health problems which are not addressed by the programme makers. It would be good if more reality programmes were about behind the scenes of making a reality programme. This would be one way audiences can learn about the process of taking part in a television programme. The more audiences know about the experience of taking part in a programme, the more they can judge the ethical treatment of ordinary people for themselves.

CRITICAL VIEWING

The key points raised in this chapter so far reflect the main findings of the audience research discussed in this book. In the penultimate section of this chapter, I want to reflect on television audiences as critical viewers. Television audiences are engaged in a critical examination of the development of popular factual television. The ability for audiences to see *through* reality TV, and by that I mean critique as well as watch stories in reality programmes, is fundamental to our understanding of the reality genre (Corner 1995). In this sense, most viewers come to watch reality TV in a default critical position.

'Critical viewing' is a term used to describe the way audiences evaluate and interpret the media. Audiences evaluate reality programmes differently according to how critical they are of the reality genre, and/or particular programmes within the genre. Audiences interpret reality programmes differently according to what critical frameworks they apply to the reality genre, and/or particular programmes within the genre. According to Livingstone and Lunt (1994: 90–1), there is something fundamentally social about being a critical viewer: 'different interpretive strategies are always expressed in a social situation ... social desirability works to support critical comments as clever, impressive self-presentation ... people's critical judgements draw on social knowledge ... [and] through their responses to television, people generate social identities for themselves and others.'

In the case of critical responses to reality TV, as illustrated in this book, audiences evaluated and interpreted reality programmes in the social situation of their homes, and in focus group settings (in other people's homes). There was a common consensus that the reality genre was 'mindless entertainment', and the majority of viewers therefore agreed with generally critical comments on the reality genre. There was less consensus that specific reality programmes were 'good' or 'bad', but overall most viewers were critical of specific programmes, even programmes they watched on a regular basis. Viewers based their critical judgements on knowledge of factual genres, how the programmes were constructed for television viewers, and shared values about the knowledge-providing role of factual television. When critically responding to reality programmes, people positioned themselves as particular types of television viewers, in this case knowledgeable viewers. In addition, when people positioned themselves as critical viewers of reality TV they differentiated themselves from the common portrayal of the reality TV viewer as stupid, or voyeuristic, or easily duped (see Chapters 1 and 5). The audience research presented in this book therefore supports the concept of critical viewing as social action, as defined by Livingstone and Lunt (1994).

Buckingham argues that 'there are significant methodological difficulties in identifying and evaluating evidence of critical viewing ... critical discourses about the media may emerge as a function of the interview context' (2000: 212). Buckingham refers to the idea of 'cynical chic' as a way of seeing critical responses to the media as socially desirable, something Livingstone and Lunt also mention in their analysis of critical viewers of talkshows (1994). Like Livingstone and Lunt, Buckingham (2000: 212) sees critical viewing as 'a form of social action which is intended to accomplish particular social purposes'. He cautions the researcher to take into account the context of the interview when interpreting qualitative data. In particular, he argues that the researcher must consider both an objective interpretation of the data (what does the data tell me?), with a more subjective interpretation of the data (what does the data tell me about the practice of researching audiences?). My own approach to the data presented in this book has been to interpret the data both in relation to what is being said, and the context to the programmes under discussion. Although to some extent viewers were critical of reality programmes, perhaps in part because they thought it chic to be cynical, it was also the case that viewers collectively and individually drew upon readily available 'critical discourses' when talking about reality TV (ibid.).

Buckingham (2000: 217) argues that 'truly critical viewing should be characterised not only by a form of principled scepticism, but also by a willingness to engage with the social reality that is represented, to relate it to one's direct experience and (if appropriate) to take action in order to change it.' We can see evidence of this type of critical viewing in the audience discussions presented here. When viewers are critical of reality programmes, they use such criticism as a means to cynically reject the 'reality' of the reality genre, and often their comments are similar to general criticism of reality TV in the media. Viewers also critically engage with the social reality represented in particular programmes, usually relating this reality to their own personal experiences. In particular circumstances, viewers may take action, based on what they have learnt as a result of critical engagement with specific reality programmes, for example with regard to an ethics of care and companion animals.

The Department of Culture, Media and Sport's Media Literacy Statement (2001) includes a definition of media literacy as:

> The ability to analyse and respond to a range of media ... and to think critically and reflectively about what has been 'read';
> The ability to weigh up how reliable the material is, whether it is fact or fiction, whether it is realistically presented or not ... ;
> An understanding of how [we] respond to and interpret experiences gained through media texts, and also that [we] are part of larger audiences, and that [our] responses are also shaped by that experience.
>
> (Livingstone and Thumim 2003: 6–7)

If we apply this definition to television audiences and factual programming we can see how the formation of critical viewing can potentially lead to the acquisition of greater media literacy. The way in which television audiences respond to ethical issues in a range of popular factual programmes illustrates their ability to think critically and reflectively about these programmes. The way in which television audiences weigh up whether what they are seeing is realistically presented or not illustrates their ability to evaluate whether popular factual programmes are fact or fiction. The way television audiences reflect on their experience of watching popular factual programmes by themselves and with other people illustrates the degree to which they are able to respond to and interpret their experiences.

Research by Livingstone and Thumim (2003) and Kirwan *et al.* (2003) on media literacy indicates young adults and older adults wish to improve understanding of audio-visual content, through formal and informal learning opportunities. The research recommends that the government establish a coherent policy to increase media literacy amongst the UK population. We need to open up our understanding of the idea of learning in order to establish a coherent policy regarding media literacy. We need to know more about how critical viewing connects with media literacy. We need to know more about how adults and children perceive and understand formal and informal learning. As Livingstone and Thumim suggest, we do not know enough about media audiences to 'develop appropriate means of both promoting and evaluating media literacy' (2003: 23). Critical reception is only one means of increasing media literacy skills. Other areas to consider are access to audio-visual media and content production (Livingstone and Thumim 2003).

In a speech by the Secretary of State for Culture, Media and Sport at a Media Literacy Seminar in 2004, Tessa Jowell asked the question 'why does media literacy matter?'[7] For Jowell, media literacy matters because there is continuous debate about the media at work, at school, at home, and in the media itself, and these debates have an impact on our lives. She states: 'I want to know whether people feel equipped to deal with the growing clamour of voices seeking their attention, and whether they feel they have the ability to sort out the wheat from the chaff, the genuine from the fake, the factual from the polemical, the objective from the biased.'[8] No matter what our opinion of reality TV, it is a common topic of discussion in our everyday lives. I would hazard a guess that reality TV is more talked about than watched. Even when 16 million people tuned in to watch the finale of *I'm a Celebrity … Get Me Out of Here!*, more people probably talked about it afterwards than would have watched the programme. I have argued in this section that television viewers of reality TV have developed critical viewing strategies, and that these strategies can be a form of media literacy. The great debate about reality TV is a useful example of how younger adults and older adults are more than equipped to deal with 'the growing clamour of voices seeking their attention', and to decide what matters to them about reality TV.

Research in television audiences of popular factual programming can help us to understand the transitional terrain of reality TV as a genre, and can enhance critical understanding of contemporary television audiences. In many ways, the story of popular factual television and its audience is a story of change.[9] If we situate the case study of popular factual television within the wider environment of policy debate about media literacy, we can see that the story of media literacy is also a story of change. In this respect, critical viewers of popular factual television indicate one possible future direction for this ongoing narrative.

CONTEXT

Much of the evidence put forward about audience evaluation of reality TV supports the claim that reality TV is significant 'to our broader sense of why television continues to be important'(Corner 2003: 298). But just how important is reality TV to audiences? If we consider the social context to television, it is possible to argue that television is important to its audience. In the UK, adults (over the age of 16), spend on average twenty hours a week watching television (Social Trends 2003). Adults spend nearly two hours of the day watching television whilst not doing anything else. Most of the people who watch television do so with other people – more than half the time we spend watching television is with household members, or friends. At 8pm on a weekday the majority of British people are relaxing after work or school, and either involved in leisure activities (57 per cent), eating or personal care activities (13 per cent), or housework/childcare (15 per cent) (Social Trends 2003). Although leisure activities include other activities apart from watching television, the fact that adults spend approximately twenty hours a week doing just that indicates that television is the number one leisure activity for the British public. Similar figures can be shown for other Western societies such as America, and Northern Europe, although Southern Europe traditionally scores lower in terms of levels of television viewing.[10]

These social trends indicate the importance of television in Western society, and the importance of television in people's day-to-day routines and social relationships. Television broadcasters have constructed the schedule according to these, and other, social trends. As I discussed in Chapter 6, it is no coincidence that popular factual programmes are more likely to be shown from 6pm to 10.30pm, and in particular from 8pm to 10pm. Over the past decade, peaktime television schedules have accommodated more and more popular factual programmes, squeezing other kinds of factual output such as documentary or current affairs into other less popular slots in the schedule (see Chapter 2). Turn on the television on any weeknight and you will find a variety of popular factual television to choose from. Not only has the success of popular factual programmes squeezed out more traditional factual programmes, but popular factual has also made life difficult for sitcom, comedy and drama.

Reality TV became popular in the 1980s because it offered broadcasters and audiences an alternative to fictional programming. Its dominance in peaktime schedules over the past decade is testament to the strength of popular factual programmes for a wide range of viewers. Television broadcasters have made time for popular factual programmes. And the ratings success of many popular factual formats indicates broadcasters will continue to prioritise popular factual in peaktime schedules (see Chapter 2).

Given the huge ratings for reality formats such as *Joe Millionaire* (USA), *The Block* (Australia), and *I'm a Celebrity ...* (UK), it would appear television audiences have also made time for popular factual programmes. We should note, however, that audiences have not made more time for popular factual programmes, but have prioritised popular factual over other kinds of programming. Robert Picard, in his analysis of audience expenditures and media use, has argued that during the 1990s there has been an increase in the number of programmes and number of hours programmes are transmitted on television.[11] One argument for the success of reality TV is that it fills a gap created by the commercial demands of multichannel television twenty-four hours a day. But television viewing has only increased by an average of two minutes per year. Picard argues that media use is related to overall time use, and time is a scarce resource. Although during the 1990s we saw a rapid increase in the number of television channels and programmes, we also saw an increase in working hours at work and at home, and more restrictions on personal and leisure time as a result of this. Therefore, although reality TV is important to broadcasters and audiences, it is important in the sense that it is on at a time in the television schedule when people want to watch television, and choose to watch these types of popular factual programmes over other kinds of fictional and factual programming.

Another point to be made is that reality TV is not that important in people's lives overall. Indeed, television is not that important in people's lives, when compared with pressing social concerns such as health or education. One of the central findings of the British Film Institute Audience Tracking Study, as reported in *TV Living* (Gauntlett and Hill 1999), is that people's lives are more important than television. Time and again when people reflect on the relationship between television and their everyday lives, it is health, or family and friends, or personal relationships that are more important to them than television. The results of a national survey on British social attitudes in 2000 indicate that health is the number one social issue people are most concerned about in terms of their own lives, and the lives of other people. Support for prioritising extra government spending on health has risen from 37 per cent to 47 per cent between 1983 and 1999 (Jowell *et al.* 2000: 17). Eight in ten people, irrespective of age, believe that the NHS should never cut down or cut out any types of health treatment (2000: 32). There is a link between health and watching television. During periods of ill health, people tend to watch more television, and as they recover they reduce the amount of time watching television in favour of other types of social activities (Gauntlett and Hill 1999).

How then do we explain the importance of popular factual television to audiences? It is a major premise of this book that when people watch reality programmes they talk about what they are seeing with other people at home, at work, at school. Popular factual television facilitates intercommunication. It sparks debate. Many of the topics addressed by popular factual television are topics about ordinary people and their everyday lives. Popular factual programmes interconnect with people's everyday lives, addressing issues people are curious about, interested in, or care about. For British audiences the most popular types of reality programmes are about issues that are relevant to them – healthcare, crime, work and leisure, personal relationships. British audiences want to see popular factual programmes where they can compare themselves and their experiences with other people and their experiences.

The importance of popular factual television to its audience will continue to change as popular factual programmes change, and as factual programmes change over time. At present, popular factual television is important to viewers because it is scheduled at a time when viewers want to watch television, and it facilitates communication with other people. Popular factual television is something to talk about, and we should not underestimate the significance of talk to the role of television in our everyday lives (Scannell 2002). But popular factual television is only important in that it speaks to the concerns of ordinary people and their everyday situations. The fact that audiences are often critical of popular factual television suggests they are not altogether happy with the way ordinary people are represented in reality programmes. Were audiences given the opportunity to become more involved in popular factual television, they would have the opportunity to change the genre for the better.

I would like to end with a personal reflection on researching and writing about popular factual television and its audience. In one way or another I have been working on the reception of popular factual television for the past five years. Much of this work, and thinking about the issues involved in the study of television audiences of popular factual programming is reflected in this book. I have found researching and writing about this topic challenging. When I began looking into this topic I did so with lots of enthusiasm, but little actual knowledge of reality TV, or the key concepts and authors in the field. Over time, and with the help of colleagues, I've 'brushed up my reality TV'. But it is still the case that researching reality TV is like trying to research a moving target. Just as you get your bearings on the latest reality format, another format steps in, and you have to change direction. I was faced with this problem when I began my audience research in popular factual television in 2000. The research was originally designed to examine audience responses to infotainment and docu-soaps, but quickly had to adapt to include the new format of reality gameshows. And once I began talking to audiences the research had to adapt again to include lifestyle formats. Thus, what had seemed like a contained audience research project into two existing popular factual formats, turned into a much larger project on a wide range of existing and emergent reality formats. In many ways, the audience took the lead in this project. There were three stages to the research – quantitative survey, focus groups, in-depth interviews with families. At each stage I had to re-evaluate my thinking on reality TV to take into account the way audiences understood the genre. They were always one step ahead of me. For audiences, reality TV is part of the landscape of factual television. When a new reality format arrives, audiences understand it in relation to other reality programmes, and other factual programmes as well. In many ways, audiences define reality TV in relation to what it is not: it's not fiction, but it's entertaining; it's not informative, but it's factual; it's not real, but it's sometimes true. Above all, I learnt to be flexible when researching audiences of popular factual television.

It is easy to write yourself into a corner when writing about reality TV. First, there is the problem of definition – what exactly is reality TV? My approach is to look at different types of reality programming and assess them each in turn as part of a broader understanding of popular factual television. And yet as I write about formats as varied as *Police Camera Action!*, *Changing Rooms*, and *Big Brother* it is all too easy to make specific points about different formats within the genre rather than to think about the big picture overall. Also, the way I might make sense of these formats is different from how audiences make sense of them, and different again from how programme makers make sense of them. Second, there is the problem of criticism of the reality genre – the 'how low can you go' syndrome. My approach is to evaluate different types of reality formats based on what audiences say about them, not what critics say about them. And yet of course what audiences say about reality TV is partly influenced by what critics say about the genre. Television audiences are reality TV's harshest critics. How best to reflect audience and media criticism of the genre? Finally, there is the problem of writing about audiences – what do audiences really mean when they say X or Y? My approach is to vary the selection of quantitative and qualitative data, cross-referencing wherever possible, and considering the context from which the data is drawn. However, audience responses to popular factual television are inherently contradictory. All too often I have found myself looking at contradictions within the data only to find I have contradicted myself when writing about the data. What I have found during the course of writing this book is that just as I struggle to write about a genre in transition, so too audiences struggle to understand their own responses to a genre in transition. I hope I have done justice to the viewing experience of reality TV, because without watching and talking to people about watching and talking about reality TV this book wouldn't exist at all.

Appendix I

Research methods

The ESRC, ITC and Channel 4 funded project used a multi-method approach, combining quantitative and qualitative techniques to gather data and subsequent analysis of television audiences and popular factual programming in the UK. The main methods used were a quantitative survey, semi-structured focus groups and in-depth interviews, and the data was collected during a particular period in the development of the genre of popular factual television (2000–2001).

The first stage of research relied on industry analysis and visual analysis. I used available television guides to assess the scheduling of a range of factual entertainment across days, weeks, months and seasons. I analysed the form and content of selected popular factual programmes, obtaining copies of individual programmes and whole series by recording live programmes, and by requesting previously aired and to be aired programmes from production companies. I also consulted production companies on programmes in production, specifically *Big Brother*. This data allowed me to produce a comprehensive account of the range and type of programmes available to viewers at particular times, and to gauge which categories of popular factual television viewers would be familiar with during the main data collection period (autumn 2000–summer 2001). The data also allowed me to navigate my way through the wide range of programming, charting existing subgenres (infotainment and docu-soaps), and responding to new developments within the genre (reality gameshows).

The second stage in the audience research involved a national survey of audience preferences for, and attitudes to, factual entertainment in the UK. This survey was funded by the Independent Television Commission (ITC), and the ITC were consulted on the design of the survey, which contained a series of closed questions relating to audience preferences for form, content, subgenres, and use of multimedia, and audience attitudes towards issues of privacy, information, and entertainment in popular factual programming. The survey was a self-completion questionnaire, and was distributed by the Broadcasters' Audience Research Board (BARB) to a representative sample of 8,216 adults (aged 16–65+) and 937 children (aged 4–15) during August 2000. The data collected allowed me to develop a source of information on the general public and their preferences for and attitudes to a range of factual entertainment in the UK. I analysed the data from a number of perspectives, looking at programme types and content, and audience attitudes, comparing this data with key demographic information relating to age, gender, class, education, households with/without children, and ethnicity. With regard to ethnicity, the sample of ethnic respondents is too small in the BARB sample to allow for useful analysis.

The third stage of the audience research involved semi-structured focus groups, where the results of the survey were used to design focus group interviews with children (aged 11–14), young adults (aged 15–18) and adults (aged 18–44), who defined themselves as regular viewers of popular factual television, and were in the C1C2DE social category. The recruitment of participants involved the use of a professional qualitative recruitment agency, and quota sampling in a variety of suburban locations. I selected these participants because the results of the survey indicated that regular viewers of popular factual television were primarily in the above categories. The primary aim of these focus groups was to explore audience attraction to different types of popular factual programming, and to understand what strategies they used to watch hybrid formats within the genre. The focus groups contained a series of open questions relating to viewer responses to subgenres within factual entertainment, the use of non-professional actors, and issues relating to information and entertainment in hybrid formats. Twelve focus groups were conducted in London, each group containing 7–8 participants, and were divided according to age, gender, and access to terrestrial or satellite/cable/digital television. I selected these groups because the data from the survey indicated that age and gender were key variables relating to audience attraction to factual entertainment, and it was necessary to consider a range of programming available across television platforms. Following an initial coding of the transcripts, I conducted a more discursive analysis that considered group dynamics as well as substantive judgements.

The final stage of the audience research involved in-depth interviews with ten families, with children of varying ages, over a six-month period (recruited from the focus groups). Four visits were made to the family homes during the period January–July 2001. Combinations of methods were used – open discussions, observation of families, and participation in watching programmes – in order to understand the social context to watching factual entertainment. In addition, key issues that arose from the focus groups relating to information/entertainment were explored further during the family visits. In my selection of interview subjects, the types of questions asked during the visits, and the timing of the visits, I was guided by a desire to follow new developments within the genre, and to understand further how family viewers responded to these developments in the home environment. Interviews were logged, and partially transcribed, and field notes written up during and after the period of data collection. The in-depth interviews provided a wealth of rich data and thick description, and allowed further flexibility for the project to assess the popularity of, and responses to, new hybrid formats and more familiar formats within factual entertainment.

Appendix 2
Research design

QUESTIONNAIRE: ENTERTAINMENT PROGRAMMES
ABOUT REAL PEOPLE

Many entertainment programmes on television are about real people. Shows such as *Airport* (BBC1), *Police Camera Action!* (ITV), *Big Brother* (Channel 4), *Family Confidential* (Channel 5) and *We Can Rebuild You* (Sky One), all involved members of the public and their personal experiences. We would like to know what you think to these types of programmes.

Q1   What kinds of entertainment programmes about real people do you regularly/occasionally/never watch? (Please place a cross in one box on each line across.)

	Regularly	Occasionally	Never
Hospitals/doctors (e.g. *Children's Hospital*)	☐	☐	☐
Building/DIY (e.g. *The Builders*)	☐	☐	☐
Weather (e.g. *Storm of the Century*)	☐	☐	☐
Motorways/driving (e.g. *So You Think You're a Good Driver*)	☐	☐	☐
Holidays/travel (e.g. *Real Holiday Show*)	☐	☐	☐
Pet shows (e.g. *Animal Hospital*)	☐	☐	☐
Homes and gardens (e.g. *Changing Rooms*)	☐	☐	☐
Real people (e.g. *Big Brother*)	☐	☐	☐
Police/crime (e.g. *Police Camera Action!*)	☐	☐	☐
Emergency services (e.g. *999*)	☐	☐	☐
Survival (e.g. *Castaway*)	☐	☐	☐
Places (e.g. *Airport*)	☐	☐	☐
Marriage/relationships (e.g. *Streetmate*)	☐	☐	☐

Q2   What do you like or dislike about entertainment programmes about real
people? (Please place a cross in one box on each line across.)

	Like	Dislike
Presenters	☐	☐
Members of the public	☐	☐
Animals	☐	☐
Stories caught on camera	☐	☐
Stories recreated for TV	☐	☐
Accidents caught on camera	☐	☐
Re-created accidents	☐	☐
Rescues caught on camera	☐	☐
Re-created rescues	☐	☐
Reactions of public to presenters/real people	☐	☐
Arguments and disagreements	☐	☐
Intrusive cameras	☐	☐
Up-to-the-minute stories	☐	☐
Information	☐	☐
Looking into other people's lives	☐	☐
Other	☐	☐

(Please write your answer inside the box.)

Like	Dislike

Q3 Here are some things people have said about entertainment programmes about real people. How much do you agree or disagree with what they said? (Please place a cross in one box on each line across.)

	Agree strongly	Agree	Neither agree nor disagree	Disagree	Disagree strongly
Real life stories are more entertaining than fiction	☐	☐	☐	☐	☐
I think these programmes are really useful as they give you all sorts of information about life	☐	☐	☐	☐	☐
These programmes give real people a chance to speak on TV about what matters to them	☐	☐	☐	☐	☐
I think true-life TV takes advantage of people who are in the programmes	☐	☐	☐	☐	☐
Programmes about real people are boring because they are all the same	☐	☐	☐	☐	☐
I don't like watching TV programmes where real people face difficult emotional situations	☐	☐	☐	☐	☐

Q4 Which ONE of the following statements comes closest to your own opinion about entertainment programmes about real people? (Please place a cross in one box only.)

I think the stories in entertainment programmes about real people really do happen like this ☐

I think the stories in entertainment programmes about real people sometimes happen like this, and are sometimes made up ☐

I think the stories in entertainment programmes about real people happen like this, but parts of them are exaggerated for TV ☐

I think the stories in entertainment programmes about real people are all made up ☐

Q5   How much do you agree or disagree with each of the following statements about the entertainment programmes about real people? (Please place a cross in one box on each line across.)

	Agree strongly	Agree	Neither agree nor disagree	Disagree	Disagree strongly
Members of the public usually act the same on TV as in real life	☐	☐	☐	☐	☐
Members of the public usually overact for the cameras	☐	☐	☐	☐	☐
I can always tell the difference between someone's actual story being caught on camera, or being re-created for TV	☐	☐	☐	☐	☐

Q6   There are three types of entertainment programmes about real people. Observation programmes are often about watching people in everyday places (e.g. *Airport*). Information programmes use true stories to tell us something, like driving, first aid, or pets (e.g. *999*). Created for TV programmes are about putting real people in a manufactured situation, like a house or an island, and filming what happens (e.g. *Big Brother*). How much do you like or dislike each type of programme? (Please place a cross in one box on each line across.)

	Like a lot	Like a little	Neither like nor dislike	Dislike a little	Dislike a lot
Observation	☐	☐	☐	☐	☐
Information	☐	☐	☐	☐	☐
Created for TV	☐	☐	☐	☐	☐

Big Brother is a nightly series on Channel 4 which began on Tuesday 18 July at 9pm, about real people who live in a house with cameras in every room. There is also a website which shows people living in the house 24 hours a day. Every week viewers vote one person out of the house, until three remain. Viewers then vote for the winner who will get a cash prize of £70,000.

Q7   Have you watched *Big Brother*? (Please place a cross in one box only.)

Yes   ☐   Please answer Question 8 onwards

No   ☐   Please go to Question 9 onwards

Q8   What do you like or dislike about *Big Brother*? (Please place a cross in one box on each line across.)

	Like	Dislike
Watching people do everyday things	☐	☐
Watching people do private things	☐	☐
Watching individual people under stress	☐	☐
Watching group conflict	☐	☐
Seeing people live without modern comforts, e.g. TV	☐	☐
Seeing people do tasks set by the TV makers and viewers	☐	☐
Seeing contestants visit the confession room	☐	☐
Seeing contestants talk about their experience	☐	☐
Suggesting tasks	☐	☐
Choosing the losers	☐	☐
Choosing the winner	☐	☐
Watching the nightly TV programme	☐	☐
Watching the live 'eviction' programme	☐	☐
Visiting the 24-hour internet site	☐	☐
Media coverage of the programme	☐	☐
Talking about the programme with friends/family	☐	☐
Talking about the programme in chat rooms	☐	☐

Q9 If you have personal experience of a certain job or particular situation, do you find a reality programme about it more interesting or less interesting: For example, if you have had an accident or illness, would you find hospital programmes interesting, or if you have a pet, would you find pet programmes interesting? (Please place a cross in one box only.)

Much more interesting ☐

A little more interesting ☐

Makes no difference ☐

A little less interesting ☐

A lot less interesting ☐

Q10a Some entertainment programmes about real people have websites where you can get information about the programme, chat to people on the programme and talk to other viewers. Have you used these websites? (Please place a cross in one box only.)

Yes, once ☐

Yes, more than once ☐

Yes, often ☐

No, never ☐ Please answer question 10b

Q10b Which ONE of the following reasons describes why you never used these websites for programmes about real people? (Please place a cross in one box only.)

I do not have access to the internet ☐

I am not interested in these particular websites ☐

I don't know about these particular websites ☐

FOCUS GROUPS

- Semi-structured, medium level of moderator involvement. Standard key topics for all focus groups, but probing questions and clips will alter with certain groups.
- Questionnaire to be filled in by all participants.

Introduction

Welcome; summary of research topic; emphasis on hearing different points of view; on their experiences and perspectives; try to not talk all at once; ask them to introduce themselves, saying name and favourite entertainment programme about real people.

Key topics

Programme characteristics

USE LIST: Entertainment programmes about real people mainly involve stories caught on camera. What do you think of the stories in your favourite programme?
Probe the characteristics, the stories, rescues and accidents, how they are told.
Probe what else they like, e.g. presenters, arguments and disagreements.

Real people

A lot of these programmes are about real people and their everyday stories. What do you like or dislike about this?
Probe if you have personal experience of a certain job or situation, are you more or less likely to watch a programme about this? Look for specific examples.

SHOW CLIP FROM OBSERVATION PROGRAMME
For young adults and satellite/cable viewers use *Ibiza Uncovered*.
For other groups use clip from *Airline*.

Actuality

Can you always tell the difference between someone's actual story being caught on camera, or being changed for TV?
Probe stage managed events.
Probe members of the public overacting on TV.
Probe celebrities, real people, and TV celebrities as presenters.

SHOW CLIP FROM CREATED FOR TV PROGRAMME
For all groups use *Big Brother*.

Information/entertainment

What's informative about these programmes?
Probe how use information in real life.
Probe whether 'information' is problematic.
Probe in relation to three clips.
Probe in relation to observation.

SHOW CLIP FROM INFORMATION PROGRAMME
For all female groups use clip from *Animal Hospital*.
For male groups use clip from *Police Camera Action!*
For mixed gender groups use clip from *House of Horrors*.

Future factual TV

What entertainment programmes about real people would you like to see on TV?
Probe long-term life expentancy of three subgenres.
Probe multimedia, and applications outside of TV.

FOR YOUNG ADULTS ONLY
Probe programmes for young adults.

Sum up and questions

IN-DEPTH INTERVIEWS

The third stage of the study into television audiences and popular factual programming comprised in-depth research in selected households. As well as enabling further investigation of issues raised by the first two stages of the research (a large-scale quantitative survey and multiple focus group discussions), the household visits provided data concerning the everyday and domestic context of watching popular factual programmes.

Methods

- From the focus group participants involved in the second stage of the research, individuals were selected as candidates for the household study. They were invited to participate if they were living in a family unit with at least one child over the age of 11 years. (All focus group participants had been selected because they were regular viewers of factual entertainment programmes.)

- Ten families were selected. (See below for an outline of their profiles.)
- Each family was visited four times over a period of six months, from January 2001 to July 2001. Every session lasted for one and a half hours and was conducted by either Annette Hill or Caroline Dover (researcher); each family was visited by the same person throughout the research.
- Visits involved all, or as many as possible, of the household members. Sessions consisted of in-depth interviews and/or observation of the families watching programmes/video clips supplied by the researchers. (See below for an outline of each session.)

Families

All of the families live in the Greater London area; social classes C1C2DE.

Family 1: 2 parents (black English father, white English mother); 4 children (aged 9–16). Household income: *c.* £40,000. Occupations: recreation duty manager; primary school administrative assistant. 4 TVs, 2VCRs and Sky Digital access. 1 PC without internet.

Family 2: 2 parents (Italian father, English mother); 2 children (aged 14 and 12). Household income: *c.* £40,000. Occupations: restaurant manager; part-time administrative assistant. 5 TVs, 1 VCR, 1 DVD player and digital access. 1 PC with internet.

Family 3: 2 parents (Cypriot father, white English mother); 2 children (aged 12 and 6). Household income: *c.* £40,000. Occupations: dry cleaning company manager; part-time personnel officer. 4 TVs, 1 VCR and digital TV access. 1 PC with internet.

Family 4: 2 parents (black English father, white English mother); 4 children (aged 2–11). Household income: *c.* £20,000. Occupations: painter/decorator; housewife. 2 TVs, 1 VCR and Sky satellite access. 1 PC with internet.

Family 5: 2 parents (both white English); 4 children (aged 8–20). Household income: *c.* £75,000 (4 working adults). Occupations: engineer; part-time care worker; estate agent; office clerk. 5 TVs, 1 VCR and cable TV access. 1 PC without internet.

Family 6: 2 parents (white English father, black English mother); 3 children (aged 16, 12 and 1). Household income: *c.* £25,000. Occupations: copier engineer; care attendant. 4 TVs, 3 VCRs; no cable/digital access. 1 PC with internet.

Family 7: 1 parent (British Cypriot); 2 children (aged 15 and 14). Household income: *c.* £10,000. Occupations: (ex-dental nurse, currently on benefits). 3 TVs, 1 VCR and Sky Digital access. 1 PC without internet.

Family 8: 2 parents (white English); 4 children (aged 12–20). Household income *c*. £55,000 (3 working adults). Occupations: builder; customer services officers (x2). 3 TVs, 3 VCRs and Sky Digital access. 1 PC without internet.

Family 9: 2 parents (white English); 3 children (aged 10, 8 and 5). Household income: *c*. £25,000. Occupations: stonemason; housewife. 3 TVs, 1 VCR, 1 DVD. 1 PC with internet.

Family 10: 2 parents (white English); 3 children (aged 15, 11 and 8). Household income: *c*. £45,000. Occupations: police officer; supply teacher. 3 TVs, 2 VCRs and cable access. 1 PC with internet.

Sessions

- Session 1: discussion of the family's viewing habits. Types of programmes regularly watched by different members; programmes watched together and separately; individual work/school/leisure schedules; when and in which room different members watch different programmes; leisure activities beyond television watching.
- Session 2: discussion of new reality TV formats and clips from *Celebrity Big Brother* and *Popstars*. Themes explored: celebrity; performance; reality. General discussion of recent programming viewed.
- Session 3: discussions around the issue of 'information', aided by a series of programme clips. The kinds of programmes and type of content and format considered informative. General discussion of recent programming viewed.
- Session 4: discussions around *Big Brother II* and *Survivor*. Themes explored: participation; performance, reality; characters; gender tastes. General discussion of recent programming viewed.

Notes

1 Understanding reality TV

1   Cozens, Claire (2003) 'Round the Clock Reality Arrives', *Guardian*, Tuesday 29 April 2003. Online. Available at http://media.guardian.co.uk/realitytv/story/0,7521,945285,00.html (accessed 27 June 2003).
2   Online. Available at http://media.guardian.co.uk/story/0,7493,787312,00.html (accessed 27 June 2003).
3   Online. Available at http://www.cbsnews.com/stories/2003/01/25/entertainment/main 537964.shtml (accessed 27 June 2003).
4   Online. Available at http://www.cbsnews.com/stories/2003/02018/entertainment/ main541100.shtml (accessed 27 June 2003).
5   In the last week of January 2003 reality programmes won 15 out of 18 half-hour time periods on Monday–Wednesday evening. Online. Available at http://www.cbsnews.com/stories/2003/01/25/entertainment/main537964.shtml (accessed 27 June 2003).
6   Tryhorn, Chris (2003) 'Celebrity Boost for ITV2', *Guardian*, Tuesday 6 May. Online. Available at http://media.guardian.co.uk/realitytv/ story/0,7521,948519,00.html (accessed 27 June 2003).
7   *Broadcast*, 13 February 2004: 5.
8   Bulkley, Kate (2003). 'I'm a Celeb, Have a Bet on Me', *Guardian*, Monday 19 May. Online. Available at http://media.guardian.co.uk/mediaguardian/story/ 0,7558,958629,00.html (accessed 27 June 2003).
9   Online. Available at http://media.guardian.co.uk/realitytv/story/0,7521,943020,00.html (accessed 27 June 2003).
10 Gibson, Owen (2002) 'Profits Roll in From Popstars', *Guardian* 19 November. Online. Available at http://media.guardian.co.uk/realitytv/story/0,77521,842831,00.html (accessed 27 June 2003).
11 See *Broadcast*, 20 June 2003: 16–17.
12 Online. Available at http://news.bbc.co.uk/1/hi/entertainment/tv_and_radio/1346936.stm (accessed 26 August 2003).
13 Online. Available at http://news.bbc.co.uk/1/hi/entertainment/tv_and_radio/1346936. stm (accessed 26 August 2003).
14 Online. Available at http://www.cbsnews.com/stories/2003/02/18/entertainment/ main541100.shtml (accessed 27 June 2003).
15 Online. Available at http://news.bbc.co.uk/1/hi/entertainment/tv_and_radio/1341239. stm (accessed 26 August 2003).
16 Online. Available at http://news.bbc.co.uk/1/hi/world/africa/3110681.stm (accessed 26 August 2003).
17 Online. Available at http://news.bbc.co.uk/1/hi/entertainment/tv_and_radio/3141021. stm (accessed 26 August 2003).

18　Online. Available at http://newsstore.f2.com.au/apps/news (accessed 26 August 2003).
19　Online. Available at http://newsstore.f2.com.au (accessed 26 August 2003).
20　*Broadcast*, 31 October 2003: 11.
21　Online. Available at http://www.cbsnews.com/stories/2003/01/25/ entertainment/ main537964.shtml (accessed 27 June 2003).
22　Vanderbilt, Tom (1998) 'When Animals Attack, Cars Crash and Stunts Go Bad', *New York Times*, Sunday Magazine, 6 December: 12–20.
23　*Broadcast*, 16 January 2004: 20.
24　*Broadcast*, 16 January 2004: 20.
25　The International Alliance of Theatrical Stage Employees wants to unionise reality programmes on US network and cable channels, in order to ensure that their employees receive the same pay and benefits as other unionised workers. This would raise the costs per hour for network reality programming. Online. Available at http://www.nytimes.com/2004/01/25/ business/yourmoney/25union.html (accessed 26 January 2004).
26　Online. Available at http://www.cbsnews.com/stories/2003/02/22/ entertainment/ main541600.shtml (accessed 27 June 2003).
27　Online. Available at http://www.cbsnews.com/stories/2003/02/22/ entertainment/ main541600.shtml (accessed 27 June 2003).
28　Online. Available at http://www.cbsnews.com/stories/2003/02/22/ entertainment/ main541600.shtml (accessed 27 June 2003).
29　Carter, Bill (2003) 'Even as Executives Scorn the Genre, TV Networks Still Rely on Reality', *New York Times*, 19 May, Section C:1.
30　*Broadcast*, 16 January 2004: 20.
31　See *The Times*, 20 December 2002: 4–5; *Financial Times*, 11 November 1999: 22; *The Observer*, 20 August 2000: 15.
32　Vanderbilt, Tom (1998) 'When Animals Attack, Cars Crash and Stunts Go Bad', *New York Times*, Sunday Magazine, 6 December: 12–20.
33　See *Broadcast*, 20 June 2003: 2.
34　Cited in 'Reality TV Takes Off'. Online. Available at http://www. cbsnews.com/stories/2003/01/16/entertainment/main536804.shtml (accessed 27 June 2003).
35　Conlin, Michelle (2003) 'America's Reality TV Addiction'. Online. Available at http://aol.businessweek.com/bwdaily/dnflash/jan2003/nf20030130_8408. htm (accessed 31 January 2003).
36　Bernstein, Jonathan (2003) 'Aerial View of America', *Guardian Guide*, 22–8 March 2003: 98.
37　Bernstein, Jonathan (2003) 'Aerial View of America', *Guardian Guide*, 22–8 March 2003: 98.
38　Bernstein, Jonathan (2003) 'Aerial View of America', *Guardian Guide*, 22–8 March 2003: 98.
39　Online. Available at http://www.cbsnews.com/stories/2003/01/16/ entertainment/ main536804.shtml (accessed 27 June 2003).
40　Ellis, John. (2003) 'Big Debate is Happening Everywhere but on TV', *Broadcast*, 27 June: 11.

2 The rise of reality TV

1　Byrne, C. (2002) 'News Corp Plans Reality TV Channel'. Online. Available at http://media.guardian.co.uk/broadcast/story/0,7493,769885,00.html (accessed 10 August 2002).

2   Hopkin, D. (2002) 'Introduction: Broadside Ballads and the Oral Tradition'. Online. Available http://www.cc.gla.ac.uk/courses/scottish/ballads/introduction_broadside_ballads_.htm (accessed 12 August 2002).
3   Vanderbilt, Tom (1998) 'When Animals Attack, Cars Crash and Stunts Go Bad', *New York Times*, 6 December: 2.
4   *Variety*, 9–15 January 1995: 55.
5   *Variety*, 9–15 January 1995: 55.
6   Source for ratings, BARB, compiled by *Broadcast*, 3 December 1994: 22.
7   Source for ratings, BARB, compiled by *Broadcast*, 3 December 1994: 22.
8   Phillips, William. (1998) 'Drama in a Crisis', *Broadcast*, 30 October: 20.
9   *Broadcast*, 30 October 1998: 20.
10 *Broadcast*, 18 May 2001: 34.
11 *Broadcast*, 30 January 2003: 17.
12 Wells, Matt (2002) 'TV to Give Terminally Ill Patient a Makeover', *Guardian*, 25 September: 11.
13 This quotation was cited in translation in de Leeuw, Sonja (2001) '*Big Brother*: How a Dutch Format Reinvented Living and Other Stories', unpublished paper.
14 See Wells, Matt (2001) 'Keep it Real', *Guardian*, Monday 14 May: 2.
15 All figures in this section are taken from press packs for *Big Brother* (Channel 4 press pack), published ratings data (BARB and Nielson), and the industry magazine *Channel 21 International*, Nov/Dec 2000 (p. 42).
16 The BARB ratings for Wednesday 11 July 2001 show that 626,000 viewers tuned in to watch E4, compared to 300, 000 viewers for Channel 5 and 400,000 viewers for Channel 4 at the same time, 11pm.
17 See *Broadcast*, 31 July 2001.
18 See *Broadcast*, 1 August 2003.
19 Quotation taken from a news release from Reuters, by Jana Sanchez, 22 March 2001. *The Big Diet* is no longer being made in the Netherlands.
20 Deans, Jason (2001) 'Viewers Tire of Reality TV'. Online. Available at http://media.guardian.co.uk/realitytv/story/0,7521,548313,00.html (accessed 12 August 2002).
21 *Broadcast*, 30 January 2004: 17.
22 *Broadcast*, 9 January 2004: 7.
23 *Broadcast*, 9 January 2004: 7.
24 *Broadcast*, 13 February 2004: 5.
25 *Broadcast*, 30 January 2004: 17.
26 *Broadcast*, 13 February 2004: 5.
27 *Broadcast*, 13 February 2004: 5.
28 Plunkett, John. (2003) 'I'm a Celebrity Copycat Claim Withdrawn', *Media Guardian*, 25 April. Online. Available at http://mediaguardian.co.uk/broadcast/story/0,7493,943008,00.html (accessed 24 February 2004).
29 I am grateful to Pam Wilson for providing me with ratings for *Big Brother 1* in America.
30 Quotation taken from Goodale, Gloria (2002) 'Reality TV's Fall Mix: Dogs, Dating and Circus Stunts', *The Christian Science Monitor*. Online. Available at http://www.csmonitor.com (accessed 9 August 2002).
31 *Broadcast*, 5 March 2004: 5.
32 *Broadcast*, 30 January 2004: 17.
33 *Broadcast*, 21 November 2003: 20.
34 See *Broadcast* Awards, 28 January 2004.
35 *Broadcast*, 5 March 2004: 5.
36 *Broadcast*, 5 March 2004: 1.

3 The reality genre

1   Holmwood, Leigh (2003) 'BBC Launches Major Shake-up of Factual', *Broadcast*, 23 February: 1.
2   Holmwood, Leigh (2003) 'BBC Launches Major Shake-up of Factual', *Broadcast*, 23 February: 1.
3   Carter, Meg (2002) 'History is Updated', *Independent*, Review, Tuesday 20 August: 12.
4   Elber, Lynne (2003) 'All-Reality TV Channel Planned for 2004.' Online. Available at http://apnews.myway.com/article/20030428/D7QMBL600/ html (accessed 3 May 2003).
5   Dignam, Conar (2003) 'Cold Steel and Silky Charm', *Broadcast*, 28 March: 12–13.
6   Deans, Jason (2003) 'Reality TV is Here to Stay'. Online. Available at http://media.guardian.co.uk/realitytv (accessed 12 March 2003).
7   Charlie Parsons, creator of *Survivor* and *Pop Idol*, calls documentary gameshows 'documentary in a controlled environment', or, more explicitly, 'producer-created environments that control contestant behaviour' (Brenton and Cohen 2003: 52).
8   Bishop, L. (1997) 'Fame or Shame', *The Journal of the Royal Television Society*, May: 6–7; Mapplebeck, Victoria. (1997) 'Voyeurs and Victim TV', *Guardian*, 1 December: 4–5.
9   Howard, Tom (1999) 'That's Edutainment', *Time Out*, 24 November: 98; Collins, Michelle (1999) 'Rage Hard, and Harder Still', *Observer*, 11 April: 2–3.
10 Cater, Meg (2000) 'From the Man Who Gave You Big Brother: Couples in Chains', *Independent*, 5 September: 8.
11 Deans, Jason (2003) 'Reality TV is Here to Stay', Online. Available at http://media.guardian.co.uk/realitytv (accessed 12 March 2003).
12 See Hill and Calcutt 2001 for further discussion of scheduling in relation to television and its audience.

4 Performance and authenticity

1   For further research in news, see Dahlgren and Sparks (1992), and Thussu and Freedman (2003), amongst others.
2   See *Heat*, 31 May–6 June 2003: 10.

5 The idea of learning

1   Ahmed, Kamal (2002) 'BBC Faces Fines Threat from Jowell', *Observer*, 5 May: 3.
2   Paterson, Peter (2000) 'Brother, What a Mess', *Daily Mail*, 19 July: 67.
3   James, Oliver (2002) 'Danger: Reality TV Can Rot Your Brain', *The Times*, 20 December: 4–5.
4   Dunkley, Christopher (1999) 'Ragbag of Cheap Thrills', *Financial Times*, 5 November: 22.
5   Wells, Matt (2000) 'Voyeur Vision Puts Contestants in Focus', *Guardian*, 28 June: 7.
6   James, Oliver (2002) 'Danger: Reality TV Can Rot Your Brain', *The Times*, 20 December: 4–5.
7   Keighron, Peter (2003) 'TV's Altered Realities', *Broadcast*, 6 June: 20–1.
8   For discussion of 'narrative lifestyle', see the factual and learning components of the BBC website (www.bbc.co.uk).

9   See Channel 4 website (www.channel4.com).

6 Ethics of care

1   Advertisement for *Joe Millionaire* on UK digital channel E4.

7 Pet deaths

1   Pet Food Institute (2002b) 'New Study Finds Pet Dogs and Cats in Over Half of all US Homes'. Online. Available at http://www.petfoodinstitute.org/reference_pet_population_releasecfm (accessed 4 April 2002).
2   The European Pet Food Industry Association (2002) 'Facts and Figures'. Online. Available at http://www.fediaf.org/Pages/figures.html (accessed 4 April 2002).
3   Pet Food Manufacturers' Association (2002) 'Pet Ownership'. Online. Available at http://www.pfma.com/petownership.htm (accessed 4 April 2002). More than 50 per cent of dogs are pedigree, and the top three popular breeds are Labrador Retriever, Yorkshire Terrier, and German Shepherd.
4   Pet Food Manufacturers' Association (2002) 'Pet Ownership'. Online. Available at http://www.pfma.com/petownership.htm (accessed 4 April 2002).
5   The European Pet Food Industry Association (2002) 'Facts and Figures'. Online. Available at http://www.fediaf.org/Pages/figures.html (accessed 4 April 2002).
6   Pet Food Institute (2002a) 'What is PFI'. Online. Available at http://www.petfoodinstitute.org/what_is_pfi.cfm (accessed 4 April 2002).
7   Advert in *The Guardian Weekend Magazine*, 30 June 2001.
8   Amphlett, Lisa (2001) 'Hungry for a Change' *The Guardian Weekend Magazine* June 30 2001: 75.
9   See Pets Pajamas, an international company which has online services (http://www.pets-pajamas.co.uk).
10   In 2001, over 2 million cattle were killed during the 'mad cow' disease scare in Europe (*Independent*, Monday 29 January 2002: 15).
11   See Kyler Laird's animal rescue online resource for a full list of shelters – Available at http://www.ecn.perdue.edu/~laird/animal_rescue/shelters (Accessed 4 April 2002).
12   For example, Thomas (1993) argues that the RSPCA was primarily interested in social reform, and used anti-cruelty legislation to control working-class forms of leisure in Victorian England (see also Franklin 1999).
13   O'Hara, Mary (2003) 'The Price of Animal Love'. Online. Available at http://www.guardian.co.uk/guardian_jobs_and_money/story/0,3605,6793 41,00.html. Accessed 20 February 2003.
14   O'Hara, Mary (2003) 'The Price of Animal Love'. Online. Available at http://www.guardian.co.uk/guardian_jobs_and_money/story/0,3605,6793 41,00.html. Accessed 20 February 2003.
15   O'Hara, Mary (2003) 'The Price of Animal Love'. Online. Available at http://www.guardian.co.uk/guardian_jobs_and_money/story/0,3605,6793 41,00.html. Accessed 20 February 2003.
16   *The Week*, 24 May 2002: 35.
17   Quotations taken from The Kennel Club Healthcare Plan promotional material, UK, 2002.

18   Quotations taken from The Kennel Club Healthcare Plan promotional material, UK, 2002.
19   Quotations taken from PetPlan promotional material, UK 2002.
20   O'Hara, Mary (2003) 'The Price of Animal Love'. Online.   Available at http://www.guardian.co.uk/guardian_jobs_and_money/story/0,3605,6793 41,00.html. Accessed 20/02/2003.
21   The Society for Companion Animal Studies (SCAS) (2002) Online. Available at http://www.scas.co.uk (accessed 20 February 2003).
22   Title taken from Carter (1999).
23   BBC1 controller Lorraine Heggessey quoted in *Broadcast*, 24 October 2003: 8.
24   Ratings compiled by Phillips (1998, 1999a).
25   *Animal Hospital with Rolf Harris* (BBC video) is based on the original transmission of the first series 29 August 1994–30 March 1995. Other animal-based series provided extra textual material, such as *Battersea Dog's Home*, a book to accompany the series (McGibbon and Long 1998), and tie-in toys for *Pet Rescue*, such as Skip, the three-legged toy terrier.
26   Quoted in Birkett, D. (2000) 'I Got Rhythm', in *The Observer Magazine*, 24 September: 37.
27   *Animal Hospital with Rolf Harris*, 1995 BBC video.
28   *Animal Hospital*, transmitted 19 October 1999 BBC1, 8-8.30pm.
29   *Animal Hospital*, transmitted 27 April 1999 BBC1, 8-8.30pm.
30   *Animal Hospital*, transmitted 27 May 1999 BBC1, 8-8.30pm.
31   *Animal Hospital*, transmitted 27 April 1999 BBC1, 8-8.30pm.
32   George, G. (1999) 'Picks of the Day', *Express*, Monday 15 February: 43.
33   *Animal ER*, transmitted 15 March 1999 Channel 5, 8-9pm.
34   *Animal ER*, transmitted 15 February 1999 Channel 5, 8-9pm.
35   It is surprising that no viewers complained to the ITC or BSC about this, or any other animal-based reality programmes. This may in part be due to the fact that the British public do not wish to be labelled as complainers (see Hill 2000b for further details).
36   Two scenes of animal mortality were shown to viewers in the qualitative research (see Appendix 1 for details). The first scene was from *Animal Hospital*, involving the death of a kitten, and the second scene was from *Animal ER*, also involving the death of a kitten.
37   See *Independent* 30 April 2001, p.7, 'The Truth about Cats and Dogs (And Hamsters and Rabbits, Too)' for discussion of parental responses to pets.

8 Story of change

1   Quote from Peter Dale, Head of Documentaries, Channel 4, in *Broadcast*, 24 October 2003: 8.
2   Rosco, Jane (2003) 'Out of Collision: The State of the Art', unpublished article: 20-21.
3   Rosco, Jane (2003) 'Out of Collision: The State of the Art', unpublished article: 21.
4   Hill/Ofcom   (2004)   'Report on Television Audiences and Factual Programming Quantitative Research', forthcoming.
5   Livingstone and Lunt (1994) also suggest similar contradictions in their examination of talks shows.
6   Thanks to Jane Roscoe for pointing out the life lessons of reality programmes.

7   Speech by Tessa Jowell, Secretary of State for Culture, Media and Sport
    to BFI/UKFC/C4 Media Literacy Seminar, 27 January 2004. Online.
    Available at http://culture.gov.uk (accessed 27/02/04).
8   Speech by Tessa Jowell, Secretary of State for Culture, Media and Sport
    to BFI/UKFC/C4 Media Literacy Seminar 27 January 2004. Online.
    Available at http://culture.gov.uk (accessed 27/02/04).
9   I am grateful to Sonia Livingstone for suggesting this phrase in her analysis
    of young adults, new media and media literacy, presented at the 2003
    Intensive Programme for Doctoral Research in Communication, 26 August–
    4 September 2003, University of Westminster.
10 Picard, Robert. (2003) 'Audience Expenditures for Media Use', 2003 Intensive
    Programme for Doctoral Research in Communication, 26 August–
    4 September, University of Westminster, unpublished paper.
11 Picard, Robert. (2003) 'Audience Expenditures for Media Use', 2003 Intensive
    Programme for Doctoral Research in Communication, 26 August–
    4 September, University of Westminster, unpublished paper.

Bibliography

Abercrombie, Nicholas, and Longhurst, Brian (1998) *Audiences*, London: Sage.

Albert, A. and Bulcroft, K. (1988) 'Pets and Urban Life', *Anthrozoos*, 1, 1: 9–23.

Allen, Graham and Crow, Graham (2001) *Families, Households and Society*, Basingstoke: Palgrave.

Allen, Robert C. (1989) 'Bursting Bubbles: "Soap Opera", Audiences, and the Limits of Genre', in E. Seiter, H. Borchers, G. Kreutzner and E. Warth (eds) *Remote Control: Television, Audiences and Cultural Power*, London: Routledge.

Almond, Brenda (1993) 'Rights', in P. Singer (ed.) *A Companion to Ethics*, London: Blackwell, pp. 259–69.

Andrejevic, Mark (2003) *Reality TV: The Work of Being Watched*, Maryland: Rowman and Littlefield.

Annas, Julia (1992) 'Ancient Ethics and Modern Morality', in *Philosophical Perspectives*, 6: 119–36.

Aries, Phillippe (1962) *Centuries of Childhood*, New York: Vintage Books.

Barker, Martin and Petley, Julian (eds) (2001) *Ill Effects: The Media/Violence Debate* (second edition), London: Routledge.

Berkmann, Marcus (1994) 'A Nosy Fly on the Ward', *Daily Mail* (25 November): 59.

Biddiscomb, Ross (1998) 'Real Life: Real Ratings', *Broadcasting and Cables-Television International*, January: 14, 16.

Bird, Elizabeth (1997) 'What a Story: Understanding the Audience for Scandal', in J. Lull and S. Hunerman (eds) *Media Scandals: Morality and Desire in the Popular Culture Marketplace*, London: Polity Press, pp. 99–121.

Bird, Elizabeth (2000) 'Audience Demands in a Murderous Market: Tabloidization in U.S. Television News', in C. Sparks and J. Tulloch (eds) *Tabloid Tales: Global Debate over Media Scandal*, London: Rowman and Littlefield, pp. 213–28.

Biressi, Anita (2001) *Crime, Fear and the Law in True Crime Stories*, Hampshire: Palgrave.

Boddy, William (2001) 'The Quiz Show', in G. Creeber (ed.) *The Television Genre Book*, London: British Film Institute, pp. 79–81.

Bodmer, N. M. (1998) 'Impact of Pet Ownership on the Well-being of Adolescents with Few Familial Resources', in C. C. Wilson and D. C. Turner (eds) *Companion Animals in Human Health*, London: Sage, pp. 3–22.

Boltanski, L (1999) *Distant Suffering: Morality, Media and Politics*, Cambridge: Cambridge University Press.

Bondebjerg, Ib (1996) 'Public Discourse/Private Fascination: Hybridization in "True-life-story" Genres', *Media, Culture and Society*, 18: 27–45.

Bondebjerg, Ib (2002) 'The Mediation of Everyday Life: Genre, Discourse and Spectacle in Reality TV', in A. Jerslev (ed.) *Realism and 'Reality' in Film and Media*, Copenhagen: Museum Tusculanum Press, pp. 159–92.

Bonner, Frances (2003) *Ordinary Television*, London: Sage.

Bourdieu, P. (1986) *Distinction: A Social Critique of the Judgement of Taste*, London: Routledge.

Bourdon, Jerome (2000) 'Live Television is Still Alive: On Television as an Unfulfilled Promise', *Media, Culture, and Society* 22, 5: 531–56.

Brandt, A. M. and Rozin, P. (eds) (1997) *Morality and Health*, London Routledge.

Brants, Chris (1998) 'Crime Fighting by Television in the Netherlands', in Mark Fishman and Gray Cavender (eds) *Entertaining Crime: Television Reality Programmes*, New York: Aldine De Gruyter, pp. 175–92.

Brants, Kees (1998) 'Who's Afraid of Infotainment', *European Journal of Communication*, 13, 3: 315–35.

Brenton, Sam and Cohen, Reuben (2003) *Shooting People: Adventures in Reality TV*, London: Verso.

Brookes, Rod (2001) 'Sport (The Super Bowl)', in G. Creeber (ed.) *The Television Genre Book*, London: British Film Institute, pp. 87–8.

Brunsdon, Charlotte (1997) *Screen Tastes: Soap Opera to Satellite Dishes*, London: Routledge.

Brunsdon, C., Johnson, C., Moseley, R. and Wheatley, H. (2001) 'Factual Entertainment on British Television: The Midlands TV Research Group's "8–9 Project"', *European Journal of Cultural Studies*, 4, 1: 29–62.

Bruzzi, Stella (2000) *New Documentary: A Critical Introduction*, London: Routledge.

Bruzzi, Stella (2001) 'Observational ("Fly-on-the-wall") Documentary', in G. Creeber (ed.) *The Television Genre Book*, London: British Film Institute, pp. 29–132.

BSC (2000) *Consenting Adults?* London: Broadcasting Standards Commission.

Buckingham, D. (1996) *Moving Images: Understanding Children's Emotional Responses to Television*, Manchester: Manchester University Press.

Buckingham, David (2000) *The Making of Citizens: Young People, News and Politics*, London: Routledge.

Busfield, Steve (1995) 'A Quest for the Sleuth', *Broadcast*, 17 March: 18.

Byrant, Christopher and Jary, David (2001) *The Contemporary Giddens: Social Theory in a Globalising Age*, London: Palgrave.

Caldwell, John (2002) 'Primetime Fiction Theorises the Docu-Real', in J. Friedman (ed.) *Reality Squared: Televisual Discourse on the Real*, New Brunswick, NJ: Rutgers University Press, pp. 259–92.

Calvert, Clay (2000) *Voyeur Nation: Media, Privacy and Peering in Modern Culture*, Boulder: Westview Press.

Carter, M. (1999) 'Pets, Vets and TV Sets', *Broadcast*, 9 July: 16–17.

Chambers, Deborah (2001) *Representing the Family*, London: Sage.

Christians, Clifford (2003) 'The Media and Moral Literacy', *Ethical Space*, 1: 1–15.

Clarke, Nick (2003) *The Shadow of a Nation: The Changing Face of Britain*, London: Weidenfeld and Nicholson.

Collins, Richard (2003) 'Ises and Oughts: Public Service Broadcasting in Europe', in Robert C. Allen and Annette Hill (eds) *The Television Studies Reader*, London: Routledge, pp. 33–51.

Corner, John (1995) *Television Form and Public Address*, London: Edward Arnold.

Corner, John (1996) *The Art of Record: A Critical Introduction to Documentary*, Manchester: Manchester University Press.

Corner, John (1999) *Critical Ideas in Television Studies*, Oxford: Oxford University Press.

Corner, John (2000) 'What Can we Say About "Documentary"?' *Media, Culture and Society*, 22: 681–8.

Corner, John (2001a) 'Documentary Realism', in G. Creeber (ed.) *The Television Genre Book*, London: British Film Institute, pp. 126–9.

Corner, John (2001b) 'Form and Content in Documentary Study', in G. Creeber (ed.) *The Television Genre Book*, London: British Film Institute, pp. 125–6.

Corner, John (2002a) 'Documentary Values', in A. Jerslev (ed.) *Realism and 'Reality' in Film and Media*, Copenhagen: Museum Tusculanum Press, pp. 139–58.

Corner, John (2002b) 'Performing the Real', *Television and New Media*, 3, 3: 255–70.

Corner, John (2003) 'Afterword: Framing the New', in D. Jermyn and S. Holmes (eds) *Understanding Reality Television*, London: Routledge.

Costera Meijer, I. and Reesink, M. (eds) (2000) *Reality Soap! Big Brother en de Opkomst van het Multimediaconcept*, Amsterdam: Boom.

Couldry, Nick (2000) *The Place of Media Power: Pilgrims and Witnesses of the Media Age*, London: Routledge.

Couldry, Nick (2002) 'Playing for Celebrity: Big Brother as Ritual Event', *Television and New Media*, 3, 3: 283–94.

Cummings, Dolan (ed.) (2002) *Reality TV: How Real is Real?*, Oxford: Hodder and Stoughton.

Dahlgren, Peter (1995) *Television and the Public Sphere: Citizenship, Democracy and the Media*, London: Sage.

Dahlgren, Peter and Sparks, Colin (eds) *Journalism and Popular Culture*, London: Sage.

Dauncey, Hugh (1996) 'French "Reality Television": More than a Matter of Taste?', *European Journal of Communication*, 11, 1: 83–106.

Davies, Hannah, Buckingham, David and Kelley, Peter (2000) 'In the Worst Possible Taste: Children, Television and Cultural Value', *European Journal of Cultural Studies*, 3, 1: 5–25.

De Silva, Padmasiri (1993) 'Buddhist Ethics', in P. Singer (ed.) *A Companion to Ethics*, London: Blackwell, pp. 58–68.

Dempsey, J. (1991) 'Hot Genre Gluts TV Market', *Variety*, 3 June: 32.

Derosia, Margaret (2002) 'The Court of the Last Resort: Making Race, Crime and Nation on *America's Most Wanted*', in J. Friedman (ed.) *Reality Squared: Televisual Discourse on the Real*, New Brunswick, NJ: Rutgers University Press, pp. 236–58.

Diggs, B. J. (1981) 'A Contractarian View of Respect for Persons', *American Philosophical Quarterly*, 18: 56–88.

Donovan, J. and Adams, C. J. (1996) *Beyond Animal Rights: A Feminist Caring Ethic for the Treatment of Animals*, New York: Continuum.

Donovan, Pamela (1998) 'Armed with the Power of Television: Reality Crime Programming and the Reconstruction of Law and Order in the United States', in Mark Fishman and Gray Cavender (eds) *Entertaining Crime: Television Reality Programmes*, New York: Aldine De Gruyter, pp. 117–40.

Dovey, J. (2000) *Freakshow: First Person Media and Factual Television*, London: Pluto.

Dovey, Jon (2001) 'Reality TV', in G. Creeber (ed.) *The Television Genre Book*, London: British Film Institute, pp. 134–6.

Dower, Nigel (1993) 'World Poverty', in P. Singer (ed.) *A Companion to Ethics*, London: Blackwell, pp. 284–93.

Dugdale, John (1992) 'Not the Nine O'Clock News', *Independent* (29 July): 13.

Elias, Norbert (1986) 'An Essay on Sport and Violence', in N. Elias and E. Dunning (eds) *Quest for Excitement*, Oxford: Blackwell.

Elias, Norbert (1994) *The Civilising Process*, Oxford: Blackwell.

Ellis, J. (2000) *Seeing Things: Television in the Age of Uncertainty*, London: I. B. Tauris.

Ellis, John (2001) '*Survivor* and *Big Brother*', *Sight and Sound*, February: 56.

Ellis, John (2002) 'A Minister is About to Resign: On the Interpretation of Television Footage', in A. Jerslev (ed.) *Realism and 'Reality' in Film and Media*, Copenhagen: Museum Tusculanum Press, pp. 193–210.

Fennell, J. (2000) *The Dog Listener: Learning the Language of Your Best Friend*, London: HarperCollins.

Fetveit, Arild (2002) 'Reality TV in the Digital Era: A Paradox in Visual Culture', in J. Friedman (ed.) *Reality Squared: Televisual Discourse on the Real*, New Brunswick, NJ: Rutgers University Press, pp. 119–37.

Fishman, Mark (1998) 'Ratings and Reality: The Persistence of the Reality Crime Genre', in Mark Fishman and Gray Cavender (eds) *Entertaining Crime: Television Reality Programmes*, New York: Aldine De Gruyter, pp. 59–78.

Fishman, Mark and Cavender, Gray (1998) *Entertaining Crime: Television Reality Programmes*, New York: Aldine De Gruyter.

Fiske, John (1992) 'Popularity and the Politics of Information', in P. Dahlgren and C. Sparks (eds) *Journalism and Popular Culture*, London: Sage, pp. 45–63.

Foucault, Michel (1990) *The Care of the Self: The History of Sexuality, Volume Three*, translated by Robert Hurley, London: Penguin.

Foucault, Michel (1992) *The Use of Pleasure: The History of Sexuality, Volume Two*, translated by Robert Hurley, London: Penguin.

Foucault, Michel (2000) *Essential Works of Foucault 1954–1984: Ethics*, P. Rabinow (ed.), London: Penguin.

Franklin, A. (1999) *Animals and Modern Culture: A Sociology of Human–Animals Relations in Modernity*, London: Sage.

Freedman, Eric (2000) 'Public Access/Private Confession: Home Video as (Queer) Community Television', *Television and New Media*, 1, 2: 179–92.

Friedman, James (2002) 'Attraction to Distraction: Live Television and the Public Sphere', in J. Friedman (ed.) *Reality Squared: Televisual Discourse on the Real*, New Brunswick, NJ: Rutgers University Press, pp. 138–54.

Garner, R. (1993) *Animals, Politics and Morality*, Manchester: Manchester University Press.

Garrity, T. F. and Stallones, L. (1998) 'Effects of Pet Contact on Human Well-being', in C. C. Wilson and D. C. Turner (eds) *Companion Animals in Human Health*, London: Sage, pp. 3–22.

Gauntlett, David (2002) *Media, Gender and Identity: An Introduction*, London: Routledge.

Gauntlett, David and Hill, Annette (1999) *TV Living: Television, Culture and Everyday Life*, London: Routledge.

Giddens, Anthony (1991) *Modernity and Self-identity: Self and Society in the Late Modern Age*, Cambridge: Polity.

Glynn, Kevin (2000) *Tabloid Culture: Trash Taste, Popular Power, and the Transformation of American Television*, Durham, NC, and London: Duke University Press.

Goffman, Erving (1963) *Stigma: Notes on the Management of Spoiled Identity*, London: Pelican Books (reprint).

Goffman, Erving (1969) *The Presentation of Self in Everyday Life*, London: Pelican Books (reprint).

Goffman, Erving (1981) *Forms of Talk*, Oxford: Blackwell.

Grant, D. (1998) *A Year in the Life of The Animal Hospital*, London: Simon and Schuster.

Grimshaw, Jean (1993) 'The Idea of a Female Ethic', in P. Singer (ed.) *A Companion to Ethics*, London: Blackwell, pp. 491–9.

Gruen, Lori (1993) 'Animals', in P. Singer (ed.) *A Companion to Ethics*, London: Blackwell, pp. 343–53.

Harris, R., Leigh, M. and Lepine, M. (1997) *True Animal Tales*, London: Arrow Books.

Hartley, John (1999) *The Uses of Television*, London: Routledge.

Hartley, John (2001a) 'Daytime TV', in G. Creeber (ed.) *The Television Genre Book*, London: British Film Institute, pp. 92–3.

Hartley, John (2001b) 'The Infotainment Debate', in G. Creeber (ed.) *The Television Genre Book*, London: British Film Institute, pp. 118–21.

Hawkins, Gay (2001) 'The Ethics of Television', *International Journal of Cultural Studies*, 4, 4: 412–26.

Hawkins, Gay (2002) 'Performing Ethics', conference paper for Visible Evidence, Marseille.

Hesmondhalgh, David (2002) *The Cultural Industries*, London: Sage.

Hight, Craig (2001) 'Debating Reality-TV', *Continuum: Journal of Media and Cultural Studies*, 15, 3: 389–95.

Hill, Annette (1997) *Shocking Entertainment: Viewer Response to Violent Movies*, London: John Libbey Media, University of Luton.

Hill, Annette (2000a) 'Crime and Crisis: British Reality TV in Action', in Ed Buscombe (ed.) *British Television: A Reader*, Oxford: Oxford University Press.

Hill, Annette (2000b) 'The Language of Complaint', *Media, Culture and Society*, 22: 233–6.

Hill, Annette (2000c) 'Fearful and Safe: Audience Response to British Reality Programming', *Television and New Media*, 2, May: 193–214.

Hill, Annette (2001a) 'Looks Like it Hurts: Women's Responses to Shocking Entertainment', in Martin Barker and Julian Petley (eds) *Ill Effects: The Media/Violence Debate* (second edition), London: Routledge, pp. 135–49.

Hill, Annette (2001b) 'Media Risks: The Social Amplification of Risk and the Media Violence Debate', *Journal of Risk Research*, 4, 3: 209–26.

Hill, Annette (2002) '*Big Brother*: The Real Audience', *Television and New Media*, 3, 3: 323–40.

Hill, Annette and Independent Television Commission (ITC) (2000) 'Quantitative Research in Television Audiences and Popular Factual Entertainment', in association with the Broadcasters' Audience Research Board, unpublished document.

Hill, Annette and Calcutt, Ian (2001) 'Vampire Hunters: The UK Marketing and Reception of *Buffy the Vampire Slayer* and *Angel*', in *Intensities: The Journal of Cult Media* (http://www.cult-media.com)

Hill, Annette and Palmer, Gareth (2002) '*Big Brother*: Special Issue', *Television and New Media*, 3, 3, August.

Hill, Annette and Thomson, Katarina (2001) 'Sex and the Media: A Shifting Landscape', in R. Jowell, J. Curtice, A. Park, K. Thomson, L. Jarvis, C. Bromley and N. Stratford (eds) *British Social Attitudes the 17th Report: Focusing on Diversity*, London: Sage, pp. 71–99.

Hoggart, Richard (1970) *Speaking to Each Other*, London: Penguin Books.

Höijer, Birgitta (1992) 'Socio-cognitive Structures and Television Reception', *Media, Culture and Society*, 14: 583–603.

Holmes, Su (2004) ' "Reality Goes Pop!": Reality TV, Popular Music and Narratives of Stardom in Pop Idol (UK) ', *Television and New Media*, 5, 2, May: 123–48.

Holmes, Su and Jermyn, Deborah (eds) (2003) *Understanding Reality Television*, London: Routledge.

Hughes, Gordon and Fergusson, Ross (2000) *Ordering Lives: Family, Work and Welfare*, London: Routledge.

Humm, Peter (1998) 'Real TV: Camcorders, Access and Authenticity', in C. Geraghty and D. Lusted (eds) *The Television Studies Book*, London: Arnold, pp. 175–97.

ITC/BSC (2003) *Television: The Public's View*, London: Independent Television Commission and Broadcasting Standards Commission.

Jerslev, Anne (ed.) (2002) *Realism and 'Reality' in Film and Media*, Copenhagen: Museum Tusculanum Press.

Jost, François (1998) 'The Promise of Genres', *The French Journal of Communication*, 6, 1: 99–121.

Jowell, R., Curtice, J., Park, A., Thomson, K., Jarvis, L., Bromley, C. and Stratford, N. (eds) (2000) *British Social Attitudes the 17th Report: Focusing on Diversity*, London: Sage.

Katz, S. (1997) 'Secular Morality', in A. M. Brandt and P. Rozin (eds) *Morality and Health*, London: Routledge, pp. 297–330.

Kilborn, Richard (1994) 'How Real Can You Get?': Recent Developments in "Reality" Television', *European Journal of Communication*, 9: 421–39.

Kilborn, Richard (1998) 'Shaping the Real: Democratization and Commodification in UK-Factual Broadcasting', *European Journal of Communication*, 13, 2: 201–18.

Kilborn, Richard (2003) *Staging the Real: Factual TV Programming in the Age of Big Brother*, Manchester: Manchester University Press.

Kilborn, R. and Hibbard, M. (2000) *Consenting Adults?* London: Broadcasting Standards Commission.

Kilborn, R. and Izod, J. (1997) *An Introduction to TV Documentary: Confronting Reality*, Manchester: Manchester University Press.

Kim, L. S. and Blasini, G. M. (2001) 'The Performance of Multicultural Identity in US Network Television: Shiny, Happy *Popstars* (Holding Hands)', 11, 2: 287–308.

Kirstein, Arine (2002) 'Decentering the Subject: The Current Documentary Critique of Realism', in A. Jerslev (ed.) *Realism and 'Reality' in Film and Media*, Copenhagen: Museum Tusculanum Press, pp. 211–26.

Kirwan, Tony, Learmouth, James, Sayer, Mollie and Williams, Roger (2003) *Mapping Media Literacy*, BFI/BSC/ITC.

Kittay, Eva F. (2001) 'A Feminist Public Ethic of Care Meets the New Communitarian Family Policy', *Ethics*, 111, 3: 523–47.

Knowsley, J. (1999) 'Lurid Scenes on Vets Show are Likely to Upset Viewers', *Daily Telegraph* (14 February): 3.

Kymlicka, Will (1993) 'The Social Contract Tradition' in P. Singer (ed.) *A Companion to Ethics*, London: Blackwell, pp. 186–96.

Langer, John (1998) *Tabloid Television: Popular Journalism and the 'Other News'*, London: Routledge.

Leichter, H. M. (1997) 'Lifestyle Correctness and the New Secular Morality', in A. M. Brandt and P. Rozin (eds) *Morality and Health*, London: Routledge, pp. 359–77.

Livingstone, Sonia, and Lunt, Peter (1994) *Talk on Television: Audience Participation and Public Debate*, London: Routledge.

Livingstone, Sonia and Thumim, Nancy (2003) *Assessing the Media Literacy of UK Adults*, BSC/ITC/NIACE.

Lury, Karen (1996) 'Television Performance: Being, Acting and "Corpsing"', *New Formations*, 27: 114–27.

McCarthy, Anna (2001) 'Studying Soap Opera', in G. Creeber (ed.) *The Television Genre Book*, London: British Film Institute, pp. 47–9.

McGibbon, R. and Long, B. (1998) *Battersea Dog's Home: Inside the World Famous Home for Dogs ... and Cats*, London: BBC.

Malim, Tony and Birch, Ann (1998) *Introductory Psychology*, London: Macmillan.

Marvin, Garry (2002) 'Unspeakability, Inedibility, and the Structures of Pursuit in the English Foxhunt', in N. Rothfels (ed.) *Representing Animals*, Bloomington and Indianapolis: Indiana University Press, pp. 139–58.

Mathjis, Ernest (2002) 'Big Brother and Critical Discourse', *Television and New Media*, 3, 3: 311–22.

Mathjis, Ernest, Jones, Janet, Hessels, Wouter and Verriest, Lara (eds) (2004) *Big Brother International: Critics, Format and Publics*, London: Wallflower Press.

Medhurst, Andy (1999) 'Day For Night', *Sight and Sound*, June: 26–7.

Mepham, John (1990) 'The Ethics of Quality in Television', in G. Mulgan (ed.) *The Question of Quality*, London: British Film Institute, pp. 50–70.

Messenger Davies, Máire and Mosdell, Nick (2001) *Consenting Children? The Use of Children in Non-Fiction Television Programmes*, London: Broadcasting Standards Commission.

Midgley, Carol (1997) 'Another Slice of Reality in BBC's Peeping Tom TV', *The Times* (18 December): 11.

Mikos, Lothar, Feise, Patricia, Herzog, Katja, Prommer, Elizabeth and Veihl, Verena (2000) *Im Auge der Kamera: Das Fernsehereignis Big Brother*, Berlin: Vistas.

Miller, Toby (2001) 'The Populist Debate', in G. Creeber (ed.) *The Television Genre Book*, London: British Film Institute, pp. 76–9.

Mittell, Jason (2001) 'A Cultural Approach to Television Genre Theory', *Cinema Journal* 40, 3: 3–24.

Montgomery, Martin (2001) 'Defining "Authentic Talk"', *Discourse Studies*, 3, 4: 397–405.

Moores, Shaun (2000) *Media and Everyday Life in Modern Society*, Edinburgh: Edinburgh University Press.

Moran, Albert (1998) *Copycat TV: Globalisation, Program Formats and Cultural Identity*, Luton: University of Luton Press.

Morgan, David (1996) *Family Connections*, Cambridge: Polity.

Morgan, David (1999) 'Risk and Family Practices', in E. Silva and C. Smart (eds) *The New Family?*, London: Sage.

Moseley, Rachael (2000) 'Makeover Takeover on British Television', *Screen*, 41, 3: 299–327.

Murrell, Rachel (1992) 'Crime Pays', *Television Week*, 3 July: 48.

National Canine Defence League (2001) *Annual Review*, London: NCDL.

Naughton, John (1994) 'The Rise of Ghoul-on-the-wall TV', *Daily Telegraph* (16 September): 23.

Neale, Steve (2001) 'Studying Genre' in G. Creeber (ed.) *The Television Genre Book*, London: British Film Institute, pp. 1–3.

Nichols, Bill (1991) *Representing Reality: Issues and Concepts in Documentary*, Bloomington and Indianapolis: Indiana University Press.

Nichols, Bill (1994) *Blurred Boundaries: Questions of Meaning in Contemporary Culture*, Bloomington and Indianapolis: Indiana University Press.

Noddings, N. (1978) *Caring: A Feminine Approach to Ethics and Education*, Berkeley: University of California Press.

Oliver, Mary Beth (1994a) 'Influences of Authoritarianism and Portrayals of Race on Caucasian Viewers' Responses to Reality-based Crime Dramas', *Communication Reports*, 9: 141–50.

Oliver, Mary Beth (1994b) 'Portrayals of Crime, Race, and Aggression in "Reality-based" Police Shows: A Content Analysis, *Journal of Broadcasting and Electronic Media*, 38: 179–92.

Oliver, Mary Beth and Blake Armstrong, G. (1995) 'Predictors of Viewing and Enjoyment of Reality-based and Fictional Crime Shows', *Journalism and Mass Communication Quarterly*, 72: 559–70.

Oliver, Mary Beth and Blake Armstrong, G. (1998) 'The Color of Crime: Perceptions of Caucasian and African Americans' Involvement in Crime', in Mark Fishman and Gray Cavender (eds) *Entertaining Crime: Television Reality Programmes*, New York: Aldine De Gruyter, pp. 19–38.

Paget, Derek (1998) *No Other Way to Tell It*, Manchester: Manchester University Press.

Palmer, Gareth (2002a) 'Big Brother: An Experiment in Governance', *Television and New Media*, 3, 3: 295–310.

Palmer, Gareth (2002b) '*Neighbours from Hell*: Producing Incivilities', in J. Friedman (ed.) *Reality Squared: Televisual Discourse on the Real*, New Brunswick, NJ: Rutgers University Press, pp. 221–35.

Palmer, Gareth (2003) *Discipline and Liberty*, Manchester: Manchester University Press.

Pence, Greg (1993) 'Virtue Theory', in P. Singer (ed.) *A Companion to Ethics*, London: Blackwell, pp. 249–58.

Pet Food Institute (2002) 'What is PFI'. Online. Available at http://www.petfoodinstitute.org/what_is_pfi.cfm (accessed 4 April 2002).

Pet Food Institute (2002) 'New Study Finds Pet Dogs and Cats in Over Half of all US Homes'. Online. at http://www.petfoodinstitute.org/ reference_pet_population_releasecfm (accessed 4 April 2002).

Pet Food Manufacturers' Association (2002) 'Pet Ownership'. Online. Available at http://www.pfma.com/petownership.htm (accessed 4 April 2002).

Phillips, W. (1998) 'Pop-fact Fabulous', *Broadcast*, 9 October: 20.

Phillips, William (1999a) 'All Washed Out', *Broadcast*, 2 July: 22–3.

Phillips, William (1999b) 'Summertime Blues', *Broadcast*, 1 October: 22.

Phillips, William (2000) 'Real Life Ratings', *Royal Television Society Journal*, January: 42–3.

Porter, Henry (1992) 'Should We Indulge This Lust for Gore?', *Evening Standard* (2 July): 9.

Raphael, Chad (1997) 'Political Economy of Reali-TV', in *Jump Cut*, 41: 102–9.

Roscoe, Jane (2001) '*Big Brother* Australia: Performing the 'Real' Twenty-four-Seven', *International Journal of Cultural Studies*, 4, 1: 473–88.

Roscoe, Jane and Hight, Craig (2001) *Faking It: Mock-documentary and the Subversion of Factuality*, Manchester: Manchester University Press.

Rose, Nikolas (1998) *Inventing Ourselves: Psychology, Power and Personhood*, Cambridge: Cambridge University Press.

Rose, Nikolas (1999) *Powers of Freedom: Reframing Political Thought*, Cambridge: Cambridge University Press.

Rothfels, Nigel (ed.) (2002) *Representing Animals*, Bloomington and Indiana: Indiana University Press.

Rowe, Christopher (1993) 'Ethics in Ancient Greece', in P. Singer (ed.) *A Companion to Ethics*, London: Blackwell, pp. 121–32.

Royal Society for the Prevention of Cruelty to Animals (1999) *Annual Review*, London: RSPCA.

Rozin, R. (1997) 'Moralization', in A. M. Brandt and P. Rozin (eds) *Morality and Health*, London: Routledge, pp. 379–402.

Salmon, P. W. and Salmon, I. M. (1983) 'Who Owns Who? Psychological Research into Human Pet Bond in Australia', in A. H. Katcher and A. M. Beck (eds) *New Perspectives in Our Lives with Companion Animals*, Philadelphia: University of Pennsylvannia Press.

Scannell, Paddy (2001) 'Authenticity and Experience', *Discourse Studies*, 3, 4: 405–11.

Scannell, Paddy (2002) '*Big Brother* as Television Event', *Television and New Media*, 3, 3: 271–82.

Schlesinger, Phillip (1978) *Putting 'Reality' Together*, London: Constable.

Schlesinger, P. and Howard, T. (1993) 'Fighting the War Against Crime', *British Journal of Criminology* 33, 1: 19–32.

Schlesinger, P., Dobash, R. E., Dobash, R. P. and Weaver, C. K. (1992) *Women Viewing Violence*, London: British Film Institute.

Schneewind, J. B. (1993) 'Modern Moral Philosophy', in P. Singer (ed.) *A Companion to Ethics*, London: Blackwell, pp. 147–60.

Seale, Clive (1998) *Constructing Death: The Sociology of Dying and Bereavement*, Cambridge: Cambridge University Press.

Seale, Clive (2002) *Media Health*, London: Sage.

Serpell, J. (1986) *In the Company of Animals*, Oxford: Blackwell.

Shattuc, Jane (2001a) 'The Celebrity Talk Show', in G. Creeber (ed.) *The Television Genre Book*, London: British Film Institute: 81–4.

Shattuc, Jane (2001b) 'The Confessional Talk Show', in G. Creeber (ed.) *The Television Genre Book*, London: British Film Institute, pp. 84–7.

Silverstone, Roger (1999) *Why Study the Media?*, London: Sage.

Singer, Peter (1993) 'Introduction', in Singer, P. (ed.) *A Companion to Ethics*, London: Blackwell, pp. v–vi.

Social Trends (1999) *Social Trends 29*, London: Office for National Statistics/HMSO.

Social Trends (2002) *Social Trends 32*, London: Office for National Statistics/HMSO.

Social Trends (2003) *Social Trends 33*, London: Office for National Statistics/HMSO.

Sparks, Colin (1992) 'Popular Journalism: Theories and Practice', in P. Dahlgren and C. Sparks (eds) *Journalism and Popular Culture*, London: Sage, pp. 24–44.

Summers, Sue (1997) 'Crime TV: Turning Viewers into Voyeurs', *Evening Standard* (25 June): 51.

Tester, K. (2001) *Compassion, Morality and the Media*, Buckingham: Open University Press.

The European Pet Food Industry Association (2002) 'Facts and Figures'. Online. Available HTTP: http://www.fediaf.org/Pages/figures.html (accessed 4 April 2002).

Thomas, K. (1983) *Man and the Natural World: Changing Attitudes in England 1500–1800*, London: Allen Lane.

Thussu, Daya and Freedman, Des (2003) *War and the Media*, London: Sage.

Thynne, Jane (1992) 'Rescue of the Ratings', *Daily Telegraph* (6 August): 25.

Tinknell, Estella and Raghuram, Pavrati (2002) '*Big Brother*: Reconfiguring the "Active" Audience of Cultural Studies?', *European Journal of Cultural Studies*, 5, 2: 199–215.

Truss, Lynne (1994) *The Times* (21 October): 47.

Turner, Graeme (2001) 'Genre, Format and "Live" Television', in G. Creeber (ed.) *The Television Genre Book*, London: British Film Institute, pp. 6–7.

Turner, Victor (1988) *The Anthropology of Performance*, New York: PAJ Publications.

Turow, J. (1996) 'Television Entertainment and the US Health-care Debate', *The Lancet*, 347: 1240–3.

Van Leeuwen, Theo (2001) 'What is Authenticity?', *Discourse Studies*, 3, 4: 392–7.

White, Mimi (2002) 'Television, Therapy, and the Social Subject; or, The TV Therapy Machine', in J. Friedman (ed.) *Reality Squared: Televisual Discourse on the Real*, New Brunswick, NJ: Rutgers University Press, pp. 313–22.

Whitehill, James (1994) 'Buddhist Ethics in Western Context: The Virtues Approach', *Journal of Buddhist Ethics*, 1: 22–45.

Wilson, C. C. and Turner, D. C. (eds) (1998) *Companion Animals in Human Health*, London: Sage.

Winston, Brian (1995) *Claiming the Real: the Documentary Film Revisited*, London: British Film Institute.

Winston, Brian (2000) *Lies, Damn Lies and Documentaries*, London: British Film Institute.

Zelizer, V. A. (1985) *Pricing the Priceless Child: The Changing Social Value of Children*, New York: Basic Books.

Index

eBooks – at www.eBookstore.tandf.co.uk

A library at your fingertips!

eBooks are electronic versions of printed books. You can store them on your PC/laptop or browse them online.

They have advantages for anyone needing rapid access to a wide variety of published, copyright information.

eBooks can help your research by enabling you to bookmark chapters, annotate text and use instant searches to find specific words or phrases. Several eBook files would fit on even a small laptop or PDA.

NEW: Save money by eSubscribing: cheap, online access to any eBook for as long as you need it.

Annual subscription packages

We now offer special low-cost bulk subscriptions to packages of eBooks in certain subject areas. These are available to libraries or to individuals.

For more information please contact webmaster.ebooks@tandf.co.uk

We're continually developing the eBook concept, so keep up to date by visiting the website.

www.eBookstore.tandf.co.uk